AGAINST MEDIOCRITY

AGAINST MEDIOCRITY

The Humanities in America's High Schools

Edited by

CHESTER E. FINN, JR.
DIANE RAVITCH
ROBERT T. FANC

With a Foreword by

WILLIAM J. BENNETT

Chairman
National Endowment for the Humanities

HM

HOLMES & MEIER
New York   London

A project of the Educational Excellence Network
of Vanderbilt University's Institute for Public Policy Studies,
undertaken with support from the National Endowment for the Humanities

First published in the United States of America 1984 by
Holmes & Meier Publishers, Inc.
30 Irving Place
New York, N.Y. 10003

Great Britain:
Holmes & Meier Publishers, Ltd.
131 Trafalgar Road
Greenwich, London SE10 9TX

Book design by Stephanie Barton

Library of Congress Cataloging in Publication Data
Main entry under title:

Against mediocrity: the humanities in America's high
    schools.
    "A project of the Educational Excellence Network of
Vanderbilt University's Institute for Public Policy
Studies."
    Bibliography: p.
    1. Education, Humanistic—United States.   2. Humanities
—Study and teaching (Secondary)—United States.
I. Finn, Chester E., 1944–   .   II. Ravitch, Diane.
III. Fancher, Robert T. IV. Vanderbilt Institute for
Public Policy Studies.
LC1011.A42   1984   373.19'8'0973   83-22819
ISBN 0-8419-0944-X
ISBN 0-8419-0945-8 (pbk.)

Manufactured in the United States of America

Contents

Foreword

The people of America are concerned about the quality of American education, and their concern has prompted an intense national discussion. Educational leaders, editorial writers, local, state, and federal officials—including President Reagan—all are debating the hows, whats, and wherefores of school reform.

The catalyst for much of this discussion is *A Nation at Risk,* the report issued in mid-1983 by the National Commission on Excellence in Education. Given the extraordinary attention being focused on excellence in education as a result of the report, it is proper to ask: what are the place and function of the humanities in excellent education? It is that question that concerns this book's authors, with whom I share the conviction that there is no sound education, no education worthy of the name, that does not include the teaching and learning of the humanities. The study of literature, history, and languages in the schools and, in addition, of philosophy, classics, and other humanities disciplines in colleges and universities must be part of what we mean by excellent education.

The focus of this volume is secondary schools, and within it will be found dozens of sound recommendations based on thoughtful analyses of current conditions in those schools. I would like to offer a few words about the importance of the humanities, their place in the schools, and the role of the National Endowment for the Humanities in the efforts represented so well by this book.

First, we must be clear about what the humanities are and what they are not. Often the humanities have suffered as much at the hands of well-intentioned but muddled advocates as they have from critics and philistines. In the last fifteen years, we have witnessed a variety of educational travesties committed in the name of the humanities. Forsaking learning in a particular discipline such as literature, history, or philosophy, eager "humanistic" zealots have imposed "humanistic education," "humane studies," and "values inquiries" upon the schools. In my experience, courses offered under these banners have largely failed to impart much knowledge; but they have succeeded in altering the public perception of the humanities. Formerly, at the mention of the word "humanities," large parts of the public would show only a glazed look in the eye, or a puzzled expression on the face. "The humanities" were assumed to be something academic and obscure. But now, thanks to educational sloppiness verging on intellectual anarchy, there is often a skeptical and distrustful attitude when one uses the term "humanities."

This should not be the case. The legacy of the authentic humanities, the *studia humanitatis* of the Italian Renaissance of the sixteenth century—the study and learning of grammar, history, poetry, and moral philosophy—and its ancient and noble lineage back to Cicero should bother no one. Indeed, the study of the humanities should please all those who believe that at least one function of education should be the cultivation of mind, imagination, and character by exposure to civilization's best thoughts and finest utterances. Plainly, the schools ought to be a place where this takes place, and the availability of universal secondary education in the United States provides the most complete opportunity for this to take place for all of our young citizens. Indeed, the secondary schools are our last opportunity to provide for everyone at least some sense of the intellectual inheritance that is part of everyone's birthright.

Happily, the National Commission on Excellence in Education did not fall victim to the contemporary colorless, tasteless, and sometimes corrupt misunderstanding of the humanities. Recognizing as it did the importance of writing, reading, and computation skills, and the need for educational practice that will build a technically, scientifically, and mathematically competent citizenry, the commission also manifested a strong and accurate sense of the humanities' important place in the schools. Of its five "New Basics," two—history and literature—are fields of the humanities. Further, the study of history and literature are recommended not only because they are useful in the development of the skills of comprehension, evaluation, criticism, and writing, but also because they are thought to be important in themselves.

Thus, students should, in the language of the report, "know our literary heritage . . . and how it relates to the customs, ideas and values of today's life and culture." The commission understood that, taught well, the humanities can offer appraisal by perspective. Further, the commission said that "students should study social studies" (one presumes this means chiefly history) so that they will be able to "fix their places and possibilities within the larger social and cultural structure" and "understand the broad sweep of both ancient and contemporary ideas that have shaped our world." It has been rightly said that a citizen remains alien to himself in a culture in which his past is denied or ignored. The commission agreed and accordingly urged disciplined study of the humanities as a guide both to better self-knowledge and to keener appreciation of the achievements of our culture and civilization.

The humanities are not an educational luxury, a collection of electives for honor students. The humanities are basic. Minimal exposure to their extraordinary capacity to advance a basic cultural literacy for all citizens is not asking too much. If this aim—cultural literacy—is put clearly before the schools and their teachers, some fundamental understanding of the ideas, events, and great works that are the taproot of our civilization can be attained. Achievable goals within the competence of teachers and the grasp of students can be articulated, as they are in this volume. But some modesty and self-restraint are required, too.

At the level of the secondary school, it is not deep musings that we need, not the intense scrutiny of profundities, but rather a basic grasp of the themes, ideas, and figures that have made our culture. First things first! As C. S. Lewis put it so well, "The task of the modern educator is not to cut down forests, it is to irrigate deserts." Where thousands of hours a year of television viewing and other cultural suppressants have left a sensibility that is often deficient, acquaintance with some of the best that has been thought and known may provide a much-needed corrective.

In saying that all students deserve some exposure to the humanities, I am not saying that this will inevitably result in an interest in the humanities. But let us invite students into the humanities by consideration of great literature, seminal history, and the importance of ideas so that, in the spirit of Plato, they at least may know what they don't know. Let us take part in a fair competition for the minds and attention of the young. We do not want our children to be strangers in a society that draws so deeply from the ideas of the humanities. Plainly, for this to occur, for the humanities to compete with other forces in shaping students' minds and allegiances, our schools must take the lead. If in later years the student wishes to reject what is in "old books," let him at least know what he is rejecting. At the outset, however, at the time the invitation is issued, let us offer him the best we have. Fortunately, the best we have is considerable, and much of it is accessible to the high school student, provided he is well taught.

The National Endowment for the Humanities surely has a role to play in furthering such thoughtful humanities education in the schools.

Since becoming chairman of NEH in December 1981, I have sought to foster greater attention at this agency to the critical area of education. For years, NEH has had a well-deserved reputation for promoting careful study of the humanities at the college and university level, advanced research at the cutting edge of all the humanities disciplines, scholarly publications, and diverse programs for the general and out-of-school public utilizing mass media and fifty-two federally funded state and territorial committees for the humanities. These efforts continue. For years, NEH has also had a Division of Education Programs. But since late 1982, that division has placed new and strong emphasis on educational excellence in the schools.

With the advice and support of the National Council on the Humanities, we have undertaken a number of initiatives. We have launched a national series of Summer Seminars for Secondary School Teachers in great works of the humanities. We have urged winners of our Independent Fellowships grants to devote part of their time to working with local schools. We have encouraged our state committees to consider programs in the schools and with teachers.

Perhaps most important, we have entirely revamped our Division of Education Programs guidelines so that they will be more responsive to the real problems of humanities education in both elementary and secondary schools and will address these problems by two emphases: teacher competence to teach the humanities, and student ability to gain at least a minimal grasp of the methods and content of the humanities. Under these guidelines we have in the past year, through the Council for Basic Education, awarded one hundred Fellowships for Secondary School Teachers for Independent Study in the humanities, and we will do so again in the year ahead. We have supported dozens of institutes and programs aimed at solid, discipline-based study for teachers. And we have supported the Vanderbilt-based Educational Excellence Network in the planning and execution of the conferences and papers that led not only to the publication of this book, but also to a variety of other activities aimed at understanding structural and attitudinal obstacles to the improved teaching and learning of the humanities in the schools.

I attended the Atlanta conference of the Educational Excellence Network's project, and Richard Ekman, Director of Education Programs at the Endowment, attended the Denver conference. The twin events were intended to foster both serious thinking about general issues facing humanities educators and actual cooperative reform efforts involving the schools, colleges, and teacher education programs at the "grassroots." Discussions at the conferences were intense, and the commitment to excellence in humanities education that these discussions evinced was heartening. The present volume contains later versions of the conference papers, revised, in consultation with the editors, in light of the discussions at the conferences.

The Endowment's support of this effort by the Educational Excellence Network is representative of our role in promoting educational excellence. In all of these efforts, we have stressed the need for teachers of the humanities at all levels and in all institutions to work together. Professors should neither patronize nor ignore high school teachers; elementary and secondary teachers should neither regard themselves as inferior because they teach in schools nor dismiss university scholars as irrelevant to the realities of schools.

The educational role of NEH, and indeed of the entire federal government, is important, but is supportive at best. We can prod, urge, initiate, and sponsor; but we cannot and should not seek to direct the discussion or implementation of programs nationwide. Effective teaching of the humanities in the schools depends a good deal less on what is done at NEH, or even the Department of Education, than on what is done by parents, local school boards, and state and local officials.

Chester Finn has argued elsewhere that a consensus for excellence in education is building at the grass-roots level all over America. We are very pleased with that consensus, as we are with the particular efforts of the Educational Excellence Network to foster it. The Network has already made substantial gains in—there is no other word—the "education" of citizens, teachers, and school administrators. We are delighted to have played a part in it.

WILLIAM J. BENNETT, *Chairman*
National Endowment for the Humanities

AGAINST MEDIOCRITY

Introduction

Chester E. Finn, Jr., Diane Ravitch, and Robert T. Fancher

Excellence in academic education for all of our nation's children is, at last, becoming a significant issue in public consciousness and debate. For nearly twenty years, the very idea of excellence was in disrepute. The conventional wisdom held that excellence was synonymous with elitism, that only a handful of children would benefit from a strong academic program, and that schools should not concern themselves with the needs of the privileged few. Behind this analysis was the assumption, often made explicit, that many children could not learn and therefore should not be exposed to the humiliation of failure, which would only embitter them and cause them to leave school early. Misconceived efforts to hold down the dropout rate led to lowered standards and to social promotion, with the unhappy result that all children received a cheapened quality of schooling without any appreciable reduction of the dropout rate. The children who had the misfortune of being considered unteachable found themselves promoted year after year without having acquired the rudiments of learning; if they held out long enough, they received high school diplomas, though not the skills or knowledge that made the certificate meaningful. Other children learned the rudiments, but did so within a context of lowered challenge, in schools where requirements for graduation had been sharply reduced, where the language of textbooks was deliberately diluted for easier reading, where grade inflation had made their A's and B's of little value, where absenteeism and indiscipline had seriously eroded the environment of learning. With the reduction of requirements, the traditional humanities in high schools suffered one of two fates: either a steep drop in enrollments, as in foreign language courses; or a splintering into multitudinous electives, as in history and English.

This troublesome state of affairs severely eroded the integrity of the humanistic disciplines. Worse, it disrupted the conditions of teaching, making it increasingly difficult to recruit or retain talented professionals in a situation where teaching and learning were continuously imperiled. In the mid-1970s, a few significant events aroused public awareness that something was terribly wrong in the schools. In two (unsuccessful) court cases, one in California, another in New York, high school graduates sued for "educational malpractice" because they had never learned to read or write. Even more important was the revelation by the College Board in 1975 that scores on the Scholastic Aptitude Test (SAT) had fallen steadily and sharply since 1964. Defenders of the status quo immediately attacked the SAT as an unreliable barometer, but further research demonstrated that scores on every other major standardized test had fallen in similar fashion. At first, instant analysts conveniently attributed the score drop to the expansion in the number of low-income and minority youngsters taking college entrance tests. However, when the College Board's own blue-ribbon panel reported in 1977, it acknowledged that the most substantial score decline had occurred *after* the demographics of the applicant pool had stabilized. While the panel was not willing to pin the blame for declining academic skills on the schools, it did acknowledge the likely influence of the lowering of standards and the lessened emphasis on critical reading and thoughtful writing.

The clearest indicator of public dissatisfaction was the fact that, by 1978, nearly forty states had adopted minimum competency tests for high school students. Though educators feared that the tests were too easy and that the minimum might become the maximum, state legislators were responding to public alarm about the condition of education. The tests they adopted were the equivalent of a consumer protection act that probably did little for the quality of education other than to guarantee that it would not be a complete fraud. Over the next five years, public discontent continued to roil as the economy slackened. In a time of high unemployment, when the blue-collar industries were particularly hard-hit, the technological competition from Japan began to loom as an economic Sputnik. Suddenly, television news programs and the newsweeklies discovered that the Japanese were leaping ahead of us in international markets because of their superior schooling in science, mathematics, and technology.

It was in this atmosphere in the early 1980s that some two dozen different study groups, commissions, panels, and task forces undertook to diagnose the problems of American education. The first of these to report to the American public was also, in all probability, the most significant. It was the report of the National Commission on Excellence in Education, a panel of educators, business leaders, and private citizens, appointed by the U.S. Secretary of Education with the approval of the President. The Commission called for a restoration of traditional educational values, for higher graduation requirements, for more time spent on teaching and learning, and for a number of drastic actions to raise the intellectual caliber of teachers. The National Commission, like other study groups, wisely recognized the importance of the humanities in any reformulated definition of schooling.

What has been most remarkable about this and subsequent national reports is that they have concurred about the central purposes of schooling in American society. First, they have acknowledged that the schools have tried without success to be all things to all people and have called for a clear recognition that the schools should concentrate on doing those things that schools do best; second, they have agreed that good schooling is for *all* children, not just for the privileged few; third, they have posited a view of education that includes not just science and mathematics, but also history, literature, languages, and the arts.

Nonetheless, there is always the danger that the current interest in science and mathematics might overwhelm the values of the less obviously useful, more contemplative disciplines of the humanities. Part of the motivation of those who compiled this volume is to reassert the continuing importance of history, literature, and language in the life of the nation and in the lives of individuals. The corruption, abandonment, and disintegration of these studies in recent years can only be cause for alarm. While we can find no exact parallel to the economic Sputnik that followed our failure in the hard sciences, we believe that there exists a broad public consensus on the values that are imparted by humanistic studies of history, literature, and language.

We believe there is general agreement that the character of our culture, the texture of our life as a society, the vigor of our polity, and the quality of our individual lives depend at least as strongly on the humanities as on the sciences—and that successful education depends on both.

Without the values and ethics, the wisdom and knowledge, the insight and context, the shared understanding and communications embodied in the humanities, we risk becoming a society that loses its balance, rather like a foolish athlete who builds up just one side of his body on the false assumption that he only needs strength in the limbs and muscles that actually pass the football or hurl the javelin. An educational system that only strengthens itself in math, science, and basic skills risks producing a generation of technopeasants*: individuals who manipulate complex machines without knowing why, who depend on other machines for amusement and recreation, who have no real intellectual interests or cultural lives, whose behavior is defined by the interaction between hedonistic cravings and externally imposed controls, who have no valid bases for judging the claims of politicians, gurus, and cult figures, and who lack any sense of a collective past or any vision of a better future.

No one, we submit, could view that prospect with equanimity. Certainly we do not, nor do the many men and women who participated in the project of which this volume is the most durable product.

We propose, then, nothing more nor less than drastically improving humanities teaching in America's high schools. In most schools, this means reforming the teaching of English language and literature, history, and foreign languages. Our purpose, though, is not special pleading for the humanities, nor indeed for school improvement as an end in itself. A well-conceived and well-taught humanities curriculum in the secondary schools is a means to larger ends: the enhancement of a free, just, stable, and secure society.

We are not content with the present condition of the humanities in American secondary education. That does not deny the presence of some fine teachers, superb curricula, and outstanding schools. Indeed, their very existence is the most persuasive rejoinder to those who mutter that what we seek is impossible, unrealistic, utopian—or simply misguided. But the pinnacles of excellence do contrast vividly with the slough of mediocrity wherein too much of the high school humanities program can now be found in too many schools. We understand that practically everyone is, in principle, opposed to mediocrity, as to sin. We realize that mediocrity is generally easier to live with than excellence—if only because it is less demanding—and is accordingly more prevalent. We believe, however, that the personal and social costs of continued widespread mediocrity in the secondary school humanities program have

---

*We borrow this term from Richard Hersh, though we use it with a rather different meaning. See Hersh, "Are American Schools Turning Out Technopeasants?", *Instructor* 92, no. 9:26ff.

come to exceed any price this nation can afford to pay, and that this assessment is shared by more Americans with every passing month.

The book that follows is neither an extended ode to the wonders of the humanities nor a "school improvement manual." The volume, we believe, offers unvarnished appraisals of the conditions of the humanities in the schools; hard-headed, no-nonsense consideration of what we can and ought to do about the teaching of the humanities disciplines; and analyses of generic educational issues that powerfully affect the humanities. The reader will find a variety of constructive suggestions and, perhaps more important, advice based on understanding the difference between generalities, which can be applied in many places, and platitudes, which can scarcely be applied at all.

The body of the book begins with an essay by Harry S. Broudy, concerned with "The Uses of Humanistic Schooling." His argument that education in the humanities disciplines is essential to an individual's acquiring "the tacit dimension" of mind—the background of knowledge that is necessary for one even to begin to think productively—is, we think, the most realistic and fundamentally important case that can be made for humanities study. Though it is not to be supposed that humanities study per se makes one wise or good, it is true, as Professor Broudy insists, that without such study one is simply not able to think at all about a great many subjects of immense importance. One lacks the necessary context to make sense of the questions and to ascertain how to go about trying to answer them.

Leon Botstein further explores the role of humanities study in the development of trained intelligence. Advocates of the humanities frequently claim that study of the humanities is crucial to the development of "the mind," but rarely do they specify why or how this is so. Together, the essays of Broudy and Botstein make this crucial case. Botstein examines the role of language in thought and suggests some ways that the humanities disciplines may be taught so as to take fuller advantage of their power to develop our command of language and thus our capacity to think.

The next three essays consider, in turn, the teaching of the principal high school humanities subjects—English, foreign languages, and history. Each combines trenchant analysis of the present condition of one subject at the secondary level—boldly daring to generalize about matters that could easily fill vast tomes if set forth in their extraordinary variety—with vigorously stated but thoughtful reformulations. Robert Fancher argues that while most high school English teachers have sound instincts, the leadership of their profession has not adequately fulfilled its responsibilities to provide a sound philosophic structure within which the secondary school English program can succeed. Fancher lays the foundation of such a structure, starting with the proposition that the foremost goal of the English program is to initiate children into what he terms "humane culture." He examines some of the prevailing philosophies of the English program, finding them individually helpful but in no case adequate for the task at hand. While resisting the temptation to develop a full-fledged curriculum, he sets forth a number of strategies that will assist the practitioner to evaluate and improve the English program.

Carlos Hortas argues that the ordinary ways that foreign languages are taught in schools hold little value for the humanistic purposes of language study. Pointing out the fundamental changes that competence in a second language can promote in our ways of understanding ourselves and others, Hortas argues that we should begin teaching foreign languages in grammar school and that we should expect no less than *fluency* in the second language from our high school graduates. To skeptics, Hortas makes the conclusive reply: Any person of normal intelligence can speak any language in the world, if only he has occasion to learn it.

Clair Keller depicts the fragmented and diluted state of history teaching in the schools. He argues that many students are deprived of the opportunity to develop the sense of time and place that history should give them. We can recover this opportunity at the secondary level by giving fresh educational legitimacy to history as narrative survey taught by methods that incorporate the soundest developments in modern "social studies" teaching.

A pair of case studies look into particular high schools to see what is being done in their humanities programs. Scott Colley examines three Tennessee schools, primarily with regard to their English programs. Gilbert Sewall looks at social studies teaching in several California high schools. A crucial lesson that emerges from both essays is that excellence is possible—and that we know this by the fact that in some cases excellence is clearly being achieved. But so, too, is mediocrity (or worse) in other cases, and occasionally within the very same schools.

These first seven essays deal directly with issues in the humanities. The next five chapters take up more general issues of schooling with attention to their impact on the humanities. Peter Pouncey presents a core curriculum for the college education of future high school teachers, and Edwin Delattre develops a vision for continuing education of those who teach through membership in bona fide intellectual communities. If Professor Pouncey's eloquent essay were heeded by the colleges that train teachers, and if school systems and teachers were to practice what President Delattre preaches, widespread criticism of the intellectual preparedness of our teachers would lose much of its force.

Gary Sykes reviews several major teacher education reform efforts of the last twenty years—Master of Arts in Teaching programs, the Teacher Corps, and competency-based education. His analyses of these reform efforts show clearly some conditions that are required for successful reform—conditions not consistently met by the efforts he examines. Beyond these specific lessons, though, he concludes that what is lacking most in teacher education reform is not ideas but a shared conviction of the value of teacher education. This reference to the lack of a shared vision of excellence provides an apt transition into the essays on teacher professionalism by Jon Moline and John Casteen. Moline argues that it is precisely because the teaching profession itself has not developed professional standards of performance which it is willing to enforce that teaching fails to qualify as a "profession" in the sense of the term that we apply to law, medicine, and the clergy. Casteen argues that the same flaw is one reason that teachers' efforts to obtain from the states greater rights to self-governance have failed. Both Moline and Casteen go beyond jeremiads, however, to describe terms and conditions that must be fulfilled if teaching is to become more professional—and both quite clearly believe that it must do this if we are to have better teaching of the humanities (or of anything else) and more effective schools.

Many participants in the first of our two conferences chided us for failing to commission a paper from the perspective of the school practitioner. We responded to this legitimate criticism by asking one of the nation's most eminent practitioners, who had attended the first conference, to take part in the second as well and to write for us an essay generally assaying the humanities in the schools. While Portland (Maine) school superintendent Peter Greer could write an entire manual on school improvement, here he necessarily confines himself to some keen observations about the humanities and the responsibilities and opportunities that administrators have for strengthening them.

In the final chapter, Chester Finn and Diane Ravitch take the opportunity to react, reflect, and recommend. Drawing on the wisdom and insights of the other participants in this project—of both the other authors and the conferees, whose experience and steadfastness taught us a great deal—and upon their own reading and experience in—and strong opinions about—the humanities in the nation's schools, they review the uses (and limitations) of the humanities, the central dilemmas that confront the schools, and the roles and responsibilities that must be assumed if significant improvement is to be made.

As will rapidly become clear, we and our colleagues have not spent our energies looking for villains to blame for the general conditions we deplore. In truth, there is plenty of culpability to go around, and no single "smoking gun" to search for, but rather a veritable armory of unwarranted assumptions and misguided ideas that have sorely wounded both the educational and general cultures.

We do, however, have many debts of gratitude to others who share both our concern and our hope (if not necessarily our every suggestion), debts that are but partially discharged by the publication of this book.

First and foremost are the authors of the essays that follow, and those of several other papers, speeches, and memoranda that enriched and enhanced the project as a whole. They met deadlines, accepted suggestions, revised, rewrote, and endured our editorial demands with goodwill and understanding. They participated energetically and sensitively in the Atlanta and Denver conferences, and each took a keen interest in the project as a whole. We would especially like to record our respect and gratitude to Dr. Benjamin H. Alexander, former president of Chicago State University and, more recently, of the University of the District of Columbia, whose stirring address to the Atlanta conferees evoked both the lofty vision and the deep compassion of that great educator, himself the grandson of a slave, and strengthened the convictions of those who believe, with him, that educational excellence in a democracy means "high but equal standards of excellence for every student" regardless of race, social class, or family circumstance. Conferees in Atlanta also benefited from the wisdom and learning of Professor David Halliburton of Stanford University, who contributed immeasurably to the participants' and our own understanding of English teaching; and from Professor Thomas Roby's extensive experience teaching the classics of the humanities to disadvantaged young people in inner-city Chicago. Denver conferees were able to discuss the difficulties of institutional change in teacher education programs with Harry Booth, Dana Professor of Religion at Dickinson College. They were treated, as well, to a captivating and moving address by Richard Rodriguez, author of *Hunger of Memory,* who spoke eloquently of the ways that we each shape our culture even as we are shaped by it. To all of these persons we owe lasting gratitude.

Second, the participants in our Atlanta and Denver conferences (identified in the appendixes) were a lively, sometimes feisty crew from every region and many states, who informed and invigorated our analyses with their own variegated experiences in the trenches of American education, with their keen insights, and with their relentless insistence on common sense. We had stipulated that prospective conferees present themselves as "teams," usually of three people, representing the three distinct domains of the education community that most influence high school humanities teaching—the schools themselves, the colleges of liberal arts, and teacher education programs. Each team was asked to submit an analysis of a problem encountered in humanities teaching in its locale and of ways that the resources of team members' home institutions could be marshaled, in concert, to ease the problem or overcome obstacles. From the applications alone we learned much—and wish our resources had allowed us to accommodate hundreds more of them. From those who were able to join us in Atlanta and Denver, we learned even more. A major purpose of the project was to encourage collaborations that would enlist school practitioners, teacher educators, university-based humanities scholars and education policymakers in joint ventures to improve high school humanities teaching in their communities. To a gratifying extent, this has occurred, and as a result there can today be found around the United States dozens of projects and activities—large and small, ambitious and modest—that were initiated, informed, or improved as a result of these conferences.

Third, we thank our fellow members of the Educational Excellence Network, a loosely knit nationwide confederation of scholars, practitioners, policymakers, and commentators united by a shared interest in the improvement of school quality at the elementary-secondary level. Based at the Vanderbilt Institute for Public Policy Studies, the Network provided the auspices under which the project operated, and many of its individual members contributed to the project's success.

Fourth, the National Endowment for the Humanities, guided by the vision and energy of Chairman William Bennett, provided far more than the material support that made the project possible. The personal interest shown throughout by NEH leaders and staff members—particularly Chairman Bennett, Director of Education Programs Richard Ekman, Myron Marty, Francis Roberts, and Carolynn Reid-Wallace—was so different from the usual bureaucratic relationship between a university-based project and a federal agency as to command special note. Though we must—and cheerfully do—assume responsibility for the results (save, of course, for Dr. Bennett's own introduction), if they have value it is due in no small part to the ideas, the energies, and the commitment of an extraordinary group of public servants.

Finally, we have benefited immensely from a competent, devoted, and imaginative staff based at Vanderbilt, including Andrea Sedgwick, Lottie Strupp, Lydia Ogden, Salli Gadini, Dot Blue, Pam Hall, Diane Sircy, and Holley Roberts.

As project directors, Chester Finn and Diane Ravitch especially want to note the superlative work of project manager (and coeditor) Robert T. Fancher, a young philosopher whose organizational skills are rivaled only by his personal energy and intellectual acumen.

WHY THE HUMANITIES?

The Uses of Humanistic Schooling

Harry S. Broudy

USES OF SCHOOLING

The purpose of this essay is neither to praise the humanities nor to bury them. They do not lack distinguished encomiasts. In times of trouble we still turn to the humanities for guidance. The question concerning their role in *schooling* is not whether they are desirable but rather whether they are postponable—a distinction, by the way, that has a venerable history. In Plato's *Protagoras,* young Hippocrates wakened Socrates at dawn demanding to be taken to the house of Callias, where Protagoras was visiting and holding court. Hippocrates was anxious to become a student of the famous Sophist, who claimed to make men better in every way, especially in the arts necessary for success in politics.[1] When Socrates quizzed the eager Hippocrates about what consorting with Sophists would do "to his soul," his young companion replied as the young always have, namely, that the long-term effects on the soul would be taken care of later, after career, fame, and fortune had been acquired.

15

Aristotle defined liberal studies as those undertaken for self-cultivation by men of virtue when free, i.e., when no longer constrained by careers and the duties owed to state and family. Clearly, in this sense, neither for Hippocrates nor modern youth in college or high school are liberal studies appropriate, and yet they have remained a more or less standard prescription for the education of adolescents, especially those destined to become members of social or economic elites. However, the link between the study of the humanities and social status has weakened; today professional studies are more direct roads to socioeconomic status than general or liberal ones, even for the well-born.

It would clarify the educational issue to distinguish the desirability of humanistic studies, however defined and justified, from their necessity. When faculties of the humanities, engineering, or law schools argue over budgets, one rarely hears denigration of the humanities. Like patriotism and high culture, they are undebatably admirable. But are they indispensable to the schooling of the young? If resources are limited, necessity supersedes desirability. Today one must argue that the humanities are indispensable to all the educated citizens in a modern, presumably democratic, and undeniably technologically dominated society.

To argue that the humanities are both desirable and necessary is a bit like claiming that a Cadillac is *really* more economical than a Chevrolet or that champagne and caviar are essential to health. It may be true, but who would believe it? However, strange as it may sound, today the educated mind really is essential and not dispensable. One must have the champagne and caviar to construe a highly interdependent, technically complicated, and precarious world. This claim is not synonymous with the attempt to sell the humanities as vocationally helpful. Some liberal arts colleges have taken this route, arguing that rhetorical skill and logical acuity will help anyone in any business or profession. This may lead to more enrollments and the continued employment of instructors, but it is more likely that professional schools (or corporations) themselves will teach the skills that their analysis has identified as essential. The general or liberal or humanistic curriculum in high school or college is hard to justify on a simple end-means analysis. This is so because these studies are not used as explicitly learned, but rather as general resources for virtually every situation in personal and professional life. It is in this use that they become indispensable. For these reasons, it seems profitable to ask how schooling is used and how the study of the humanities fits into these uses.

In previous writings, my colleagues and I have distinguished four distinctive uses of schooling:[2]

The first of these we call *replicative*. This occurs whenever a former student *recalls* something that he learned, in pretty much the form in which he learned it. Things learned by rote memory or habituation often come under this use, in postschool life; and recall tends to occur on the basis of standard "cues"—i.e., in the sorts of situations for which we were taught the items. "Replicative," then, means remembering what you learned, more or less when you are supposed to. A simple example would be any computation in comparative shopping: one remembers that eighty (cents) divided by sixteen (ounces) equals five (cents per ounce).

The second use of schooling is the *associative*. The notion of association is familiar: various items, including images, information, and ideas, become associated in one's mind, so that thinking of one calls up others. In this way, each item takes on a *context* in one's thought: when one thinks of that item, one thinks of it *as associated with* all sorts of other things. Seeing a flag at half mast, for instance, conjures images of death and statesmanship, public service and community grief, and of the deaths of persons like John Kennedy, for whom flags were dramatically lowered.

The third use of schooling is *interpretive*. Whenever we have to translate an experience into a set of concepts, we are exercising the interpretive use of our schooling. Explanations are the most common sort of interpretation: e.g., "Snow (an item of our experience) occurs because moisture high in the atmosphere freezes," invokes concepts of atmosphere, altitude, and the process of freezing to explain the cold white stuff that is falling. Evaluations and definitions are also typical types of interpretation, "What he means by that is . . . " or "That is good because. . . . "

Finally, there is the *applicative* use of schooling, in which one applies what one has learned to a situation, usually to solve some sort of problem or to effect some sort of change. The applicative use requires that one be familiar with the phenomena that constitute the situation, with the principles that explain them, and with the relevant technology that uses the principles to affect the facts. This should not be interpreted too "practically," however. We may use knowledge to get more knowledge or to invent instruments of investigation, and these are just as "applicative" as, say, using scientific principles and knowledge of local demography and geography to bring under control a sanitation problem.

A particular response to a situation may involve more than one use of knowledge. Thus the applicative presupposes some use of the other three, but these do not entail the applicative; the interpretive usually involves some of the replicative and associative, but the reverse is not necessarily the case.

Borrowing the notion of "tacit knowing" from Michael Polanyi, I hold that the associative and interpretive uses of schooling may be regarded as tacit. Certain school learnings, in this view, would function even though not recallable at will. And these, characteristically, include the learnings of the humanities.

If school studies are assessed on their replicative and applicative uses a decade or so after end-of-course examinations were passed, one finds most of what was studied as general education is either forgotten or not applied. The easy and, unfortunately, not uncommon inference is that it was a waste of time to study them in the first place. By contrast, skill training and professional curricula produce lasting and useful results. This is to be expected; for what can be recalled for long periods is what has been repeated frequently, and skills and professional knowledge are constantly repeated in use. Application entails not only the knowledge of principles of a discipline or disciplines, but also an intimate familiarity with the phenomena of a field of practice plus a technology that enables principles to become agents or causes of change. On these criteria the humanistic studies are bound to fail.

The humanities function instead through their associative and interpretive uses. We think *of them explicitly* while studying them in school, but in life we think and feel and act *with* them—tacitly, without being able to recall many of the details. The results of humanistic studies are largely context-building resources (logical, linguistic, and imagic) for association and interpretation. We may call the results of such context building either "patterns" or "structures" of mind, if that clarifies the point. These interpretative resources form the underlying framework with which we find orientation in dealing with information and problems.

Not only is the retention of course work in the humanities—or indeed in any courses not repeated and reinforced frequently—low and uncertain, but that such work is applied is even harder to demonstrate. In virtually every value domain and especially in those of the moral, intellectual, aesthetic, and religious, the humanities are supposed to be applied to the conduct of life. Indeed, the humanities are, in no small part, accounts of such applications, or attempts at application.

However, the claim elicits too many counterexamples to be convincing. It would be difficult, for example, to lay the horrors perpetrated throughout the centuries up to and through the Holocaust to lack of formal study of humanities. Goering pilfered the finest works of art he could lay hands on, and Hitler was a master of rhetoric.[3] It is almost a cliché that for conduct to follow doctrine (or even example) requires psychological and societal reinforcement that schoolwork does not usually provide. Furthermore, there is no lack of exemplary character and conduct by peasants and untutored saints. About the only examples of applying the humanities are to be found in the professional scholars who use them for teaching and research in their disciplinary specialities, in some members of the clergy in their sermons and counseling, and in a few old-fashioned orators.

To be sure, if language training and mathematics are included in the humanities or the liberal arts, there is a clearer case for application. Language usage is not only valuable in communication and persuasion, but is also a mark of social status and intelligence. Mathematics, of course, has a similar applicative value; but that the study of Latin and Greek classics, or even modern classics, in literature or history or philosophy or the fine arts is applied in an analogous way is doubtful indeed. For one thing, as will be discussed, to apply such studies requires an allusionary community that no longer exists, even among college graduates. The telling quotation from Milton or Tennyson or Yeats makes little impact on those who have never heard of these poets. Even biblical allusions fall flat on an audience that has not made the acquaintance of even the most familiar Bible stories.

The allusionary base is a store of symbols, images, signs, and languages *with* which we commonly think, feel, speak, and act; it is what goes without saying. Whatever the source of these materials, the participants in the culture take it for granted that the allusionary base will function to supply associations and interpretations. Some portions of this allusionary surround are shared by all members of the community; some are distributed by gender, age, status, or occupation. Its formal constituents are usually provided by tuition of some kind—initiation rites, schools, and the like. And here one comes upon a critical change in the composition of the allusionary base. The development of the various disciplines by scholars, from the time of the Sophists on, introduced contents to the allusionary base that could not be picked up informally. This intrusion of scholarship into the culture divided the community into those who were initiated into a scholarly discipline and those who were not. Even more disturbing was the introduction of norms that did not always or even usually coincide with those of the informal sector of the culture. Each scholarly discipline came under the authority of a guild, the members of which developed, promulgated, and purified that scholarship. A rough working definition of the educated mind, therefore, might be the acceptance of these scholarly disciplines not only as sources of materials to think and feel *with*, but also as authorities for the norms of the good, the true, and the beautiful.

The alleged failure of the public schools to integrate minority group children into the school system is better explained by the discrepancies in the allusionary bases of these groups than by genetic or racist hypotheses. When these dicrepancies are large, many remedial measures that theoretically ought to work do not. However, the mitigation of this diversity is derogated as the "melting pot" mentality by the educational left. Nevertheless, the melting pot does simmer away. Willy-nilly, the mass media, mass marketing, mass sports, and mass popular music exude a homogenizing influence that not even the most self-centered cultural enclaves can wholly exclude. A Greek, Chinese, Pole, or Hispanic who has lived in the United States for five years or more is immediately spotted as a "foreigner" on a return visit to the mother country. This is so even though the visitor can speak the mother tongue and has retained a fondness for childhood foods and perhaps even a strong distaste for the Americanisms he has acquired. It would be surprising indeed if the allusionary base were not so affected. But such "melting" at the edges is a slow process, and where economic and social discrimination make it even slower, the impact of the public school is discouragingly meager.

Education, formal schooling, in and of itself, does little to that part of the allusionary base which is formed by folkways and mores. Rather, formal schooling deals with the explicit organization of experience in the manner of the arts and sciences. But education develops an allusionary base of its own—that of the educated mind, which cuts across the customary class lines and even across the cleavages of cultural diversity.

Some of the context-building resources are cognitive structures with their respective entities, relations, and modes of inquiry. The several disciplines are distinguished by these structures, which, as has been suggested, were learned explicitly as testable end-of-course products. But without frequent repetition in daily life, these become tacit, and the details fall out of the schemata that make up the structure. Some of us who no longer can recite the table of chemical elements are tacitly aware of the notion of elements, atomic weights, and the properties of acids, bases and so forth. We may also be aware of recent developments that have changed the concepts of chemistry, even though we cannot recite them. History, literature, and language also have cognitive structures, and each leaves its skeleton, so to speak, in the context-building allusionary base *with* which we think.

Still another sort of content belongs in the context-building resources provided by schooling. Images—meanings of words and sounds and shapes—have been deposited by literature and the other arts. American travelers have frequently remarked that on their first visit to Rome, Athens, or London what they perceived was filtered through the imagic expectations built up by early school studies. (Indeed, if the perception did not conform to these expectations, they were inclined to doubt the genuineness of the reality rather than of their imagic expectations.) It is only a small stride from images to feelings and attitudes and from these to norms and preferences.

Tacit knowing is manifested not only in cognitive contexts as deposited by the study of the analytical subjects, but even more in evaluational lenses, stencils, and schemata. Norms are formed by the study of all disciplines including the literary, historical, philosophical, and aesthetic studies. After all, value norms are the objects of the humanities and of any subject used humanistically.

Yet as with the conceptual schemata, we are hard put after our school days are over to recall the details of the studies that still function in our daily life. Although the distortions time has imposed can sometimes be revealed by expert introspection or psychoanalysis, there is a sense in which not *having* to recollect the original experience is characteristic of the associative and interpretive uses of what was originally learned.

In urging the importance of the disciplines for associative and interpretive uses, there is a temptation to take the scientific subjects as models. Their logical structure is clear and the consequences of not mastering them no less so, not merely for good thinking, but also for good technology. There is a clear distinction between commonsense science and the educated kind. A parallel with the humanities is more difficult to "sell." Do art, philosophy, history, and religion purify or improve the accumulation of images, ideas, beliefs, and feelings? If the study of the humanities is indispensable to the educated mind, we must answer in the affirmative. Surely disordered feelings and value norms can be more dangerous than naive chemistry or physics.

But to make the case, it is necessary to dwell on how imagination and intellect create a whole new realm of being, the being of *possibility,* of what might be and what ought to be. How, for example, did such simple and direct physiological functions as feeding become dining, copulation become love, the need for shelter turn into architecture, and the impulse to fight into heroism? The record of these and similar transformations is the domain of the humanities; they provide the contexts for ordered feeling.

Inasmuch as associative and interpretive contexts are by definition tacit, i.e., not ordinarily at the focus of attention, it is difficult to describe them precisely. Lenses, stencils, and structures are figures of speech that convey what is intended. Each discipline provides its characteristic sort of stencil or lens that shapes and organizes whatever phenomenon is discerned through it. The educated mind can be characterized as one that uses these stencils with facility.

Humanistic study, then, can be said to provide the cognitive, imagic, and attitudinal contexts *with* which the citizen confronts the world. Training in vocational skills will not function in the same way, as becomes evident when a profession is forced by circumstance to expand the context of its practice beyond customary bounds. Medicine, law, industry, and engineering today operate in contexts that go beyond the particular skills and concepts of entry training embodied in their curricula. This is hardly surprising in an interdependent world made ever more so by electronic communication by mass media that influence not only information, but (even more) the images by which the public orders its feelings. If these considerations do not make the case for the humanistic studies in the secondary school, it is difficult to imagine what would.

Indirectly, the commitment of schools to a program of general education based on the scholarly disciplines solves or evades the thorny issue of cultural pluralism. As has been noted, the contexts (lenses, stencils, etc.) derived from the disciplines carry an authority that is not primarily or even significantly political. They are not culture-bound as are the mores, folkways, manners, and other interesting traits of diverse cultures. We cannot demand that the dominant culture of a society impose its peculiar folkways on all others; but the scholarly disciplines can be offered to all rational human beings and especially to the children they send to a public school. Perhaps these contexts define the genuinely public school.

CURRICULUM DECISIONS

What subjects shall count as humanities? The National Endowment for the Humanities has responded with more inclusiveness than some would like, yet any systematic inquiry that reflects on the human condition can make a bid for membership. The two-culture quarrel is still alive. The designation "College of Liberal Arts and Sciences" on many a university campus dodges the issue. Are the sciences liberal arts or not? Are science courses taught in the College of Liberal Arts and Sciences humanities but those taught in the College of Engineering not? Is a doctoral seminar in the history of medieval Britain humanistic or professional?

The comments I have made on the uses of knowledge have stressed the *use* of studies rather than their *subject matter*. In this view, literature, when studied for application, whether it is to improve reading or virtue, is not a humanistic study. Conversely, astronomy and biology, when studied for interpretation and understanding, are humanistic.

There is a sense, however, in which the fine arts, literature, philosophy, and history have firmer claims to the humanities designation than do the sciences. This is so because they deal more directly with attitudes and judgments. Science, in emphasizing predictable results, negates freedom, creativity, and autonomy, qualities that form the very essence of personhood.

Nevertheless, the sciences are also the products of the human mind, and among the most brilliant. They are the products of the imagination, which traffics in ideas of what could and ought to be. Humanistic education helps us to understand the differing manifestations of the human psyche, including the sciences, and to interpret life *with* the resources of all of them. It is only when the sciences are converted into tools for the control of behavior that the study of them as humanities comes into question.[4]

Accordingly, curriculum decisions involve choosing materials from the arts and the sciences and organizing them for humanistic use in post-school life. These choices are naturally contingent upon available time, the nature of the student body, and the characteristics of the teaching staff.

In making curriculum choices, "the classics" make a distinctive claim on the curriculum. A classic is usually a work that has withstood long and intense criticism; it has had a heroic career. It may also have been the climax of a long development or a bridging work between two phases of development of a discipline; or it may have been (although not realized at the time) a seminal work that anticipated the future in a creative way. Sometimes it has survived because of superb elegance or lucidity of form, as when we speak of classic simplicity. But classics as exemplars also have unusual pedagogical value. They yield unusually good returns for the time invested in their study. Above all, they have contributed so much to the allusionary store of the culture that they tend to be equated with that culture. Not to introduce students to that allusionary base and not to make it a resource for their associative and interpretive activity may be the most unwise of educational investment strategies.

However, the classics are not easily assimilated. They are old, and they assume an allusionary base of their own—one unfamiliar to later generations. To reinstate its images and symbols takes time and demands of the teacher expertise, patience, and imagination. But it pays. These are the windows to the past, and hence to the present that that past has shaped.[5]

The choice of materials for a sequential curriculum requires a joint effort by scholars and teachers. The authority of the "consensus of the learned" rests with the scholars, and only those who have participated in this consensus through formal study are entitled to exercise it. It is overly simple merely to require a degree in a subject for qualification as a teacher. The teacher also represents humanities study not as a vestibule to professional scholarship, but as an education that a citizen will use for explicit learning and, associatively and interpretively, in the formation of habits and qualities of mind. This is the decisive distinction between scholars and educationists. Only the scholar can speak authoritatively on this or that item in a discipline; only the scholar can pass judgment on the cogency of a theory or the adequacy of the research. However, scholars may not understand the ways in which the nonspecialists utilize the findings of the respective specialties to construe, say, newspaper and television accounts of events. Too often, the professional scholars in the disciplines disdain the educationists. Yet their own naivete, if not downright ignorance, of the conditions that obtain in public school instruction should be an embarrassment, not a source of arrogance. As for the educationists, after all allowances are made for the difficulty of teaching the young in schools that cannot select their pupils, it still remains crucial that their authority come from scholarship. It will not suffice simply to be "caring," "loving," and "creative," or to possess a bagful of survival tricks (sometimes called teacher competencies).

The scholars are correct to fear watered-down versions of their disciplines, and the educationists have to recognize that the designation "general" or "liberal" does not warrant diluted and flabby surveys of a field. Schooling *for* humanistic uses does not justify making these *uses* the object of study, either. On the contrary, for a school study to become useful tacitly, it has to be learned explicitly. We learn the structure of physics by working hard on the basic concepts and the detailed, particular experiments from which they were derived and by which they were tested. We use these concepts in later life associatively and interpretively by forgetting these details while retaining their structure. That is why curriculum selection is so important. For practical reasons, the contents have to be limited. But the way in which they are studied has to remain true to their disciplinary structures and cannot evade their demands upon the learner.[6]

Just how deep and extensive the detail need be for this purpose is a highly sophisticated judgment. The degree of detail most suitably employed in teaching a unit on the internal combustion engine would vary considerably for a physicist, an automotive engineer, and an auto mechanic. The challenge is to determine what one would teach for use by an "educated" automobile owner. Even so with the humanities. The trick is to impart the resources of a discipline, not as one would impart them to an incipient research scholar, but as they are needed by the "educated" human in his personal, social, and civic life.

TEACHING THE HUMANITIES

Do the humanities call for a special type of teacher? And, if so, special in what way? In the mode of one's training or in its contents? If the views I have expounded on the peculiarly humanistic uses of schooling, namely, the associative and interpretive uses, have any cogency, then the type of teacher commonly found on college faculties may not be the appropriate model for the high school teacher. And the fairly typical college graduate with a secondary teaching certificate may not be appropriate either. But, the bright graduate of a good college with a major in one of the liberal arts and no other immediate career plans is not necessarily the answer either.

We might paraphrase Quintilian's formula for the orator, "A good man skilled in speaking," to read, "A well-educated person skilled in teaching," provided we are willing to specify the meanings of "well-educated" and "skilled in teaching."

To do so requires breaking down "well-educated" into, first, the usual requirements of general education at the baccalaureate level; second, mastery of the contents of the humanistic materials to be taught; and third, cultural resources *with* which to teach. There will be some overlapping among these areas of a "well-educated" teacher's study, to be sure. One cannot generalize from the random collection of courses prescribed for degrees and certificates to grand analyses of teacher education; but some care will have to be taken to make up the deficiencies of most baccalaureate education of prospective teachers, especially deficiencies in those areas that have to do with the social, political, economic, and philosophical contexts of the school. Furthermore, there are studies cognate to a teaching field that are important for the teacher, but that do not ordinarily find their way into ordinary baccalaureate majors. The study of drama and dramatic technology may be a first-rate cognate study for the prospective English or history teacher, just as the history of metallurgy has been an interesting cognate field for the study of some of the fine arts.

"Skilled in teaching" usually refers to techniques of classroom control, the assignment of lessons, recitations, testing, and the like—the things that "methods courses" are supposed to provide the beginning teacher. One school of thought holds that these tricks of the trade are no more than common sense, proverbial wisdom, and simple apprenticeship. Another school argues that psychology provides scientific justification for one method over another; that teaching, in short, is a form of behavior control. The difference between these two views is radical. If teaching is a knack, then it is not a profession. For a profession claims the right to guide practice in a domain of experience by virtue of general principles, principles that not only generate rules and methods of practice, but provide the reasoning that sustains them.

My own analysis of the teaching process—into didactics, heuristics, and philetics—does not claim to be the result of systematic research, though some empirical evidence supports it.[7] It is based, rather, on rough intuitive distinctions that seem to capture some important characteristics of the ways knowledge is transmitted in school and used in nonschool situations.

The replicative use of schooling emphasizes *didactics*. A carefully wrought lesson plan covers the topics to be taught for long-term retention and accurate recall. The most systematic and reliable knowledge we have about pedagogy has to do with didactics. There are ways of disguising and sweetening the drudgery of didactic teaching and learning, but there is no way of eliminating it. Every discipline, however abstract, calls for rote learning of its terminology and its constants. Not all teachers and pupils take to didactics equally well, but some prefer it. It is orderly and reassuring in its clarity of purpose, methods, and criteria. One knows where one is, where one is going, and when one has arrived.

Yet a persistent criticism of traditional teaching of the humanities is that didacticians kill their very spirit. "Spirit" covers such characteristics as "critical thinking," "appreciation," "creativity," "inspiration," "imagination"—all presumed to be incompatible with systematic study and orderly school keeping.

Teaching by discussion, induction, discovery, dialogue, debate, and various inquiry procedures I call *heuristic*. Clearly, the associative, interpretive, and applicative uses of schooling resemble heuristic teaching more than they resemble the rote learning of didactics. Heuristic teaching makes complex demands on the teacher as well as on the student. Deprived of the orderliness of didactics, the sense of bewilderment, randomness, and loss of direction can be threatening. To keep discussion free and yet relevant; to follow an argument through the confusion of many voices and views; in short, to use it for critical thinking, requires a *facile but highly disciplined* mind. Such thinking develops only when exercised on problems with the logic of inference; when comparisons are finely honed and distinctions are tested for differences. Plenty of exercise is afforded by the subject matter of the humanities, but tests of interpretation and association on contemporaray materials are essential. The danger of heuristic teaching is confusion. Only the vigil for logical and substantive relevance to the topic of discussion prevents discussion from degenerating into noisy irrelevance. The price of good heuristics is difficulty of evaluation, strain in covering the material, and frustration on the part of some pupils. Socrates made his partners in dialogue uncomfortable. Good heuristics assume or pray that the didactics will be taken care of elsewhere; by homework, outside reading, or some other teacher. Without didactics, heuristics is just so much babble.

Good didactics and heuristics cover much of what is meant by "skilled teaching," but neither one nor both necessarily provide for what may be called *philetics*. Philetics is derived from the Greek word for love, covering a broad spectrum of relationships between pupil and teacher—from casual friendship, to adolescent crushes to sexual attachments. If we exclude gross physical aspects (as Plato urged) of this relationship between the youth and the older mentor, we get something akin to the "love of the ideal" that inspires both teacher and pupil. From Socrates to Mr. Chips, from the "Paper Chase" to "To Serve Them All My Days," the philetic component of teaching supplies its drama and distinctiveness. Even the negative aspects of a concerned mentor—sternness, severity, perhaps a certain rigidity—can also bring about positive results.

In studying the humanities, teacher and pupil are living through an experience that is more than an acquisition of skill and knowledge. Somehow, the teacher is expected to *be* what he or she teaches, or at least give a convincing imitation of it. Elite private preparatory schools used to choose teachers with teacup as well as scholastic competence. They were supposed to exemplify the roles that the young would assume in society, or at least the manners and mores of those roles. The humanities being among the "finer" things of life, their teachers were also to exemplify the finer forms of conduct—indeed, much finer than prevailed outside the school. The confidence of the pupil that what was being taught, however the manner, was in the long run a manifestation of love of the best *for* the pupil, has always been regarded as the most important ingredient in the humanistic teacher-pupil relationship, i.e., the philetic relationship. Perhaps the most important factor in philetics is credibility. Does the teacher exemplify the virtues his or her subject professes? How scientific in spirit is the science teacher? How humane the humanities teacher? This intangible can have tangible results, both for pupils and teachers.

Unfortunately, few teachers or pupils are equally at home with didactics, heuristics, and philetics. Most of us can do passably well with all three, but very few are equally good (or perhaps equally bad) in all three. The triple-threat paragon of the classroom is rare indeed. Hence we have to rely on a mix of faculty and pupils over the years to match learning and teaching styles. Whether the mix should be left to chance, or whether there is not some way in which superb didacticians, heuristicians, and philetic teachers can be deliberately matched with corresponding students in some appropriate sequence and pattern are questions I leave to the ingenuity of school administrators.

Although the knowledge base for training in the skills of pedagogy is neither strong nor extensive, school psychology is a serious and fruitful research enterprise. Furthermore, some teaching methodology (for example, the case study) is more than fad. There is no inherent theoretical or practical impossibility to assembling case studies that can serve to stabilize and standardize classroom practices, or to devising analogues to clinical study and internship in medicine or business or law to round out the teacher's professional training. In short, there can be a genuinely professional preparation for teaching. The difficulty does not lie in lack of intellectual resources but rather in the lack of any rational incentive for people to undertake it when market conditions give no sign that the choice of such training is rational. In our society, professional careers demand a high investment of time and cognitive strain. The preparation is long, and it demands study at a high level of abstraction. This is true whether the profession be law, medicine, engineering, or university teaching and research. The return on the investment is remuneration, prestige, social status, and psychic satisfaction.

Neither in the investment nor in the return is school teaching in the elementary or secondary school professional.

We must ask what level of preparation we require from teachers in the humanities. That is much the same as asking what level of professionalism we seek. How high is that level, and how much is the public willing to pay for it? Either we demand of teachers the investment that a genuinely professional preparation requires, and then make that investment worthwhile, or we continue to make do with a more or less random collection of courses and a meager dose of practice teaching. We might get by with the latter sort of teacher training if a monitoring class of professionals were in the schools to oversee beginning teachers, but such a class is precisely what the school establishment lacks. Supervisors and principals can help, but they do not stand to the classroom teachers in the same relation as does the engineer to the machine operator, the physician to the nurse, or the architect to the builder. Perhaps the schools cannot or will not people all the classrooms with personnel at the professional level, but until a few of them are on every school staff, we shall have to rely on occasional miracles for the kind of results we profess to want.

An M.A. in the subject matter may not do the trick either. Instead of completing the preparation of the humanistic high school teacher, it may be the prelude to the college professor manqué, and a disgruntled one at that. A master's in the teaching of the humanities would complement the baccalaureate major if it stressed the sorts of considerations with respect to the uses of schooling proposed in this essay—the considerations of providing schooling not for incipient research scholars but for educated human beings who can teach our children as we want them to be taught.

NOTES

1. Later, Cicero, discussing the training of the orator, i.e., the orator as legislator and lawyer, raised the question in classic form as to the place of the liberal arts in a professional school.

2. Broudy, B. O. Smith, and Joe R. Burnett, *Democracy and Excellence in American Secondary Education* (Chicago: Rand McNally, 1964). See also my essay, "Tacit Knowing as a Rationale for Liberal Education," in *Teachers College Record* 80, no. 3 (February 1979), 446–462.

3. Alfred North Whitehead once noted that the Renaissance witnessed a remarkable pursuit of beauty, but that it was a pursuit by bandits.

4. Vico may have been right to differentiate the externality of the givens of nature and the internal origins of human activity, but the understanding of the

externals of nature is not less instigated and sustained by the activity of mind. Insofar as all thought is human, the distinction between the *Naturwissenschaften* and *Geisteswissenschaften,* as far as their humanistic import is concerned, loses its decisiveness.

5. There are many prescriptions and formulas for studying a classic such as the *Iliad* or the *Divine Comedy.* The footnotes are a clue to the method and hint at the scholarly erudition needed to decode the work. Some of these aids are necessary to avoid embarrassing anachronisms and wildly unhistorical interpretations. However, if a great work of art or literature or philosophy cannot speak directly to the reader, its usefulness as an educational resource, especially for general education, is limited. In one collegiate experiment, it was found that for an average upper-division class, three hours a week for thirteen weeks were needed to reach the stage when the classics named above were speaking directly rather than being translated. Only then could it plausibly be claimed that the work was revealing another culture through its own eyes.

6. We do not know and often cannot trace the changes that an item entering consciousness undergoes over the years. The analog of fermentation and distillation is a tempting one; and although untrustworthy, it is nevertheless true that vintners do not bottle the mash, without which there would be no wine.

7. Rodney A. Clifton, "An Empirical Evaluation of Three Orientations Towards Teaching: Philetics, Didactics, and Heuristics," in *The Modes of Teaching,* R. R. Magsino and J. R. Covert, eds. (Washington, D.C.: University Press of America, 1977). See also Donald S. Seckinger, "The Teaching of the Social Foundations: Didactics, Heuristics, or Philetics," *McGill Journal of Education* 9 (Fall 1974), 213–224. Also, my "Three Modes of Teaching and Their Evaluation," in *The Evaluation of Teaching,* ed. William J. Gephart et al. (Bloomington, Ind.: Phi Delta Kappa, 1976).

Language, Reasoning, and the Humanities

Leon Botstein

When we speak of teaching the humanities, we ought to imply thereby teaching the whole range of disciplines that constitute the humanities— history, philosophy, literature, languages. But in the high school, relatively little of the humanities is taught at all. Usually there is English—or, as has become fashionable in education circles, "language arts"—and a bit of history as part of "social studies." At most schools some foreign language is taught to some students; but is is not at all clear that the methods used in most such courses add much to the students' understandings of what it is to use language, of how language informs thought, or how our substantive views about the world are embodied in the very grammar and vocabulary of language. Even to try to talk about teaching the humanities is schools is, then, something of an odd task.

For at least some seventy years several canons of secondary education orthodoxy have militated against the notion that study of the humanities ought to be at the heart of every person's education. One such belief is the notion that the humanities are beyond the abilities of most students. Another is the notion that the humanities contain little of cognitive worth, when measured by an obvious standard of utility. This notion is manifest whenever the humanities are alleged to be "luxuries" or "matters of taste."

In fact, study of the humanities is not beyond any person of normal intelligence, provided he or she commands some intelligible form of language, spoken and written; and far from having little cognitive value, the humanities disciplines are crucial to the development of intelligence, which in turn is at the heart of any sense of utility.

This essay offers a complex program: how the humanities disciplines might well be taught in the schools if their essential function in the development of students' minds is to be encouraged. That function is indicated, as is why study of the humanities is not beyond any normal student who, upon entering the classroom, commands enough language to carry on normal and often complex conversations. Implicit—and on occasion explicit—will be criticisms of a number of normal ways of doing business in the schoolrooms; but the primary aim is not critical. Rather, the aim here is the constructive one of encouraging teachers to help students learn to think well—whoever those students may be.

In the high school curriculum, the binding characteristic of the several sorts of study grouped as the humanities is the use of language. The command of language—its structure, its elements, its words, and its grammar—through writing, speaking, naming, declaiming, arguing, persuading, commanding, describing, interpreting, and reading is at the heart of any successful study and teaching of the humanities. In the high school curriculum it is initially in the humanities subjects that language plays a crucial role in students' classroom performances. This is neither surprising nor bad. It is not surprising, for the language of the humanities derives from "ordinary" rather than specialized or "ideal" languages, "natural" rather than artificial ones. In contrast, the language of the sciences is usually technical and theoretical. Despite the dependence of science on mathematics and non-ordinary theoretical claims about reality, a serious command of ordinary language is essential for the development of intelligence for all careers and endeavors in life. Every scientist's or technician's mastery of a technical language presupposes command of ordinary or natural languages. The inseparability of language use from thought can therefore occasion a unifying theme and a fruitful curricular and pedagogical strategy for high school humanities programs. In each of the subjects of the humanities, we must give attention to both the common language at the heart of all the humanities as well as the more suspect specific modes of language discourse. As we do so, we must make students critically conscious of language; awaken them to its dynamic and historic character, to its wonders and mysteries; teach them to use its power and engage its complexity. Last, we must arm them with the aesthetic and reflective capacities to command language as the essential instrument of self-expression and analysis, the route to comprehending and interpreting the thought of the world, past and present.

Three general pedagogical approaches—which should be used together—will be explored as a potential high school humanities curricular strategy devoted to teaching language-as-instrument-of-thought. First is the philosophical, in which language is viewed as the mechanism by which claims and inferences are made and questioned, true and false assertions disputed, arguments dissected, and words and phrases understood in terms of knowing, supposing, describing, performing—the acts and the situations for those acts that language makes possible; in other words, the ways in which cognition takes place.

Second is an etymological approach, in which individual words or phrases of particular importance are studied in depth. Initially one can talk about the roots of words, the origins of words, and the changes that have overcome word use in various phrases, sentences, and situations, all as an avenue to understanding current uses directly under study. This approach illuminates historical changes in structures of perception and belief. It introduces the student to a sort of archaeology of ideas. This avenue of study creates a bridge to teaching the skill of interpretation by enabling the student to perceive intentions and meanings in texts and to distance him- or herself consciously, in the act of reading, from the words on a page. The student encounters the varieties of understanding and meaning that a text can inspire and struggles with what appears to be the *objective* text and the spectrum of plausible *subjective* understandings, starting first with one's own.[1]

Neither of these approaches is dependent upon any great prior sophistication on the part of students. The philosophical approach assumes only, at the outset, the students' everyday language, their ordinary grammar, vocabulary, and usage. It builds in complexity from the students' common uses of languages. Likewise, the etymological approach can easily start with particular commonplace syllables and words. The two approaches are connected: the philosophic technique of questioning the uses of ordinary speech leads to an interest in the constituents of language, in words and their history. This in turn leads into the history of ideas and thinking. Once the student becomes aware (critically) of the fascinating and complex significance of actual and potential ways of speaking and encounters the historic career of speaking and writing, he or she begins to reflect back again on everyday usage. In this way we can teach language's dynamic, still evolving character—its continuing power.

The third and final approach is aesthetic. It is both parallel to and derivative from the philosophical and the etymological. In the aesthetic approach, language is taught and used as an "open-ended" means to the student's expression of ideas, wishes, opinions, and observations on whatever subject is under scrutiny. The free exercise of writing is encouraged. The intent of this approach is to assist the student's evolution of a distinct—but, in due course, aesthetically disciplined—way of expression and to encourage the student's desire to command writing as a personal tool. The student, individually, begins to extend the tradition of speaking and writing and contributes a new body of written work to be considered, first by peers and teachers. The matter of style is raised in this approach. Style emerges only as an aspect of saying and believing something; as integral to the content of students' work defying the false notion of style as the almost arbitrary "clothing" of ideas. Hence the notion of "aesthetic" discipline becomes an element in the development of intelligence.

THE PHILOSOPHICAL APPROACH

"After all," wrote Ludwig Wittgenstein, "one can only say something if one has learned to talk. Therefore in order to want to say something one must also have mastered a language; yet it is clear that one can want to speak without speaking. Just as one can want to dance without dancing."[2] This observation offers the starting point for the philosophical dimensions of teaching language in the high school. Students seem to want to say something; they command a quite complex ordinary language. Yet they usually keep wanting to say more than they actually do or even think they can. There is invariably some distance between the fluidity and eagerness of the most ordinary of passing conversation among peers, in the halls or over the telephone, and what students present to teachers in even the most successful teaching context.

However, usually it turns out that even in schoolwork (after the fact) a student "wanted" to say something other or more than he or she did. The connection between the student's unexpressed desire to present ideas and the successful attempt to do so (and the prior motivation to want to) is the student's common ordinary language—which, in the instance of peer talk, often suffices, but in the case of quite demanding uses, especially in writing (inquiry about one's language, feelings, beliefs, opinions, one's hopes and fears), does not. A vague image of how to say something often is lodged in the student's mind. The student is captive to the inability to move from the "image" of saying something elaborate, extended, and serious to the confidence and the capacity actually to do so.

The solution does not lie in more sophisticated vocabulary or fancy information. The starting point (and the end point, ironically) for the teacher is the student's quite ordinary, if banal, speech. The first illusion to penetrate (held, unfortunately, by many teachers as well as students) is the romantic notion that thinking is a silent, inner feeling that either cannot be expressed, or "loses" something when put into words. Students and teachers persist in the view that, despite its messy prose and linguistic confusion, a paper still shows that it "contains good ideas." They imagine that the student says more than he actually says: they do not recognize that only what one can *say* can one *think*. They do not recognize this, perhaps, because they have not realized that *ideas,* even unspoken, have linguistic form. Once this is realized, though, the student, using ordinary talk, can be led to generate and express thoughts about much more than he or she ever imagined. The student can also be led to reflect on what, in fact, he or she is saying, doing, or implying as he or she engages in and expands the range of everyday talk—the intricate logic of ordinary language.

Every student does, in fact, ordinarily engage in at least prototypical discourse characteristic of humanities subjects. Students hear and tell stories, whose quite-well-understood meanings lie in symbolic and indirect uses of words and images. They make historical claims constantly, if only about what happened last week or last year. In the ordinary ability of a student to speculate on what so-and-so did at some point in the past lie the tools of historical inquiry. In every "Why did you do that?" and in every commonplace explanation offered in reply, lie the roots of ethical discourse and philosophical analysis. The problem with students is not that they lack resources to understand the questions of the humanities subjects and to pursue those questions, or even that these activities are foreign to ordinary life. The problem is that too rarely do students or teachers understand the relations of language to thought, or the nature of ordinary language and its relation to sophisticated thinking.

With the philosophical approach, one begins in the classroom to look at acts of ordinary speech that lend themselves readily to expansion into the sophisticated, complex discourse of the humanities. In whatever subject one teaches, one may start by asking the students simply to talk and by leading them through analysis of how what they say reveals how they think and how they might then reflect further on how they might think. In history, perhaps, one simply asks students to tell of an incident in the past, then draws attention to the logic of the telling, the words used to indicate various sorts of inferences, various sorts of evidentiary relations between the different parts of what is said. One may then have students write down such ordinary narratives and dialogue exchanges and analyze their writing, with an eye toward the same sort of understanding of the revelation in language of how they have thought. One uses peers as the

critical audience. Then one is ready to move into texts. When the move into texts is made, of course, one does not drop reference to ordinary language. Constant reference to parallels between the discourse of the text and the student's own ways of talking are necessary, both to enable the student to understand fully what is going on in the text and to clarify the contrasts with his or her own intellectual perspective.

Through this whole process, the student is brought to realize how much more he is able to do than he thought. When the student thinks that ideas have to "come to him," and then be put into words, but ideas somehow don't come; or when he thinks that understanding the text is a mystical process of decoding a set of symbols on a page, and then the arrangement of letters fails to excite the expected mystic revelations; or when he thinks that he knows much more than he can say but just "isn't good at expressing himself"—at these times it is no wonder that the student despairs of understanding. And when the teacher shares the same misconceptions, there should be no wonder that teachers become convinced that some students just cannot learn or that verbally or conceptually oriented subjects are beyond students not from advantaged social backgrounds. The advantaged student often may have a superficial awareness of how language works and how to read texts, because people and activities in his background have taught him this. The less advantaged student simply does not know how much he knows or is capable of knowing.

The approach urged here, if done well, can build the student's confidence. Only with increased confidence in her own speaking and writing *as* embodied thinking, a command of language, of academic subjects related to ordinary language, can the student be led to move easily in the discourse of the discipline. The student must know herself *to be able,* if she is *to try.* In the early stages of the approach urged here, the key is not to crush the student's confidence with overly severe criticism—though one must, if this approach is to work at all, be firm in insisting that a searching, critical analysis of one's talk be done. Only with increased care and confidence in *speaking as thinking and doing* will motivation and more (far more) competence in thinking be nurtured.

Argument and questioning must be sustained and as regular as daily jogging or training for a high school sports team. It also needs to be as cooperative. The student can be brought to a critical awareness and linguistic facility, both remarkable and sophisticated in nature, starting and ending with how actual language does and ought to work. Austin provides the commanding insight of this way of teaching: "First, words are our tools, and, as a minimum, we should use clean tools: we should know what we mean and what we do not, and we must forearm ourselves against the traps that language sets us. Secondly, words are not (except in their own little corner) facts or things: we need therefore to prise them off the world, to hold them apart from and against it, so that we can realize their inadequacies and arbitrariness, and can relook at the world without blinders. Thirdly, and more hopefully, our common stock of words embodies all the distinctions men have found worth drawing, and the connections they have found worth marking, in the lifetimes of many generations. . . ."[3] It is Austin's final assertion that teachers of adolescents need most to keep in mind. Language is the business of the humanities; its grasp will empower our young students who are at the brink of taking their proper place in the sequence of generations. They come to us from all sectors of our population, rich and poor, despite obvious deficiencies, with considerable facility and complexity in language use. It is the teacher's task to uncover the consequences of their language use, inspire critical reflection on it, and extend considerably the student's command of language.

THE ETYMOLOGICAL APPROACH

Of the three primary strategies of teaching the humanities through language, the etymological approach concentrates most on single words. Their meanings and their uses, their exact placement in phrases or sentences are studied. Clearly, there is some overlap with the philosophical approach, since the varieties of uses and import of words are discussed. The significant distinction to be drawn, however, is between this etymological approach to language teaching, on one hand, and vocabulary building through usage or memorizing of definitions (both in themselves not bad things to do), on another. What is suggested by the etymological approach is a search into the roots of the words, both in the traditions of English and American usage and in foreign languages. Historical changes can be key, especially in their varied contexts. The student learns how a word was used at a different time. The historical roots of the words are then discussed in ways that reflect residues in meanings in texts under study.[4]

This etymological approach, like the philosophical, raises the student's general cognitive ability by raising his understanding and command of language. Once one establishes the origins of a word and its syllables, and chronicles, with examples, the career of the word, a bridge is built to questions central to the sort of understanding characteristic of the humanities. Not only can one ask what Pericles meant by "freedom" and "excellence," say; but also what clues does a contemporary contrast with his usage tell us about Pericles and ourselves? What do the meanings of words, as signs for feelings or beliefs, tell us about the world view of any group of people, past and present, who employ a particular language? The student might hear echoes of prior meaning buried in the roots of a common word. The student can locate ancient resonances that a word still carries. Without a discussion of roots and the career of usage, such insight would not be possible.

We too frequently slide over changed meanings and merely inform the student what a word (even a quite common one) now used differently or now not at all (why not?) meant, in, let us say, Shakespeare's day. Why have certain words become archaic, or uses obscure and forgotten? An opportunity is missed for teaching about Shakespeare's world and our own, and about alterations in habits, attitudes, and values. In searching for roots in "loaded" words, residues of literal meanings can be hints to the underlying significance and use of those words. What pictures are conjured up by certain words, and how have those pictures been forgotten or altered?

In overused significant and clichéd words (e.g., "voluntary," "free," "liberty") the origin and shifts in usage and meaning provide insight into different ways of assuming crucial things about humans, our nature, and our social and political association. Even in our customary practice of replacing one word with another as supposedly an approximate equivalent—a thesaurus-like view of words as a matter of style and rhetorical eloquence—actual contrasts in buried meaning and current emphasis can be illuminated. For example, contrast "to be at liberty" and "to be free." Why can one be "libertine," or "liberated," and yet not be quite the same thing as "free?" Why is "at" used with liberty and "be" with free? Word expansion and contraction into different parts of speech and the significance of such linguistic alterations can also be studied.

In American history, word usage and emphasis in the creation of phrases and slogans are keys to how matters of justice and right, for example, were once viewed. What implicit remainder and visible changes exist in our current political debates? The instruments for this approach are texts that, studied in sequence, can uncover the history of word meanings in political discourse. The next stage would be for the teacher to encourage an examination of the current use of comparable key words by students. The same can be done with literary texts in descriptions of characters, their motivations and actions. Compare past and present usage of, for example, words like "original" and "creative," "arbitrary" and "logical," when applied to figures in novels and short stories.

This etymological approach, when applied to, let us say, "spirit," "genius," and "essential," leads us deeper into the history of thought. The mind-body problem, the belief in ideals, the claims of materialism, all appear. Furthermore, the legacies of natural right theory and social contract theory come into view. The discussion of simple words of daily life can provide a window not only into the history of daily life and social-groups but of the assumptions behind social institutions—hospitals, jails, churches, schools, banks, markets, stock exchanges. Words like "civilization," "civility," "civilized," and "cultured" (as in a pearl?) open up anthropological claims, issues of cultural evolution, assertions of a social psychological nature. Using a limited set of texts and a few words, the teacher can open up large vistas in the humanities.[5] And—for those who deny the "relevance" of academic humanities to ordinary life—we note that this is an inherent movement in awareness of even ordinary language.

Imitation can be employed as a useful teaching technique. The student can be asked to write using key vocabulary in ancient ways, approximating archaic colloquialisms. The student becomes sensitive to the altered meanings by trying to use them in old ways. The contrast—as well as the character of current everyday usage—becomes clearer this way. The student can imitate rhetorical and literary styles in addition to word use.[6]

The student can be asked to discuss situations in which particular words change their meaning; situations in which onlookers might get different impressions. Issues of rhetoric and style in the service of a strategic use of language in a particular context can be raised, including those of the sound and pace of language use. Ample opportunities to read closely classic examples of rhetoric and cultivated styles must be provided. They can be used to spur active imitation centering around particular words and phrases. How have clichés emerged, and why do they retain their function?

Freud observed that the mind contains ancient memories and modern realities side by side, requiring a variation on archaeological excavation. However, the mind is not like a village in which, over time, shacks are destroyed only to be supplanted completely by new buildings. Like the mind, language, in individual words, retains memories of past usages in the present. In words, in the constituents of words, in speech and in texts, past and present stand side by side albeit in fragments, some looking back and others pointing forward.[7]

The student is now on the brink of moving on to a key skill of the humanities: interpretation. This skill is bound up with reading. The etymological strategy helps to inspire the reading of texts initially in a historical mode, as expressions of intention and communication in worlds gone by that can be partially reconstructed. From individual words in phrases, that reconstruction builds to meaning generated by larger passages. It is crucial for the teacher to remember that generalizations or other interpretive concepts need not be placed initially in front of the student. Too often, textbooks and classroom teachers interrupt the student's capacity to reconstruct and interpret actively through reading, by providing for the student ready-made conclusions that the student simply verifies by reaching into an original document merely for surface correspondence with textbook assertions.

By starting with words, then moving to sentences and to larger sections of a text, the student can generate, through careful critical reading, interpretive conclusions well beyond those a textbook wants to hammer home. The key is, of course, to offer the student original texts extensive enough to present a coherent point of view but short enough to be studied in great detail. A letter exchange (e.g., Justice Holmes with Harold Laski; Mozart and his father) or a speech (e.g., the Lincoln-Douglas debates, selections from the seventeenth century in England or the French Revolution) can be starting points. Larger arguments divided into manageable forms or particular chapters and discrete sections can come next (e.g., selections from Montesquieu, aphorisms, the shorter dialogues of Plato).

Following this mode of analytical reconstruction through the reading of texts and focusing on language use, the student can move into the analysis of forms. Here the significance of genre, the structural framework, and the rhetorical cast of a work are discussed. Historical examples and current models can create strong contrasts. Autobiographies, letter exchanges, words of scientific description and explanation, speeches, state papers, diaries, journals, biographies, documents of travel, novels, plays, newspaper articles, poems, works of political argument, history books, all should make an appearance. The student can compare the form of presentation, the use of devices and conventions. Students begin to witness the heritage, the continuity and the extension, by imitation and alteration, of traditional forms of cultural expression.

After the formal approach, the teacher can move into the widest and most challenging arena: how one teaches the student, in reading, to confront the language, ideas, and views of a text, and to formulate a worked-out interpretation that he or she is willing to argue and defend. What does a passage or an entire work say as we read it now? The impact of the philosophical teaching approach becomes visible. Setting aside for a moment the fact that Rousseau wrote in the eighteenth century, or that Henry James finished a novel over eighty years ago, what do their texts seem to say? It is startling how much can be gleaned by the student from the text (even without access to a body of prior insight and information helpful in decoding meaning). The student should not read modern commentaries first. The student must be taught to extract meaning from the text himself. How many kinds of readings might be justified? Why? How does one justify one's reading of a text? Furthermore, how does what we think and know influence what we deem significant in what we read?

For example, how have generations of readings of the Constitution changed how we understand it? Are we not only influenced by what the text seems to say to us; what we believe the framers intended; and what, in our context and culture, we assume its words and phrases mean; but also by the career of constitutional interpretation? What meanings have been "sewn" into the text? The "reception" of a text can often be barely separated from our sense of the "original" even as we begin to read it for ourselves. The First Amendment to the Constitution and any of the Bill of Rights are cases in point. The student must make sense of the ideas of the Bill of Rights by reference to the text. The student must be challenged to present his or her own views on those assertions. But we are dealing not only with the original authors, but with our national legacy of *accepted* and debated readings that has somehow been absorbed into the language of the text itself. Restoration, reconstruction, and interpretation can become identifiable, distinct skills of reading.

Students then not only begin to grasp the possible meaning of an "original" intent and "historically valid" reading, but they encounter the gradual detachment of the text from its own birth. Most critically, the student joins in on the process of reinterpretation and rewriting of significant texts and their central claims. Reading becomes not only a task of problem solving and puzzle completion but the creative generation of serious meaning.

Another useful example is a careful reading and discussion of the first lines of the Declaration of Independence, focusing on assertions like "We hold," and phrases like "self-evident," words like "endowed" and "equal." A view of man, of "truth," of what constitutes a "scientific" argument, of nature, of history, of how one seeks to convince someone of the contrast between mere personal political opinion and alleged human certainties can be revealed. What is the structure of the Declaration's argument? What are its assumptions? All this is asked of the text itself, without the usual barrage of general statements found in American history textbooks. The student learns how to read historically, critically, and actively; to grasp a set of beliefs and assumptions perhaps foreign to his own. He or she can use this analytical, interpretative, and critical skill on texts of greatness and gain insights far stronger than any gained from reading generalizations cast in the modern prose of a textbook writer.

A central teaching assignment is asking the student to recast a text in his or her own words. Asking for a detailed presentation, clarification, and summary of a text is an indispensable teaching technique. This use of the *explication de texte* mode of teaching reading in America has untapped advantages. Two criteria should be used when a student is asked, for example, to present a written *précis* of the argument in "Federalist No. 10" in his or her own words. First, a reasonable correlation between the text and the student's presentation must be found and defended. There are canons of accuracy and plausibility in one's view of the meaning and structure of argument in a preexisting text. The student is not asked to repeat or condense. Rather the student is asked to remake the argument and reveal its bases and development. Second, the student then applies philosophical analysis to discern what the writer seems to mean and what critical questions might be raised. By comparing the original with one's own version, not only are one's precision and insight as a reader enhanced, but one's self-knowledge, one's recognition of one's ówn assumptions, inferences, claims, and impressions of meaning and belief on the same and comparable issues, is clarified. In this process of writing about texts, strictly in terms of presenting and clarifying meaning (not writing from the text in an amorphous, tangential, or personal way), and reconstructing precisely and in detail the arguments of a given text, sensitivity to rhetorical devices, style, logic, essential assumptions, short-cuts in defense, strengths or weaknesses in argument of the original and of one's own beliefs become clearer.

The reading aloud and memorization of passages are also to be recommended. Hearing how the original sounds (even in the case of one's own writing) and witnessing matters of location and emphasis, phrase by phrase, word by word, as they have impact on a listening public are a help in learning how to read and interpret. In the process of reading writing aloud, one feels and recognizes Wittgenstein's insight: "Speech with and without thought is to be compared with the playing of a piece of music with and without thought." Reading aloud is a special and illuminating form of speaking words and can reveal when there is thought and when there is not. By writing about what one reads, and by reading along both text and commentary, students can more quickly avoid "playing" a piece of thinking (in the sense of music) thoughtlessly. The faculties of discernment and judgment crucial to the humanities come alive, not only to the eyes and the mind, but to the ears as well.

THE AESTHETIC APPROACH

The third and final strategy for teaching language as thinking in a high school humanities curriculum is, for lack of a better term, called the "aesthetic" approach. The first step in this approach is to ask the students to keep a journal every day in which they write whatever comes to their minds over the course of thirty minutes, initially without particular reference to subject matter, word order, grammar, syntax, spelling, or sequence of thoughts. In this way the students compile a notebook of thoughts and phrases comparable, in its ideal form, to the sketchbooks of composers or painters. In most cases the students will realize (some at first and most later) that for their thoughts to be comprehensible, even in a fragmentary and spontaneous format, grammar, spelling, and syntax are crucial. As the students progress in the philosophical and etymological parts of the curriculum, that sensitivity to the essential rules of language will no doubt increase. The purpose of "free writing" in this portion of the curriculum is to encourage the students to use language regularly and consistently in written form for the full range of their feelings, reactions, and experiences. This writing ought to remain private, even though it may well be done in class at a scheduled time when all students are asked to make their journal entries.[8]

However, the students should be asked each week to write up some aspect of their journal entries (or some other part of their thoughts and feelings) without reference to a particular assignment or subject, in a form that can be shown to teachers and peers. Students should be encouraged to use their journals as the raw material. The length of this assignment is short. The students should then be asked to read each of these writings aloud, to correct it, rewrite it, and expand on it. At the end of a given period of time (every two weeks, for example) the students are asked to complete and submit one of these very short pieces of writing (a page or two) without errors. These pieces of writing should then be circulated to other students. The point here is to show the students that their thinking and writing can be of consequence and have meaning for others. The achievement of an effective use of language, therefore, becomes more than a private experience or a necessary aspect of survival in one's school.

These exercises, when performed regularly and reviewed consistently and critically by teachers and peers, can lead a large number of students to original writing of poetry, fiction, and "self-motivated" essays. This clearly should be encouraged and the results made public in the school community. This approach to writing will also encourage the writing of journalistic pieces for school magazines and newspapers. Some students may be encouraged to interview members of the adult and student communities, write family histories, work on local and regional histories, using interviews and anecdotal remembrances rather than social-scientific research as the basis for their writing. All such projects have a link to the personal origins of the journal writing and short personal paper exercises.

It must be remembered that these excercises occur simultaneously with philosophic and etymological approaches. As students develop confidence and facility in writing and thinking, greater focus and discipline can be required of the regular journal writing. Still starting exclusively from their own individual interests, students are nonetheless taught to write coherently, clearly, and effectively. This strategy offers the opportunity for the teachers to teach the skills of rewriting and editing. Students will also realize that the first effort at writing something down may have to be organized to give effective voice and the proper form to what they want to say, that thoughts develop only through active effort—and that they do *develop* as they are worked over.

In order for this approach to work—for the students to be genuinely encouraged to employ writing as a daily instrument of personal expression—the teachers must participate actively. Too many teachers of writing do not write themselves. They, like their students, must display finished work that can be commented on and responded to by students. They should keep a journal in school as well and write in the thirty-minute journal-writing session too. They must, by their own examples, give courage to the students, not only to write but to have their writing read and commented on by others. All adults who write realize that what they produce always undergoes critical review, editing, and even rejection. It is not reasonable for the adult community to try to inspire the regular, committed employment of writing among the far-more-vulnerable adolescent if they, as adults, do not practice what they seek to encourage. No serious music teacher would attempt to teach an instrument without playing one him- or herself. No artist would seek to teach drawing without doing it as well. If a command of language about matters we all can talk about is a common objective for all of us, there is no technical or pedagogical barrier to teachers demonstrating that command in whatever way they see fit to do so. It need only be visible to the students.

The aesthetic approach, conducted in tandem with the previous strategies, encourages development of the motivation to engage and command language. Too many observers and critics of the contemporary scene have commented on the triumph of visual stimuli (television and video games) and nonverbal ways of expression in our culture to bear repeating such comments here. The crucial insight for the purposes of teaching the humanities in high school is that speaking, writing, and reading are skills whose decline cannot be reversed among our students merely by more clever approaches to in-school teaching. If the roots of the decline in literary interest and clear and powerful thinking among students are beyond the school, then the school must confront those deeper roots by addressing the challenge of motivating the student to employ language in the first place. Since language is at the heart of the humanities, and since without language there is no thought, the teacher can ill afford to circumvent a strategy that can create the emotional impetus and a sense of need to command language.

The aesthetic approach suggested here can make the students realize that without language they cannot give voice to their own thoughts and feelings. This approach also reinforces the view explicit in the philosophical approach that they *already* possess quite a sophisticated repertoire of insights and ideas in their command of actual, ordinary language. The free writing system can help overcome reluctance and fear in beginning to write. The aesthetic approach, by relying on regular, open-ended free writing, enhances motivation by making students realize that even in silence and passing conversation they actually command a powerful linguistic tool. By using language more extensively, they see how thoughts emerge from language and not before it. No "remediation" for anyone is required; only effective and improved practice. Each student uses his own resources without fear of failure but with the acceptance of active criticism. From the regular practice of expanding and correcting journal entries into pieces of finished prose, the elaboration and extension of the student's linguistic facility quickly becomes the obvious next objective.

After several years of high school, as a result of this aesthetic approach, the student should have accumulated a body of his or her written work. The student can be justly proud of such work. The sensitive question beneath this approach, and the philosophical and etymological approaches as well, is whether these goals can be accomplished with the least talented and more disadvantaged student. The answer is yes. The aesthetic approach most clearly underscores the assumption of all three approaches—that all of us can and should participate in them. Not all students will reach the heights of critical skill attainable with a serious command of language. But no students are incapable of improving their language by making it function as a tool of thought. They will use it, in one way or another, more extensively and thoroughly throughout their lives. Schools can ill afford not to try to improve, in the case of every student, the way he or she speaks, writes, and reads. Of all the three approaches, the aesthetic approach helps most to reconcile the democratic obligation to encourage each student to give voice to what he or she thinks or feels, with the intellectual demand that we apply high standards of criticism and excellence to all uses of language.

A teaching strategy that centers on language can become the key element of a humanities program in high school. It requires the creation by schools and teachers of a language and thinking curriculum without an initial reliance on preexisting textbooks. It demands, in addition, far more time devoted to language use in the students' day in school. This strategy also makes it clear that the issues and materials of the humanities— literature, history, philosophy—are easily linked together, albeit not in a conventional manner. By starting with the ordinary speech of high school students, utilizing the actual language and human situations of everyday life, teachers can build a bridge between past and present, between our intellectual tradition and current and future thinking. At its best, this curricular design can achieve a critical command of language among students that can reduce misunderstandings, clarify their thoughts, and extend their imaginations. The more we cultivate our students' power of imagination, the ease with which they communicate with one another, the more certain we can be of the quality of our cultural and political future. What more can we ask of the teaching of the humanities in our high schools?

NOTES

1. See *Daedalus (Winter 1983), Reading: Old and New,* particularly the articles by Eugene Goodheart and Stanley Fish.

2. Ludwig Wittgenstein, *Philosophical Investigations,* 2d ed. (Oxford: Basil Blackwood, 1958), p. 109e. Much of the discussion here is drawn freely from Wittgenstein. Hereafter cited as Wittgenstein, *PI.*

3. J. L. Austin, "A Plea for Excuses," in *Philosophical Papers,* third ed. (Oxford: Oxford University Press, 1979), pp. 181–82.

4. See ibid., pp. 201 ff, 260; see also George Steiner, *Martin Heidegger* (New York: Viking Press, 1979), pp. 15, 23ff.

5. The works of Norbert Elias, Karl Mannheim, and Michel Foucault are worth consulting in this respect.

6. See Karl F. Morrison, *The Mimetic Tradition of Reform in the West* (Princeton: Princeton University Press, 1982), especially the preface, the last two chapters (14 and 15), the epilogue, and the appendix.

7. Sigmund Freud, *Civilization and Its Discontents* (New York: W. W. Norton, 1961), pp. 16–17.

8. Much of this discussion is drawn from the work of Peter Elbow, especially as it was adapted and extended in the process of creating Bard College's Workshop in Language and Thinking and "The Institute in Writing and Thinking" at Bard now headed by Paul Connolly.

TEACHING THE DISCIPLINES

English Teaching and Humane Culture

Robert T. Fancher

If there exists some consensus among educators as to what high school English teachers are supposed to do and how and why, or if there exists some widely held philosophical foundation that stabilizes the English curriculum, one would be hard-pressed to locate either. The leadership—perhaps we should say, the visible, *official* leadership—of "the profession" consists of a rich array of behaviorists and romantics, utilitarians and aesthetes, ersatz social workers and scholars manqué, social activists and academic opportunists, and assorted other souls. Many of them are thoughtful, hard-working, concerned educators and scholars; but it is not to be wondered that they do not always reach consensus, that such agreements as they do reach may not last long, or that not all their putative constituents track every twist and turn of official doctrine.

Where these educational leaders lead, practitioners simply may not follow. The major influence on teachers seems not to be "the leadership of the profession" so much as their own high school and college English teachers. Ninety percent of high school English teachers were "majors" in

English, and they spend well over half of class time teaching what they judge to be English literature, most adopting objectives and using methods derived from their own education. The "leadership" is not always happy about this. Alfred Grommon, when president of the National Council of Teachers of English (NCTE), asked, "How can institutions and school districts help teachers keep from returning to outmoded concepts, materials, and methods of teaching soon after they have completed their preservice preparation?"[1] Arthur Applebee, author of many NCTE publications, was straightforward in his assessment of why teachers use traditional methods:

> . . . To the extent that the teacher remains unsure of his own professional skills, he will probably continue to cling to those methods and materials with which he is most familiar, leaving professional leaders to protest as in the past at the slow and difficult pace of change. . . . [2]

One supposes that most classroom English teachers do a better job at teaching than their ostensible leaders do at leading. Still the confusion of leadership has serious consequences. Translating the fruits of sophisticated scholarship into forms that are accessible to and useful for adolescents is no easy task, and the harried classroom teacher needs help in performing the task. Teachers need a clearly conceived, critically examined understanding of what secondary school English teaching is supposed to do. When the leadership is busy trying to expand the turf of the English program beyond anything that has to do with language or literature per se or trying to "do research" using social science methods that they may not understand and that may not be well suited to an inquiry into English teaching, when there is a tacit agreement that the tasks of English must be identified with *some* ideological or social agenda and then the argument becomes *which one,* or when the leadership in fact sets itself apart from and over the teacher—as Grommon and Applebee did—then we must worry that the tasks of formulating a comprehensive, sound philosophy of English teaching and of translating mature scholarship into appropriate forms for high schools will not get the attention they require. Classroom teachers, who often lack time, resources, and institutional support for these tasks, are left to catch as catch can. Some do an admirable job. Others do not. Some barely try.

English programs, like all major endeavors, need a philosophical base if they are to be conducted coherently, effectively, and with foresight, if decisions are to be made rationally rather than on an ad hoc basis, and if anything of definite character and lasting worth is to be accomplished. The view underlying this essay is that the fundamental purpose of secondary schooling is to initiate youngsters into humane culture, nurturing in soon-to-be adults the qualities of intelligence, wisdom, and grace that distinguish a free, civilized society. English teaching occupies a place of honor and urgency within this fundamental project of schooling. When we articulate what is meant by "humane culture," and when we factor into our thinking fundamental principles of acculturation, we can develop a philosophical framework that is sufficient, I believe, both to synthesize what is best in the various partial perspectives that have constituted warring camps among English policymakers and to address the pedagogical needs (and wonts) of the classroom teacher—whose first concern, after all, is effective teaching, not allegiance to an educational ideology.

The Tasks of English Teaching

The notion of "humane culture" does not refer to what the "better classes" do in their tuxedos in their spare time, nor to an artsy-craftsy, Book-of-the-Month Club, cocktail-party milieu. Rather, humane culture is a web of social institutions and practices that engender in the individuals who populate a society habits of mind and spirit that make for kindness, grace, and wisdom in the doings and dealings of that society. A culture that is humane—one in which a fair number of citizens display a fair amount of kindness, wisdom, and grace in a fair percentage of the events of their lives—is an achievement, not a "natural" happening. It depends upon the cumulative efforts, over many generations, of the society's intellectual, moral, spiritual, political, and aesthetic leaders and upon the dynamic, creative conservatorship by which each generation reinvests and then passes to the next the fund of cultural learning that has been amassed by these efforts. Schooling is a major part of that conservatorship.

In most schools, the English program more than any other is charged with stewardship of education for the sake of "humanity." Certainly it possesses the richest resources for exercising this stewardship. Enrichment, sophistication, and discipline of the verbal imagination are entrusted primarily to English. Knowledge of human character and of social facts and patterns is to be gained in English classes, principally through the study of literature, in far greater degree, diversity, depth, and detail than in any other high school course. The English teacher more than any other is charged with imparting command of the intricate logic of discourse that language embodies and grammar codifies, overseeing processes of writing and rewriting, and thus teaching students to organize their thoughts and to reflect upon them for improving their organization and cogency, and nurturing a sense of style and aesthetic discipline in one's verbal activities—which is, after all, the sort of aesthetic sensibility that all of us deploy every day in listening, talking, reading, and writing.

We must start from the recognition that children possess minds that are pliable and largely unformed—or uninformed. The point of schooling is to shape these pliable minds. If, as I have asserted, the point is to further humane culture, then the task of secondary schooling is to shape young minds by teaching the best that generations of poets and prophets and scientists have created. Each generation, in the hoary image, "stands on the shoulders" of its forebears. This is not out of reverence for the past—indeed, we may well be extremely critical of the past, once we have acquired knowledge necessary to judge it clearly—but out of sheer efficiency, if not necessity. The only ways of understanding and the only knowledge we have at the outset of adulthood are those that previous thinkers have created. Not to appropriate this knowledge as one's starting point is to undermine all efforts at improving the quality of our lives. If a generation had to start from scratch and had to experience the world in more or less primitive terms, rather than as shaped by the understanding of those who have already wrestled with the perplexities and mysteries of experience, that generation would have to reinvent not merely the wheel but the very rudiments of civility and insight.

Two distinctions are in order. The first is between the kind of people that we want in our society and the specific traits and abilities we can reasonably aim to produce through schooling. The second is between what we expect schools to do and what we expect their English programs to do. In a free society, schools are not—and ought not be—given the authority to oversee the "complete" development of the "whole person." Parents have some rights and responsibilities, and all sorts of civic and religious organizations have roles to play in the development of the person. Nor are high school English programs properly called upon to furnish all the schooling of the child.

The distinctions are important because they are often overlooked. In an official statement on teacher preparation, for example, the National Council of Teachers of English noted, apparently approvingly, that English has come to be thought of as "whatever one does with language (maybe even: with symbols)."[3] This is certainly excessive. There is hardly anything that humans do that does not require the use of language, at least if it is to be done in distinctively human forms—even eating involves recipes and, save when dining alone, rudimentary conversation concerning the passing of dishes! From the facts that language shapes every human response (since the ways we conceive of what is happening to us are always in terms of the language that we command, and our possible reactions are envisioned in those same terms) and that the English program has a primary responsibility for teaching language, it does not therefore follow that the English program has jurisdiction over every human response.

The fundamental task of the English program is to educate the imagination. All disciplines contribute to this process, of course—minds do not divide neatly along disciplinary lines. We must be careful in explaining what we mean by "the imagination" and by "educating" it; but even at a commonsense level, we can understand that the world of literature is an "imaginary" one and that the processes of thought for which we use the symbols that constitute language take place "in imagination"—thinking is seldom confined to recognizing what is present before us but is always suffused with ideas and information brought to consciousness only by imagining. It is only slightly misleading to say that language is the principal medium of intellectual imagination, and that intellectual imagination is the principal power of the human mind. To those to whom we entrust stewardship over shaping the language of the young and providing them with imaginative worlds through literature, we entrust a great deal.

"Imagination" is a type of activity, not a "faculty" of mind distinct from the rest of the intellect. "Imagining" is something that a person, with a whole mind, does. He brings to imagining all the contents of his mind (and heart), and he takes from it all the things that one may take from any activity of mind—including guidance for action. The crucial fact about imagination on which the possibility of a humane culture rests, and which justifies schooling as a means of fostering humane culture, is that imagination may be informed by, and may issue in, knowledge, and that the imagination may shape emotion and aspiration and thus guide action and temper response. It is because imagining is a sort of thinking, and that thinking can influence action and feeling, that we are able to make ourselves behave civilly, graciously, and with considered foresight.

To that extent, one can applaud the insights of "affective" education: the schools, and the English programs especially, do have serious responsibilities for students' emotional development—but this is because thinking shapes emotion and emotion must be shaped *deliberately* (i.e., by deliberation) if it is to be humane. What distinguishes humans is not that we feel, but the ways in which feeling may be articulated, enriched, and molded by understanding. "Purely academic" study of literature indeed has little place in high school, if by that term we mean literary study that focuses only on the technical aspects of texts, without regard to the dimensions of feeling rendered by the characterizations and action. At the same time, asking the student, "How do *you* feel about what happens to so-and-so" is at best a way to start literary study, not a sufficient end. The student must learn, through the writer's rendering of the affective dimension of his subject, what he did not already know about what humans can feel and why and the effects such feelings may have. Never should we disjoin the analysis of literature from the analysis of what it is to be human.

"Educating the imagination" is fundamentally intellectual. It consists of "stocking" the mind with the concepts and facts with which imagination works; of equipping the person with the skills and traits that allow a rich and fruitful imagination; and of cultivating the qualities of mind that enable the person to deploy his skills and knowledge with power and grace. These concepts, facts, skills, and habits are the creation of a culture, the discoveries of generations of thinkers and seekers, and they do not occur "naturally" to anyone. All of the components of culture, including knowledge, are human creations, not objects lying around for children (or adults) to stumble across. If children's imaginations are to be educated, it will be accomplished through processes of acculturation, not by the unfolding of innate tendencies or the adventitious discoveries of one person's experience.

We can distinguish three aspects of an educated imagination: its content, its processes, and its form. The three, however, cannot be separated: the processes by which one things are governed as much by the relations of the items that he thinks about and by his beliefs about those items as they are by any general, formal process of imagining. For example, one who wants to imagine a perfect friend will have the shape of his thought determined by what traits he believes can be conjoined in one person, by his beliefs about himself and about what qualities in another would complement his own, and thus by a great host of beliefs about human psychology. One item would follow another, and each possibility would be accepted or rejected, on the basis of these "substantive" notions as much as on "logical" or other "procedural" grounds.

It is especially important for teachers to recognize the interdependence of content, process, and form. To try to isolate one of these and teach toward improving it alone is to doom ourselves to frustration and failure. We will never teach children grammar, for instance, by teaching them only the rules of grammar, because much of grammar is embodied not in formalisms but in specific words themselves, and these in turn embody that grammar because of beliefs that we hold about the world. Consider the student who writes that "Much tasks awaits to be completed." How will we correct this? We would have to teach the child that "much" is a term that designates amount, not number. We would have to make clear the (very difficult) distinction between amount and number. And we would have to teach the child that tasks are things that come in numbers, not amounts. Then we would have to show that if we speak of "tasks," we must have a plural verb. If, however, we choose to say "much work" rather than "many tasks" the singular verb is fine. But we must decide which of these phrases to use! Thus, correcting this error involves attention to meanings of words ("much" and "tasks" cannot go together, given what each means); to categorical distinctions between sorts of things ("substances," which come in amounts, and "items," which come in numbers); to categorizing what it is the child wants to talk about ("tasks" falls into the "items" category); to applying a formal rule about agreement in number between subject and verb; and finally to stylistic concerns.

Having stipulated their inseparability, we can still distinguish the content, the processes, and the form of imagination.

THE CONTENT OF IMAGINATION

Roughly, the content of imagination, insofar as the English program is concerned, is the body of concepts, doctrines, characters, contentions about reality, and other "content" of literature and the analysis of literature. Writers of poems, plays, novels, and stories do not write simply to evoke responses to be "appreciated" or to provide pleasure and entertainment, but to make claims about how the world is and how it ought to be. We cannot think that Faulkner, for instance, wrote *Light in August* to provide us with a pleasant experience or simply to "express" his own feelings. He wrote *Light in August* to reveal truths as he saw them. Every important literary work addresses important questions and makes claims about them. These claims are the source of much of the best knowledge that humanity possesses. Most often, "classic" works are classics because of the depth and penetration of the visions of reality that they contain. By teaching the student the body of knowledge—or as much of it as the short time in high school allows—that people of literary genius have created, we raise dramatically the quality and accuracy of the imagining that he may do. To refuse to regard and teach our literary heritage as a repository of knowledge and wisdom is not only to engage in falsehood but to squander the richest resources of our culture and to fail miserably at our responsibilities to our students.

Most teachers of my acquaintance do teach literature as containing important ideas, some of them true, and as revealing dimensions of reality that we would overlook had not writers of genius exposed them. But this is one of the distressing points of divergence between what teachers actually try to do and what their leaders would have them do. Arthur N. Applebee cites as one of the major problems facing English teaching: *"Teachers of literature have never successfully resisted the pressure to formulate their subject as a body of knowledge to be imparted."* He also claims that *"the acknowledged goals of the teaching of literature are in conflict with the emphasis on specific knowledge or content."* These "goals," in his view, are "values and perspective."[4] Now, why the acquisition of values and perspective is thought even to be possible without knowledge or why the study of the content of a work of literature conflicts with gaining values and perspective from it is not made clear. In any case the contention is false. It is only by attention to *what in fact* a text says that we can derive *anything at all* from it. We cannot learn "values" from Flaubert unless we understand what he says, and this we cannot possibly understand without closely attending to the content of such texts as *Madame Bovary.* We cannot learn perspective from Hemingway unless we understand what he says, and again, this can be done only by learning what he says. The notion that one can learn anything worth knowing without attending to the content of what is said is simply silly.

Applebee also insists that we should not conceive of our literary heritage in terms of certain "Great Books," but in terms of "a continuing dialogue on the moral and philosophical questions central to the culture itself."[5] In a fundamental sense, this is true: great books are great because of what they say about enduring issues, and we should study them not as idols but as sources of wisdom and knowledge, as the best thinking on the central issues that is available to date. We study them to appropriate them to our own thinking. But we cannot learn what these books say if we do not attend to what they say. We can gain no insight from them unless we treat our literary heritage as a "body of knowledge." It seems to me, as it seems to all those teachers who have "never successfully resisted" the notion, that unless our literary heritage does constitute a body of knowledge, we have no reason whatsoever to claim any power for the study of literature. Why study what has not, in its thousands of years of existence, created any body of knowledge? Why believe that this is an activity worth continuing? If English cannot claim to provide knowledge, we will attract neither the intellectually curious, who will study history of the sciences instead, nor the vocationally inclined. We should not wonder if administrators regard as a "frill" a subject judged cognitively vacuous by its leaders.

PROCESSES OF IMAGINATION

The processes of the imagination, insofar as the English program is concerned, are primarily linguistic and, hence, logical. A person cannot entertain thoughts for which he does not have symbols. So far as verbal imagination—and hence discursive thought—is concerned, one cannot think in more complex and intricate terms than his linguistic ability allows. The linguistic forms that words and grammar constitute allow articulation, not in the sense of *expressing* thoughts that exist independent of articulation, but in the sense of forming thoughts in the first place. Insofar as a student is to be capable of clear, complex, comprehensive thoughts and ideas, he must have made second nature the apparatus of language that allows him to hold in mind, in usable order, diverse facts, concepts, and relations.

It should be clear that—notwithstanding to whatever extent there is some "universal grammar" or to whatever extent our genetic endowment to be language-users creates similarities in all speakers—languages are cultural creations into which children must be initiated. Our language embodies many concepts, theories, and beliefs that have long outlived the treatises in which they were first noted, and now exist independent of their sources. Our linguistic resources, the conceptual equipment with which we are able to think, include the cumulation of the best thinking that has occurred in our culture—though, of course, it includes much bad or archaic baggage, too, which can be distinguished only by those who have mastered the language. Language will change as new ideas enter our culture or as old ones are forgotten. (Sadly, too many words live longer than the concepts behind them and become virtually meaningless; one thinks of the debased use of the term "fantastic," which has fallen from an informative term describing a certain air of capricious unreality to a mindless exclamation.) With changes in language come—or go—changes in possibilities for thought. Any ten-year-old American child can think with ease of some things that never could have occurred to Plato, for instance, simply because that child is the heir to a language informed by two thousand years more thinking—including thinking inspired by Plato's own contributions. Schools and teachers have a responsibility to students to teach them the best language that we currently can—the language of the most sophisticated, careful thinkers of our culture. One also hopes that the students will join the process of improving the language, weeding out the bad and archaic and adding the freshly expressive.

Several strange notions are mistakenly thought to follow from the fact that language is a cultural creation rather than a "natural" (or supernatural) possession. One is the claim that "forcing" students to learn "standard" English is a sort of "cultural imperialism" in which a child is forced to give up his own culture and to take on the thought patterns of an alien one, simply by virtue of the fact that the speakers of the "dominant language" are also representatives of the "dominant culture." Another is the notion that "since one culture is as good as another," one language must be as good as another. A third is the idea that since language is changing and dynamic, there are no such things as rules of language that must be mastered.[6] These common misconceptions impede teachers' efforts to educate powerfully the imaginations of children.

Nowhere in the world have the speakers of the richest and most precise language been the dominant culture. Insofar as the "dominant culture" of a place has spoken the sophisticated language of the reflective—actually, a pale imitation of it—it has been because the dominant culture has had access to schools and teachers that has been denied to other members of the society. A serious student of language, who recognizes the origins of many of our most important words, will rarely find that these words have been invented by members of the "dominant" culture per se. More often, one finds that important changes in language have resulted from the thinking of people who stood apart from or ahead of the culture of the time. Aristotle's distinction of form and substance, for instance, drew not upon the "dominant" culture of Athens but upon the intellectual heritage dating from Thales. That Aristotle was an Athenian is true, obviously; but one simply cannot make a case that he created the words that he did and that they have entered our language because he was a well-born Athenian.

The "dynamic, changing character of language" does not argue against canons of correct usage. Rather, it requires that we must consciously preserve such advances in precision and subtlety of language as generations of logophiles and creative thinkers have brought into being if we are not to lose the capacity to think the thoughts those usages allow. It means that present and future changes of words can be either advances or regressions in the power of our language. What it does not mean is that there is anything to be gained by failing, or refusing, to attend to accurate, sophisticated language. No longer should only the "dominant culture" have access to the fund of words and grammar that the intellectual pilgrims and prophets of our heritage have created. Those who have learned these words and these patterns of usage but would deny them to others insure themselves an elite status in the society. This we should not countenance. Every person should be initiated into that aspect of our heritage constituted by the best language that exists, even though—as we have insisted—"the best" includes much that needs improvement. Students who have not mastered language have little ability to distinguish its better and worse elements.

It will be claimed, of course, that we cannot distinguish "dialects" as better or worse. Persons who believe this must have limited knowledge, limited capacities for self-awareness, or a general obtuseness. As the Italian Communist Antonio Gramsci recognized,

> If it is true that every language contains the elements of a conception of the world and of a culture, it could also be true that from anyone's language one can assess the greater or lesser complexity of his conception of the world. Someone who only speaks dialect, or understands the standard language incompletely, necessarily has an intuition of the world which is more or less

limited and provincial, which is fossilised and anachronistic in relation to the major currents of thought which dominate world history. His interests will be limited, not universal. . . . It is at least necessary to learn the national language properly. A great culture can be translated into the language of another great culture, that is to say a great national language with historic richness and complexity, and it can translate any other great culture and can be a world-wide means of expression. But a dialect cannot do this.[7]

Languages or dialects have different capacities. *In principle* there is no reason why any dialect could not *develop* to the level of a "great national language." But it is simply false to claim that every one *does in fact* attain to this level.

THE FORM OF IMAGINATION

The third dimension of imagination is the form or style of one's thinking. "Style" is a much-used word, and its uses range from the relatively trivial—meaning only "fashionable," as in stylish clothes or hair styles—to much weightier uses, as in "Picasso's style." I use the term as a precise analogue to the notion of "literary" or "artistic" style, and I mean by it the aesthetic form of one's habits of thought. Alfred North Whitehead, mathematician, physicist, and philosopher, had this to say:

> Style, in its finest sense, is the last acquirement of the educated mind; it is also the most useful. It pervades the whole being. The administrator with a sense for style economises his material; the artisan with a sense for style prefers good work. Style is the ultimate morality of mind.
>
> . . . With style you attain your end and nothing but your end. With style the effect of your activity is calculable, and foresight is the last gift of gods to men. With style your power is increased, for your mind is not distracted with irrelevancies, and you are more likely to attain your object.[8]

Style is surely the last thing that we are *successful* in acquiring, for it is the most pervasive of the "shapings" that education gives us; but it is not a last-minute *addition* to learning. Rather, one's "style" is the fundamental shape of his processes of thinking and feeling; it is a cumulative acquisition built up over years of study.

No one who has benefited from the fruits of a serious education will quarrel with Whitehead on this point. To try to discuss anything with persons who consistently miss the point or indulge in irrelevancies, to read arguments that are "flabby" and loose, to have to depend on people whose ways of thought lack the efficiency and order of a sense of style— these are as frustrating as any of the minor trials of daily life, and they may at times lead to major trials. The emotional, moral, and intellectual gains that accrue to a mind informed by aesthetic discipline are among the most important elements of enhancing one's quality of life. There is nothing "precious" or dandified about this. A fine athlete, a champion driver, an assembly line foreman all show style in every judgment of how the elements of their activities are put together. The thinker shows it whenever he judges what bears on what and how significantly. That mathematicians and physicists consider the elegance of a theory or argument an indicator of whether it is likely to be true is sufficient evidence of the cognitive value of style.

What this means for the English teacher is that we must demand for students only the best in literature, and we must evaluate students' writing (and speaking) for all the standard features that distinguish efficient, powerful, clear writing from sloppy, vague, and flabby writing. The notions that students can be given poorly written works to read because the content is interesting and that students should be indulged in the styles that they find most immediately amenable are born of failure to realize the crucial role of aesthetic discipline in determining quality of thought. The "higher order cognitive skills" must—and in fact do, whether or not we care to acknowledge it and adjust our teaching accordingly—include the style with which relevance is judged, diverse materials are juxtaposed in mind, and inferences are made. We encourage such style by immersing students in fine writing and by insisting on fine writing from them. We undermine it by recommending and approving mediocrity.

Not the least value of studying great writing and of trying to write in formal, established genres is the gain one makes in sense of style, with consequent gain in power of articulation and thought. We are all imitators when first we begin to think. If we are ever to think well, we can do worse than to begin by imitating great writers and trying to conform to genres whose power is evident. If we are truly to initiate students into the best thinking that is open to them, we must immerse them in the finest writing, and we must demand that they write, and write, and write. Only then will students do enough writing ever to develop the ability to think clearly, logically, and expansively, in a style that economizes thought and fosters soundness. Only the most egotistical or ambitious of us will write profusely without being forced to by teachers—and we will write poorly unless forced to write well. For learning to write well, like learning to think well generally, is difficult work. It requires submission of the self to the rules and resources and established truths that constitute a culture standing beyond and over the self and containing criteria for showing wherein we fail. It requires a discipline that simply does not "come naturally." Even so with reading difficult works, the works of "great literature." A discipline, a willingness initially to suspend one's judgment in recognition that what is being said may be beyond the jurisdiction of one's present competence, is essential to good reading and to developing greater powers of reading. We must not dismiss what is "beyond us" if we are ever to be able to read it. We must submit to the arduous, insecure process of learning; and this we do only by discipline. Students will learn this only if teachers teach it to them. They will form the habit of doing it only if teachers lead them to. But the disciplines of reading and writing are the disciplines requisite for thinking well. Teachers must impart these disciplines to students.

CURRENT PHILOSOPHIES OF ENGLISH TEACHING

Three "curriculum models" represent the main currents in the contemporary thinking of English teaching's leaders.[9] One is the "heritage" model. The heritage model tends to be "academic" and to focus on the culture of the students' society. Discipline, rigor, and care of thought are its watchwords. As Barrett Mandel has well expressed it:

> In the heritage model, the underlying assumption is that the way to acquire skills and knowledge is to submit to something larger than one's self, that is, to the culture. . . . For the heritage teacher, there is value in surrendering one's ego-bound sense of relevance to a more informed or enlightened sense of what truly endures.[10]

The "heritage teacher" tends to see the individual as part of the larger sweep of things, finding meaning in his relations to larger forces, trends, and groups. The point of learning literature and language is to join one's culture and to participate fully in the life of this larger source of meaning. Among the advocates of a heritage curriculum we are likely to find scholars and aesthetes, rather than social reformers.

The latter are more likely to advocate the "process model." The emphases in process teaching are on the child's own discoveries and "free" or "open" classrooms. The fundamental idea is that children develop best when allowed to develop at their own respective paces, in directions of their own choosing, toward values that they discover on their own. Rather than emphasizing the "larger" groups of which the child is a part, the process teacher is apt to decry the insidious influences of these larger groups, which are seen as "imposing" on the child or "coercing" him. Process advocates Barbara and Gene Stanford identify three principles of process teaching:[11] concern with the whole person rather than with intellect alone; recognition of the developmental processes of adolescents, which leads to a theoretical background for the curriculum drawn from developmental psychology (rather than from the logic of the subject matter); and placing a higher value on the individual student's opinions concerning his growth than on standards established by the community or society. The process teacher is more concerned that the student develop social and personal skills than intellectual prowess. As the Stanfords, apparently in all seriousness, put it:

> In a curriculum based on the developmental concerns of adolescents, English, along with history, mathematics, and science, would definitely be considered "frills" that one might elect during free time on Fridays if the essential tasks of peer relations, identity development, sex-role definition, and relations with the opposite sex were being achieved satisfactorily.[12]

The Stanfords acknowledge that few communities would allow such a curriculum in its pure form, and they offer what is actually a fairly sensible curriculum as a means of pursuing process concerns within a traditional academic framework. Other process thinkers are not so catholic. It is within the process framework that we are to understand Applebee's aversion to "content" and "knowledge." Process thinkers tend toward a Romantic belief in the innate wisdom of the child, and they also tend to be "liberal" in their social values. Indeed, we find Applebee *identifying* literature with progressivism and claiming that there is an inherent tension between literature and convention[13]—as if most novelists, poets, and dramatists shared the same sorts of social or political philosophy. This, of course, would be news to Faulkner, Eliot, Pound, Wilder, cummings, and Steinbeck.

The "competencies" model is openly behavioristic and aims at establishing in students observable "competencies" through a curriculum based on discrete, carefully defined tasks that students will master, each at his own rate. The tasks are to be carefully "sequenced" so that when one task is mastered, the student moves to the next, adequately prepared to master it. Like process thinking, the competency model is based on certain theories of developmental psychology. While process teachers take Carl Rogers as their chief intellectual patron, competency theorists are apt to trace their roots to Thorndike and to the many behaviorists, such as Skinner, who have addressed educational issues.

We should not pretend that these three "approaches" are wholly reconcilable in ways their several advocates would approve. It is logically impossible both that the source of the meaning in persons' lives is submission to a heritage and that it comes from eschewing "external" standards. The two cannot both be true, at least not without substantial qualifications. Likewise, the orderly discipline of the competency model is incompatible with the spontaneity and freedom of the process curriculum.

Any rapprochement among the three approaches requires that we recognize that each is only a partial perspective and that when its limited truths are generalized into a complete theory of the child and schooling, they become false. If the half-true generalizations are reduced to their proper domains, so that they cease to be such sweeping claims, each becomes true. Indeed, it is the truth of each perspective *within a limited domain* that gives it the credibility with people of good will that it holds.

The heritage model—to which some readers may have erroneously relegated this essay—is correct in holding that knowledge and value are social and historical. The only knowledge that we have, again, is that which has in fact been won. The values that have been found adequate for guiding countless millions of lives and the institutions that support them deserve a preliminary presumption of trustworthiness. Only insofar as a person submits his own development to the canons of thinking and judgment embodied in social, professional, artistic, and intellectual institutions does he appropriate as his own the only learning that we have. But the heritage model is wrong in expecting the student to find the meaning of his own life in exclusive adherence to this or that "historical force" or in understanding his place in the "larger scheme of things." He may or may not. One of the ways that we may relate ourselves to our heritage is by opposing some or all of it. And we may even change "the larger trends" in unpredictable ways by our own efforts. It is true, then, that the student must appropriate his heritage. It is not true that he must find it adequate and worthy of reverence or find the meaning of his life in participating in its continuation.

The process teacher is surely right in insisting that pedagogy and the curriculum must address the needs of students and must be framed in light of developmental psychology. He is correct in insisting that a student should be judged by standards appropriate to his stage of development. Any student worth his salt will have the wildest and (to adults) most frightening ideas when his immaturity, his naivety, his adolescent need to define himself as different from his parents, and exposure to new and far-reaching ideas are combined. Students must be allowed to think such thoughts freely. Part of what that means is that "correctness" of interpretation of literary works, for instance, will matter less initially than a serious attempt to think through the material. What the teacher must do is use this sincere engagement with the text to teach the child to read the text closely and to base interpretations on what is really there—all the while recognizing, as the process theorists insist, that the crucial consideration is guiding the student at a pace and judging him by standards that do not crush his exploration and creativity. It is rumored that Alfred North Whitehead, while teaching at Harvard, gave primarily A's and F's, with no "gentleman's C's." The point, he said, was that students who thought carefully and imaginatively should not be discouraged because at a given point they happened to be muddle-headed. Students who did not think at all were given F's, even if they memorized texts. Whitehead's scheme probably is not one that should be universalized; but the spirit that led him to adopt it is well taken.

We must emphasize, though, that the point of allowing students to think wild thoughts freely and of taking care not to crush creativity is a *developmental* point and that the teacher must guide this development. Active, creative thought alone has little to commend it. The reason that we value active thought and individual creativity is that they are necessary—but not sufficient—conditions of intelligent action and new discoveries. Other necessary conditions include adherence to logical and evidentiary canons, accumulation of a substantial body of facts, principles, and experiences, and ability to be self-critical. The teacher who encourages "free" thinking, where that means thought free from the demand that it be intellectually responsible, does not serve the student well. The point of allowing students to think immature thoughts without immediate censure is that this gives the teacher the opportunity to lead the student through processes of self-criticism, in which the student learns a good deal about how to think. We short-circuit our opportunities to teach when we alienate the student by too-swift and too-authoritarian censure of his childish thoughts or when we stop him from thinking by convincing him he is incompetent anyway. We must remember that the thinking of the immature and incompletely educated is immature and incomplete; that we cannot teach an adolescent everything at once, so that we cannot expect to make the student a mature thinker overnight; but that we must be no less attentive to teaching the student to think well than to encouraging him to think at all. We must remember that teaching is a process, in which different stages of immaturity (hence error) must be tolerated, each in its turn, and in which development from one stage to another can surely be retarded, accelerated, or prevented altogether.

The essential trouble with the "competencies" approach—serious humanistic criticisms of behaviorism aside—is that we do not yet possess anything that vaguely resembles a sound psychological rendering of literary study and of the processes of composition and language acquisition that allows for the clearly defined and carefully sequenced "tasks" of the competency curriculum. We may also doubt that such a psychology will ever exist—since there may be more randomness, creativity, and idiosyncracy to human development generally and English study particularly than a behaviorist model can accommodate. It is clearly the case that sequences of "competencies" that are now offered resemble nothing so little as they resemble operant behaviors. The "competencies" approach is at least partly optimism and partly pretense.

At the same time, the competencies model recalls for us some basic principles of teaching and learning. It reminds us that we need to analyze carefully the various things that we are trying to accomplish, to determine which of them most students must learn first if the others are to be learned well, and to design evaluations of students around sequential mastery of the objectives. What we do not need to do is try to design "behavioral" objectives for what is not behavior, e.g., understanding or creating ideas and perceptions.

RECOMMENDATIONS ON THE CURRICULUM

The notion of English teaching as educating the imagination unites the positive aspects of all three approaches. Abstractly, this is easy to see. The question is how this synthesis could actually take place in the curriculum and the classroom. I offer a few suggestions, well aware that they are stated generally and must therefore be adapted to the style and emphases of each teacher.

First, the literature curriculum should be organized around the crucial themes and questions that animate human life in our culture—including how to relate to other cultures, of course. Students, unlike scholars, do not urgently need to know the history of literature—who developed which technique or genre, who influenced whom, when, and so forth. Too often, heritage advocates think there is some peculiar significance to chronological order. Chronology is indeed important in history, but not necessarily in literature, simply because the best literature is timeless. We appropriate our heritage no less fully by reading *Oedipus Rex* and *Death of a Salesman* in the same semester than by reading them in different courses in different years.

Second, the teaching of literature must concentrate on close, active reading of texts. Surely it is true, as some have overemphasized, that any great work of literature has many meanings, and that the meaning a particular person extracts from it depends in part on his own interests and concerns. This suggests that teachers should be open to students' finding in the work themes and doctrines that the teacher had not planned to address or indeed may never before have seen. However, that does not mean that students should be allowed to impose on texts content that simply is not there or to ignore substantial portions of texts in developing interpretations. An author's message or messages are bound up with the integrity of the work as a whole. To interpret a work in ways that ignore major parts of it, or to inject into the text things that are not there, is to distort the work and thus to garble whatever insights are incarnate there. Some people's creative deformations of texts yield more insight than the text ever contained, of course—but few scholars have that genius, and most seventeen-year-olds are more likely to learn important things by deciphering something of what a text says.

Teaching literature based on close reading of texts, in a spirit of intellectual adventure that allows students to find claims and interpretations that the teacher had not planned to bring out, requires that the teacher be both intimately familiar with the work and capable of thinking through the text quickly in response to students, finding textual matter either to support or to challenge the students' views. This is a much more demanding task than talking expansively about how students "feel" about texts. The question that the teacher must always be ready to address is this: How do I use this student's response to teach him how to read, and thus learn from, texts? How do I use this student's response to push him into deeper and more critical engagement with the claims of the author and with his own reaction to those claims? We ask this question because of our initial assumption that the great works constituting our literary heritage contain more wisdom than most of us can generate on our own. The point is to teach the student how to extract some of that wisdom so that he can put it to use in his own thinking.

We must recognize, though, that themes raised in literature sometimes demand a wider ranging discussion than can be securely based on the texts alone. Adolescents often want to discuss the issues in general, not merely in reference to the text. This is well and good. But in such cases, the text should be used to anchor and focus discussion. When reading *The Grapes of Wrath,* for instance, students will likely want to talk about what kinds of responsibilities people have for each other and how these responsibilities relate to social, economic, and moral systems. This often enough moves into a wide-ranging discussion of capitalism versus socialism or of responsibilities that override social convention. Such discussion begins to move out of the realm of the bull session and into the realm of education when the teacher can tie the issues involved not to vague generalizations about life in general but to what Steinbeck has to say about them and whether what he says is powerful, persuasive, and revealing. If we do not like what Steinbeck has to say, we can follow his book with one by an author whose point of view is different. We only confuse matters, and undermine the notion that literature provides insight into crucial issues, if we do disregard what a text says on the issue under discussion, or use the text only to get people talking.

Third, we should try to organize the study of each theme in terms of increasing sophistication of the treatment the theme receives from one work to the next, and we should be sure that students understand the less complex work before we move to the next. This does not mean that the simpler literary works should be mediocre or simple-minded. Indeed, as I have insisted, students should be immersed only in the best literature—and there is far more of that than any high school curriculum can hold. What it means is that works of "classic simplicity" should preceed works that deal with the same issues and themes in more convoluted and intricate fashion.

Fourth, we must teach language and writing not as isolated "skills" to be mastered but as integral parts of the process of thinking. This does not mean that we cannot focus on these disciplines. Indeed, if we focus on mastering the correct linguistic forms of expression, so that we can relegate them to "second nature" and not give them constant attention in our composing, we gain much in efficiency of thought. "Competency" learning has its greatest value in teaching the mechanical supports of composing, and we should take full advantage of them—realizing that no one ever generated a thought on the basis of memorized grammar and vocabulary, but that no one ever made himself clear in formulating complex thoughts without drawing upon the resources of grammar and vocabulary.

Teachers should recognize the expressive power of "dialects," but they should not be mesmerized by it. We all know that at times a regional or ethnic expression surpasses in pungent aptness anything that has heretofore entered into our common language. This is well and good. Moreover, we should not make our students into prigs who go about correcting the formal errors of their parents. We should teach our students that usage should always be pitched to the purpose for which we speak, that some usages do not require great precision, but that for purposes of sophisticated, accurate thinking and communication the correct use of "standard" English is usually essential. Teachers certainly should not teach students to scorn the patois of their neighborhoods; but we should teach them language of more rigor and richness, too. All of us whose backgrounds have bequeathed both a "local" or ethnic dialect *and* a command of advanced language remain "bi-dialectical." We *certainly* use both dialects, each as occasion demands. We should expect neither more nor less from our students.

Fifth, students should write and write and write, and rewrite and rewrite and rewrite. Nowhere as in writing is the student called upon to muster in imagination a sense of his audience, so that he can envision what he must say in writing to make himself clear; to formulate and to organize thoughts; to make his thoughts into "objects" for evaluation, in the form of publicly readable words on paper for which he is accountable; hence to submit the works of his imagination to the standards constituted by the community of thinkers; to consider fully what he really does and does not think; and to confront the shape of one's own thinking directly. Moreover, nowhere as in a student's writing does the teacher have such an opportunity for individualized teaching. The student's papers and the teacher's comments on them should constitute an ongoing dialogue, through which the teacher learns things that the student thinks and cares about that the student might never voice in front of his classmates.

Finally, the English curriculum should be organized around its literary component. Literature contains the substantive ideas, novel insights, richness of vocabulary, power of linguistic structure, paradigms of style, and forms of intellectual discipline necessary for educating the imagination. The activities that the authors of literary works engaged in while creating them, after all, are precisely the activities of observation, reflection, evaluation, and so forth that we are trying to nurture in students, and all of our attention to language and composition is ancillary—though essential—to this. While we shall certainly need separate attention to rules of grammar and to learning structures of the composition process, these can be woven into, not set off from, literary study. We may, perhaps, study grammar one week in four, or two days a week, or whatever proves most workable. But each round of study should focus on certain carefully delineated grammatical forms, and attention should be paid to examples of these forms in both the literature studied and the writing done subsequently. We may reasonably expect students to master a few grammatical principles at a time, if we present these clearly, then "drill" and grade students, so far as grammar is concerned, only on uses of those principles (and ones learned earlier) for a period of several days or weeks, within a context in which these principles are in fact used expressively—i.e., within the reading of literature. We cannot reasonably expect adolescents to memorize a large number of abstract grammatical rules at once and to translate them into practice simultaneously. Similarly, vocabulary items should be drawn from works to be studied, and memorization of definitions should be subordinated to discerning how each word, used as it is in the works studied, means and what it expresses.

Writing should be of at least three different sorts: analysis of literary works studied; the student's own thinking on the themes studied; and the student's own creations within the genre of various works studied. Through analysis, the student both learns to learn from a text and gains specific knowledge to be used in his own thinking. In works expressing his own thoughts, the student puts what he has learned to work, with a freedom that is not available when trying to comprehend what someone else has said on the subject. And in trying to create works of his own in the genre, the student is required to draw together everything that he has been taught and to try to accomplish everything that he is expected to learn to do. As should be obvious, these types of writing are to be graded with different degrees of severity. We must insist, if tactfully, that students base what they write about texts on what is in the texts; this is a prime source of intellectual discipline. As the student is called upon to risk more self-exposure, though, the teacher's concern is as much with nurturing engagement in the activities of thinking as with intellectual discipline. As the child matures, we insist on greater discipline in his own writing—and surely we begin from the first to prod gently toward logical coherence, adequate research, and responsible self-criticism. All education requires a blend of freedom and discipline; and for adolescents, who are only beginning to learn to be separate individuals with minds of their own, we must allow much freedom in the creation of their own works.

Within these principles, an infinite variety of specific curricula can be designed. What is important is not that we all teach the same works, in the same order. What is important is that we educate the imaginations of our students, so that all can participate in the best thinking that is possible for members of our culture, at this point in our common life.

NOTES

1. Alfred H. Grommon, "A History of the Preparation of Teachers of English," *English Journal* 57, no. 4 (1968), 501.

2. Arthur N. Applebee, *Tradition and Reform in the Teaching of English: A History* (Urbana: National Council of Teachers of English, 1974), p. 215.

3. NCTE Standing Committee on Teacher Preparation and Certification, *A Statement on the Preparation of Teachers of English* (Urbana: NCTE, 1976), p. 1.

4. Applebee, pp. 245–248.

5. Ibid.

6. The *classicus locus* for these misconceptions is "Students' Right to their Own Language," adopted by the Conference on College Composition and Communication in 1974 and printed in *College English* that year.

7. Quoted in Geoffrey Partington, "Gramsci and Education," *Educational Philosophy and Theory* (Australia), Summer 1981, 35.

8. Alfred North Whitehead, *The Aims of Education* (New York: Macmillan Company, 1929; Free Press paperback, 1967), pp. 12–13.

9. See *Three Language Arts Curriculum Models,* Barret J. Mandel, ed. (Urbana: National Council of Teachers of English, 1980).

10. Ibid., pp. 8–9.

11. Ibid., p. 139.

12. Ibid., p. 141.

13. Applebee, p. 249.

Foreign Languages and Humane Learning

Carlos R. Hortas

In 1915, most American high school students studied either a modern foreign language or Latin. Thirty-six percent of all high school students were studying a modern foreign language at that time, 37.3 percent were studying Latin, and the majority of students enrolled in a modern foreign language had previous training in Latin. Clearly, many Americans felt that a person was not truly educated unless he or she knew at least one foreign language. Today only 15 percent of all high school students are enrolled in foreign languages courses (including Latin and Greek), and only 8.4 percent of the total college population elects to study a foreign language. Only one-third as many high school students are enrolled in Latin classes today as in 1915, even though today's high school population is ten times larger.[1] Of particular significance to today's enrollment figures is that most students in language classes are enrolled in first- or second-year courses.

It is a fact that in order to graduate from college, earn a living, and generally satisfy their daily needs, most Americans have no need of any language but English. It is a fact that relatively few people have any need at all in business or personal life for working fluency in any language other than our own—or *could have* any such need: few of us can be multinational business people, diplomats, or world travelers. And it is a fact that our society tends not to assign value to experience or knowledge that has no immediately apparent dividends. One might be tempted to think that the decline of language study in our nation's schools is a sign of wisdom, a sign that subservience to old visions of education has been supplanted by education devoted to more pressing matters, hence to education more efficient for improving our lives. One might be tempted to think such a thing. But one would be wrong.

WHY STUDY LANGUAGES?

When one questions the need for foreign languages in the curriculum, it would be good to remember that language is perhaps the central human activity, other than those activities associated with the continuance of life itself, such as nourishment, reproduction or sleep—and those fundamental processes could not take place in distinctively human forms without language, if only because conversation and communication are essential to learning them in civilized forms. Language, therefore, is properly central to a study of humanity.

The study of foreign languages leads to an understanding of the ways in which the particular constraints of individual languages shape the exchange of information and ideas. The language that we use predisposes us to experience things in particular ways and may predetermine for us certain modes of observation and interpretation.[2] Language is not only a bearer of meaning; every language helps to shape thoughts.

This point is crucial, for most people seem to think that the existence of many human languages is no more significant than the inconvenience that we cannot all talk to each other readily. Most people, it seems, think that the existence of many languages means only that different peoples utter different sounds or draw different graphic symbols to refer to the same things. If these general impressions were true, there truly would be no need to study foreign languages other than strictly utilitarian ones. We would need to understand other languages only if we needed to talk to the native speakers of those languages. *The very fact that so few people understand how radically language shapes thought and experience, and hence how language gives shape and substance to one's ways of dealing with the world, is the strongest possible argument that failure to study languages has dire consequences.*

Since any language shapes the speaker's thought and experience, knowledge of a second language is liberating. By understanding that any cultural viewpoint is shaped by the way a language structures what its speakers think and feel, we may begin to realize that *we* are products of a culture and that our thoughts and beliefs are shaped by the characteristics of our own native language. Thus, a second or foreign language offers a fresh perspective from which to view the world and speak about it.

A foreign language not only provides liberation from cultural provincialism but a greater degree of consciousness of the activity of language itself. For one thing, understanding another language and developing the ability to use it correctly leads to the realization that each language has its own set of rules. When an Italian, for instance, answers a question in a way we would not expect an English speaker to, our knowledge of how languages work will allow us to realize that the Italian is not necessarily answering incorrectly or stupidly; he may simply be behaving according to a whole different set of rules. If we understand his language's rules, we may even understand his specific response correctly. Such an appreciation for language must lead to greater understanding among peoples, and can lessen the likelihood that one will be scorned or vilified because of linguistic or cultural differences.[3]

The very question that we often ask one another to better understand the truth, "What are the facts?" becomes misleading if we do not make allowances for the different ways in which languages foreign to us frame their "facts." As Benjamin L. Whorf puts it: "Facts are unlike to speakers whose language background provides for unlike formulation of them."[4]

Of course, beyond general appreciation of how language works, knowledge of another language also allows one to read foreign literatures and to understand the ways in which other languages depict life and express aesthetic subtleties and the peculiarities of human behavior. One becomes aware of the ways in which a foreign language does things differently from English, how words and parts of speech are positioned differently, how such positioning may result in a different effect on the reader. We may become aware that the ways in which words are engaged by each other, the ways they speak to each other in a foreign language create distinctive organic relationships that cannot fully be expressed through translation. Through reading the classics of another language, we learn not only that culture and language are intimately related, we learn the culture of that language. A person who must always have recourse to an English translation is a person who has learned the lyrics to a song without knowing the accompanying melody.

Never in the history of the world has there been a nation of such rich ethnic and linguistic diversity as ours. One out of every fifty Americans is foreign born; far more are second- or third-generation Americans. English has never been the only language spoken by the American people. European languages have coexisted in North America for several centuries. Spanish explorers had established their language in parts of the South and the Southwest long before the founding of the first New England colonies. English itself is a Germanic language mellowed by its contact with old French, and owes its lexical strength to its appropriations from Latin, French, and other European languages. Thus, foreign language study is an avenue toward improving our knowledge and appreciation of the richness of the English language. In the words of Yale President A. Bartlett Giamatti:

> The demise of foreign languages [as a subject of study] is part of a larger assault on literacy, part of a larger decline in the capacity to handle any language at all. It is, I believe, a fact that in the last fifteen years, certainly the last ten, any American college student who knew anything about the dynamics of English—its struts and cables, its soaring spans, the way it holds together and works—knew it by analogy from the grammar of a foreign language. (It is true, the old cliché, that says a foreign language necessarily deepens one's grasp of one's native language. And what is true about language tends to be true of culture.) All the general worry about students' capacity to structure and to express their thoughts in English must include the current sorry situation with foreign languages.[5]

The study of languages, then, develops in the student an understanding of what it is to be a language user, a human being; an appreciation for the subtleties and precision (and imprecision!) of his own language; a general "cosmopolitan" outlook; and an ability to acquire an immersion in the culture of another land. To the claim that language study is useless, because most people in the "provinces" may never see a non-English-speaking alien—the answer is simply that the claim is false. The study of languages is useful not merely for the would-be diplomat or world traveler. Language study is essential for anyone who would be humanely educated. In fact, the less likely it is that a particular student will ever "have a use for a foreign language"—in a simple utilitarian sense—the more important it is that that student be taught foreign languages in school. For the students who will, in due course, engage in commerce with people and literature of other lands will pick up from their associates and reading something of the "cosmopolitan" attitude, the understanding of differences between the ways that people think and speak. The student who will never have any significant contact with non-English-speaking people will never encounter the substantive facts about other languages, other ways of thinking, and the workings of language if he is not given them in school.

But of course, we must be careful not to overpraise language study. Only if it is done properly can we claim for it these virtues.

THE SORRY STATE OF LANGUAGE STUDY

Language study is not carried on very well in most American schools. The current sorry situation with foreign languages in these schools is suggested by enrollment figures; but it becomes dramatic when one considers the low level of proficiency attained by those high school students who study them. According to Congressman Paul Simon, "Tests show that only 17% of those who study a foreign language wholly within the United States can speak, write, or read the language with ease."[6]

Languages, in general, require study over a long time, and the lack of articulation between primary, secondary, and college instruction militates against the success of foreign language education. High school instruction in foreign language may be too little too late; most students take no more than two years of foreign language in high school, and for most it is their first exposure to a foreign language. A more fundamental problem is the lack of teacher competence in foreign languages. One of the main reasons students so often fail to continue the study of a foreign language beyond the first two years is that the courses they take are taught in a dull, tiresome style, and much of the instruction is in English rather than in the foreign language itself. A recent survey of high school language teachers showed that the amount of time spent in first-year classes learning to use the foreign language to communicate was less than 5 percent of total class time.[7]

Many of our teachers are not fluent in the language that they teach. Thus, they are inadequately prepared for their positions and cannot fulfill their professional obligations. A future teacher may graduate from college with a major in a foreign language yet be unable to meet even the minimal rating for proficiency in the language of her major. According to a 1967 Harvard study, *college seniors* majoring in a foreign language clearly exhibited higher mean scores in foreign language skills than did foreign language *teachers* enrolled in National Defense Education Act Language Institutes. A report by the Ford Foundation attributes the lack of the development of first-class competence in foreign languages to the low level of language teaching in the United States.[8]

Teachers must be alive to their teaching responsibilities, and they must become more fluent in a foreign language before any successful attempt can be made to increase the foreign language requirement in the nation's high schools. If we increase the number of years a student should study a foreign language, we must also insure that there be an adequate supply of teachers able and trained to bring the student to that level. Moreover, financial and other career rewards must be improved in order to attract first-rate individuals to the teaching profession and away from fields that now offer superior career incentives and more lucrative salaries.

WHAT SCHOOLS SHOULD REQUIRE

Because the "dividends" of foreign language study are not readily apparent *prior* to one's study, any significant improvement of Americans' linguistic facility will require reinstating foreign language requirements.

Before we reinstate a universal foreign language requirement, however, we need to define our educational objectives in terms other than years of study. The completion of a foreign language requirement should not be measured primarily in terms of time spent in the classroom or chapters covered in a book, but in terms of skills attained and degree of functional competence. We need to measure a student's ability to make active use of a language, not just his passive recall of verb endings and vocabulary. The language requirement, then, must be cast in terms of the quality of language learning. Some school systems and language teachers may resist the imposition of quality controls—particularly since, if we are to teach languages with a view toward inculcating real competence in our students, teachers must submit to proficiency exams in language, and passing such exams must become preconditions for teacher licensure, certification, and employment.

A set of desired levels of attainment developed by the U.S. Foreign Service Institute has served as a model for guidelines recently developed by the American Council on the Teaching of Foreign Languages.[9] These guidelines are not only useful in measuring student attainment; they are also of value in improving articulation between middle schools, high schools, and colleges. Making proficiency the yardstick for placing students in a higher or lower foreign language class would result in the grouping and promotion of students on the basis of their command of active language skills and not just on the basis of time spent in the classroom or material covered. Thus, articulation could be based clearly and unambiguously on increasing levels of skill.

If we are serious about graduating students with a reasonable command of a foreign language, we must realize what "reasonable command" means. We must require of teachers that they teach their students to do the following: (a) to understand a native speaker of the language, (b) to carry on a normal conversation with a native about world affairs, people, sports, literature, (c) to read newspapers, periodical literature, and books in the language with reasonable comprehension, and (d) to be able to write a short essay or a simple personal or business letter in the foreign language.

Most students who have taken even four years of a foreign language in high school are unable to perform at this level. This is no argument against requiring such a level of proficiency. If foreign language study is to be a serious discipline from which we expect intellectual and personal enrichment, then our goals and expectations must be much higher than they have been in the past and are at the present.

Americans have never been as accomplished at languages as we ought to be, so in bemoaning lax contemporary standards we must be careful not to pretend that there was once a golden day of language study in the United States. Nonetheless, things are worse with language than they once were; and we would do well to try to understand why. In the 1960s and 1970s, colleges dropped foreign language entrance requirements and graduation requirements in response to demand from student activists and faculty in favor of greater "academic freedom." All requirements were viewed as "constraints" that limited free choice, and their abolition allowed students a greater voice in determining their own curriculum. In the long run, the weakening of requirements has resulted in freedom of choice for undergraduates, but it is perhaps a freedom that they are not ready to exercise responsibly. At many colleges in the country a student may graduate not only without a foreign language, but also without a natural science or even, in some cases, without ever taking a college-level English course.

The erosion of academic requirements at the college level has had its effect on the high school curriculum. When the majority of colleges no longer required a foreign language as either an entrance or graduation requirement, high schools were quick to follow suit. Why? Because a high school education today is not regarded as an end in itself. Instead, it is a means to prepare students for college; we even call the more demanding high school courses "college prep" courses. The high schools, therefore, seem to have no convictions about what should constitute a rigorous and sound program of studies, independently from what the colleges may think.

When colleges decided not to require foreign languages as preconditions for admission, foreign languages became "elective" subjects in the high school curriculum. This change in the status of foreign languages in the high schools may also be attributable to arguments based on "relevance." However, I am convinced that the example of the colleges was really what persuaded the high schools that foreign languages were no longer to be considered central to the educational enterprise.[10]

Now it is high time for those responsible for educational policy at the secondary school level to have the courage of their own educational convictions and to decide curricular issues based on educational merit, not on the example of colleges. The schools have the responsibility to teach foreign languages, whether or not colleges do, because all students need the benefits of language study—not only those students who go on to college.

Language requirements should not be confined to "college preparatory" curricula, then. Notwithstanding the recommendations of the National Commission on Excellence in Education, there is nothing excellent about limiting language study to two years of work provided for the college-bound in their late adolescence. With only two years of work, no student is capable of reading the literature of another culture or understanding the complex ways in which one language shapes and forms thought differently from another. Two years of high school work, pursued by ordinary methods, is good for little more than making students pretentious. Surely if language were required only for those who go to college, and if we could somehow insure that those students go to colleges that would require the students take at least two more years in the same language, we would accomplish something. But we can guarantee none of these collegiate requirements, and it is silly to create high school requirements that will not bear fruit unless colleges cooperate.

In truth, language requirements should begin in elementary school and they should be for all students. Any student of normal intelligence is capable of learning any language, if he is capable of learning language at all. By the eighth or ninth grade, the student should be reading and speaking the language with some ease. The high school years should be devoted to learning the culture and habits of mind embodied in the language and literature of another land and to beginning study in a second or third language. This would be geniune excellence—and, in fact, it would be enjoyable. Memorizing verb endings, crucial though it is, should not be seen by students as the substance of language study. Rigorous learning of the mechanics of a language is always ancillary to learning to read, speak, and think with the language. When students realize that studying languages has a "payoff" in the ability to explore another culture, we may reasonably expect that they will find the hard work of learning the mechanics worth doing.

A language program sufficient to produce high school graduates with the level of competence for which I am calling would necessarily take a long time to put in place—at least twelve years, obviously, if we started the first batch of this program's students when those students entered first grade. In the early years of such programs, we may expect problems with finding enough teachers to staff large numbers of programs of this sort. This problem would be self-correcting, though. As children emerged from such programs fluent in a second language they would thereby increase the "teacher pool." A nation whose high school graduates were multilingual would have no more difficulty staffing language programs than English programs.

Realistically, we would have to hope at best for a few school systems to make a fifteen- to twenty-year commitment to such programs as "pilot" programs. As the programs proved their worth, more schools could be expected to follow the lead of these experimental programs. Public support should be forthcoming. With the exception of those who eschew anything "foreign," Americans would, I believe, be delighted to see our children reading, writing, and speaking fluently a second language. Of all the high-minded recommendations for educational excellence contained in current political and educational debate, surely this recommendation for multilingualism is the most workable of all. There is no way at all that anyone can deny that every person of normal intelligence is capable of learning any language. To claim that some languages are beyond the ken of normal students is to say that the speakers of that language are all brilliant. No one that I know would be willing to say that about any language.

NOTES

1. See Sandra B. Hammond and C. Edward Sebold, *Survey of Foreign Language Enrollments in Public Secondary Schools* (Washington, D.C.: U.S. Dept. of Education, 1980), p. 11.

2. Edward Sapir, *Selected Writings of Edward Sapir,* David G. Mandelbaum, ed. (Berkeley: U. of California Press, 1949), p. 10.

3. See Mills F. Edgerton, Jr., "On Knowing a Foreign Language," *ADFL Bulletin* 11, no. 1 (September 1979), 22–26.

4. Benjamin Lee Whorf, *Language, Thought, and Reality* (Cambridge: M.I.T. Press, 1956), p. 235.

5. A. Bartlett Giamatti, "On Behalf of the Humanities," *ADFL Bulletin,* 10, no. 4 (May 1979), 11.

6. Paul Simon, *The Tongue-Tied American* (New York: Continuum Publishing Corporation, 1980), p. 5.

7. *Northeast Conference on the Teaching of Foreign Languages: Our Profession: Present Status and Future Directions,* Thomas H. Geno, ed. (Middlebury, Vermont, 1980), p. 44.

8. Simon, *The Tongue-Tied American,* pp. 124–125.

9. *ACTFL Provisional Proficiency Guidelines* (Hastings-on-Hudson, New York, 1982).

10. See Peter A. Eddy, "Attitudes Toward Foreign Language Study and Requirements in American Schools and Colleges," *ADFL Bulletin* 11, no. 2 (November 1979), 8.

Improving High School History Teaching

Clair W. Keller

Nearly one thousand students, teachers, professors, and parents jammed the auditorium and patiently waited through a few short remarks by invited guests. Then the anxious waiting was over; the director stepped to the podium and began announcing the winners. "Third place, in the essay category for the Senior Division, from Ames High School in the state of Iowa, with a paper entitled: 'The History of Soper's Mill,' Chris Smith!" A loud cheer went up. The cheers continued as third-, second-, and first-place winners were announced for essays, performances, media presentations, and projects for the Junior and Senior Divisions. Cheers for history? We must be dreaming.

But it was not a dream. In fact, it happens many times each year at more than four hundred district, state, and national History Day contests.[1] No one can witness a History Day contest without sensing real enthusiasm for history. People do care about history, and learning it can be exciting and rewarding—not just for those students lucky enough to be involved in History Day, but for every student.

PROBLEMS WITH HISTORY IN THE SCHOOLS

While history in the high school curriculum may not be exactly alive and well in the 1980s, it is not quite dead—and may, indeed, be on the verge of finding new vigor. For despite the continuous attempt by "social studies" advocates during the last half century to replace history with more contemporary-oriented courses, history courses, especially American history, have demonstrated surprising staying power. Unfortunately, though, this does not mean that history is being taught, for much of what passes for history is not history at all.[2] Only history's *place* in the high school curriculum is relatively secure.

For quite some time, social studies advocates have aimed to replace history as the heart of social studies with various sorts of ersatz social science. Many social studies educators would, like the late Edgar Wesley, eliminate history as we know it from the curriculum. In a 1967 article entitled "Let's Abolish History Courses!" Wesley argued that history met no ". . . needs that pupils can appreciate." History, in his view, should be changed from a course to a resource. "No teacher at any grade level, however, should teach a course in history as content. To do so is as confusing, unnecessary, frustrating, futile, pointless, and as illogical as to teach a course in the World Almanac, the dictionary or the Encyclopedia. The content of history is to be utilized and exploited—not studied, learned, or memorized."[3]

Wesley's article might well have served as the intellectual backdrop for recent curriculum proposals in New York, which resembled an attempt to eliminate history. Contemporary "Wesleyanism" is also evident in a proposal by the Social Science Education Consortium. This curriculum proposal, called SPAN (Social Studies/Social Science Education: Priorities, Practices, and Needs)[4] grew out of a National Science Foundation study of social studies education from 1955 to 1975. SPAN put forth an agenda for reform that would radically alter the social studies curriculum within the schools, recommending that it be organized thematically around social roles, ". . . through which most young people and adults participate in the social world—citizen, worker, consumer, family member, friend, member of social groups and self." The seventh- through ninth-grade courses would abandon chronology in favor of topical treatments of social roles. The secondary grades' course *structure* would be retained, but with a different emphasis. The tenth-grade "world cultures" course would be organized around social roles. The United States history course at the eleventh grade would focus on the same topic, though within a chronological framework. U.S. government, with its focus on citizenship, would remain a one-semester requirement at the twelfth grade. A series of interdisciplinary electives and social action courses focused on one or more societal roles would also be offered. Discipline-based courses would be made available, as well, "particularly for college-bound students."[5] While SPAN seems to suggest a radical departure from the present social studies curriculum, it could also be seen as echoing the *Progressive Education*'s agenda of the 1930s and, perhaps, the "Seven Cardinal Principles" of 1918.

Even courses that do deal with history have, in many schools, been broken into innumerable "minicourses" on a hodge-podge of topics that have little integration with each other or comprehensiveness as a curriculum. This balkanization of the history curriculum resulted from several important influences during the 1960s and the 1970s. In part, it shows a sincere and well-meaning response by history teachers to the demand that the traditional history course include minorities. This demand, especially by blacks, struck a responsive chord among curriculum planners and seemed to be best met at the time by creating special courses or units. Few teachers knew enough to incorporate sound Black history into general history courses. Thus specialists in "Black studies" were hired to teach separate Black history courses. Colleges also provided new courses on Black history or the black experience, courses that many high schools emulated. Other minority groups demanded similar treatment, until the whole year of high school American history often became a baffling concatenation of minicourses on Blacks, Indians, Chicanos, other ethnics, and women.

Along with the demand for specialized courses, there also arose a desire by curriculum reformers to make school more "relevant." Students, they argued, wanted schools to be responsive to what these reformers presumed were student needs, or even to students' uninformed notions of their own needs. The mood shifted away from the concept of a teacher-supplied core curriculum or set of basic requirements toward a curriculum based on demand, where students developed their own courses of study. This view reflected what Tom Wolfe has called the "me generation" attitude. In an effort to become more relevant, some schools went into the business of offering minicourses (six- or nine-week units) on a wide variety of subjects. Course requirements for graduation and entrance were eliminated or drastically cut at all levels of education.

The minicourse approach contributed to a pervasive presentism insofar as unit topics were studied without reference to historical context. The relations among social, economic, and political events went unnoticed. As a result, certain events were given weight far beyond their historical significance, while others were slighted. This could only result in a distorted view of the past.

In addition, federally funded social studies curriculum development projects during the 1960s and the early 1970s advocated a methodology that encouraged abandonment of a survey approach in teaching the various disciplines in favor of the inquiry method. The inquiry method, out of necessity, relied on narrowly delimited area and case studies. Which problems and cases were to be studied was decided on the basis of what issues were currently interesting to curriculum specialists. The Revolutionary War, for example, was studied through the concept of loyalty because loyalty is what the authors of one social studies project called a persistent issue.[6] By focusing on the concept of loyalty, though, the central question of the American Revolution—why the colonists decided to abolish their colonial status—managed to get lost. Historical roots of the conflict were often ignored in favor of more "relevant" issues.

Increasing specialization within the scholarly discipline of history also contributed to fragmentation of the traditional survey course. The "new history" with its emphasis on quantification and narrowly defined topics, has balkanized history studies even further than political pressures on schools have. As a consequence of the increased array of course offerings at the college level, it has become more difficult for students to take a broad course that integrates these topics. Hence, prospective teachers have too little experience with which to integrate these fragments into survey courses to teach at the secondary level. Instead, teachers concentrate on specialized units and topics in which they feel adequately prepared. Lack of adequate preparation may also explain why, when survey courses are taught at the secondary level, teachers may slavishly follow the textbook. They do not know enough about the broad sweep of their field to do otherwise.

As social studies have pushed history away from its central place in the curriculum, and as minority history, beguiling electives, the inquiry method, and specialized scholarship have fragmented the history programs that still exist, students have been deprived of the chief benefits of history study. History is, simply, the collective memory of mankind, and all people need to partake in this memory. History is the account of how the human species developed over time: its triumphs, its tragedies, its patterns of life in different cultures and eras. Knowledge of history is one of the things that distinguish civilized people from barbarians: the civilized person is one who has learned, and continues to learn, from the experience of past generations. Those who are without knowledge of history are cultural amnesiacs: they cannot know who they are, because they do not know whence they came.

The study of history should develop in students a sense of historical time: seeing events in relations of cause and effect, influence and reaction, repetition and origination; understanding the interplay of the many aspects of political, artistic, intellectual, economic, and social life; gaining a sense of both change and endurance. Students must develop a sense of time and place—what we usually call "perspective," though the word has become so common that it is hardly expressive now. A person who lacks perspective has no basis for judging the significance of current events. Some events that seem of enormous importance to the untutored dwindle when seen in historical perspective—and some apparently innocuous happenings reveal their true portent. A person who lacks historical perspective cannot distinguish social practices that are dying from those being born or the transient from the enduring—indeed, it is hard even to recognize that these distinctions matter, if one has no perspective on the processes of change.

The reasons that "social concepts" courses and balkanized history curricula cannot provide these traits of mind are not hard to identify. The contemporary orientation of "social studies" and the usual emphasis in such courses on generalizations about societies leave the student without any rich lode of information about the past. (Concrete facts, after all, are the source of history's power to illuminate the human condition.) Balkanized history gives one partial, hence distorted, perspectives. A scholar is surely justified, for myriad reasons, in specializing in a carefully defined topic, and he has the expertise to do his work in perspective—precisely because he is a scholar who has learned a great deal about a great deal more history than the area that is his research specialty. But youngsters do not have the background that makes responsible specialization possible. The child, for instance, who learns little of the history of race relations in this country because that subject is dealt with only in an elective course on Black history that he does not elect, is poorly prepared to make responsible decisions on matters of racial justice. A child in Hispanic studies who is taught more about the Mexican-American War or the history of U.S. dealings with Puerto Rico than about the American Revolution or the Civil War is poorly prepared to understand the shape of this nation. If students are to be given a sense of perspective, they must be given a balanced, integrated narrative of the whole social fabric of our country and its diverse heritage.

We cannot be surprised at an electorate that refuses to rise above special-interest politics if our schools teach only special-interest history. Students with no sense of the ways our many histories combine into the history of a single country cannot be expected to have much sense of the public interest. For they have been taught that there are only private interests, and that one has common cause only with those whose private interests coincide with his own.

ON TEACHING HISTORY WELL

One remedy for the maladies described is for history teachers to reinstate an appropriately modified version of the chronological survey approach to teaching history. History loses its sense of time and place when taught any other way. "Appropriately modified" means that the manner in which we conceive of history and the methods through which we present it must accord with the reasons we study it in the first place.

When history is taught as "Here is how it was"—the traditional recounting of a matter-of-fact pretense at certainty and clarity—at least three undesirable things happen: students never learn that historical knowledge always rests on active integration of diverse evidence and inference beyond what is clearly known; they fail to see that one must know and utilize some general truths about how the world works in making the inferences and integrations that constitute historical knowledge; and study itself becomes dull, routinized, and passive. Though true intellectual work never ceases to be demanding, just as physical work is always tiring, it can be rewarding and even enjoyable, if done well. In history teaching, classroom work (and homework) should reflect how thinking gets done—though without the arrogant pretense that the student is himself a full-fledged historian, as if adolescents were supposed to be able to duplicate through "inquiry" in a couple of years the fruits of generations of mature scholarship! Rather, teachers should lead students through a survey of the period and place that the course covers, but do so in ways that reflect patterns of genuine historical judgment.

An illustration may help. Suppose that, at the beginning of a study of the Revolutionary War, we want to examine causes of the war. We start by asking students how we might find out what caused it. If we could go back in time, to whom would we need to talk? What information could we expect each to have? What factors about the involvement of each of these persons should we consider in evaluating his testimony? When would this person be in a position to tell us the most? Since we can't go back and talk to these people, what sorts of artifacts should we look for that substitute for interviews and provide corroboration or rebuttal of the testimony that we are likely to glean from other sources? What characteristics of humans might have to do with the start of the war? Why do people want to be free from various kinds of situations? What sorts of things prompt people finally to decide to act on a risky desire for freedom? Then we ask which of these human traits might be relevant to the American colonists. Once we have laid out all of this background, we are ready to guide students through serious study of texts—both texts from the period, which serve as "evidence," and textbook accounts, which can be evaluated critically as to how well the relevant questions that we have identified have been taken into account.

The strategy of teaching in this manner I call "the complete lesson," in that it includes not only inquiry but guided, disciplined learning. The complete lesson consists of three types of activity. First, students acquire data in any number of ways—reading, listening, or observing. But obtaining data is not sufficient if students are going to do more than regurgitate it. Consequently, in the second or application phase of the complete lesson, students use data to develop some kind of product. This product may be written or oral preparation for a class or group discussion, an essay, a project, even a dramatization. The activity works best, however, when students use data to make a decision or defend a position. During the final phase or analysis, students, guided by the teacher, review and evaluate the thinking used in the development of their products. If, for example, a group of students has staked out a particular explanation of the colonists' break with Great Britain, the teacher might raise the following questions: What assumptions about human nature are implied in your decision? What data did you find most useful in reaching your decision? Are there other data that you could have used? If so, what? Did all colonists hold the same opinion? How would you know? Were the reasons for colonial independence similar to more recent independence movements? Would you say your reasons for why the colonists wanted independence reflect latent or manifest events?[7]

A crucial proviso must be emphasized. The transition from speculating about ideal historical sources to the reality of using actual documents and evaluating textbook accounts allows the teacher to make clear the inferential, fallible nature of knowledge; but in so doing it also allows for precluding the mistaken notion that, since knowledge is tentative, one opinion is as good as another. The teacher must be clear and emphatic that historical judgments are not equal, that some are ruled out completely by evidence while others fit the evidence, as credible presumptions about human behavior, more or less well. Students must learn not only that knowledge involves making active judgments, but that judgments must be based on evidence, that a solid base of information is necessary for making any reliable judgment at all, that "background" knowledge is crucial to making judgments, and that rules of logic are decisive in weighing the probable truth of any opinion. This method rests not on a romantic notion that adolescents can somehow "figure out for themselves" what it has taken legions of mature scholars decades of serious study to discover. Rather, it is based on the premise that teaching any student any body of knowledge must reflect the structure of thought, must employ the best available techniques, and must respect the content of the subject as well as its methodologies.

THE HISTORY CURRICULUM

A radical revision of the scope and sequence of the history/social studies curriculum is needed in most schools, if we are to nurture in students both the habits of mind and bodies of knowledge that result from solid history study and sufficient familiarity with social science "concepts" that have too often been substituted for history. There is no reason that students should not have both; surely all people can harvest the fruits of the social sciences, and all need to be able to think clearly about the organization and functioning of societies. Current curricula, though, jumble these with history in ways that defeat our attempts to teach either well.

We do well, experience convinces me, to conceive of the last six years of schooling—grades seven through twelve—as the span of the social studies/history curriculum. Across these six years we can integrate a coherent selection of courses that meets the legitimate concerns of social studies advocates, provides extended and serious study of history, equips the student with the knowledge that he needs to be a functioning member of a democracy, and matches the curriculum with normal patterns of intellectual development in children.

In the seventh and eighth grades, students should study material "more concrete" than the economic, political, and sociological abstractions that inform most American or world history courses. We do well to begin with study of the students' own community and to pay special attention to those aspects of community life that are familiar to the child, though not particularly well understood by him. The seventh- and eight-grade years are good times for "local history" exercises—of which the *Foxfire* series is the best known, and quaintest, example. While courses rooted in such exercises at the senior high school level too often usurp more advanced work that is essential to understanding our country and to participating responsibly in our culture, in the early years of post-primary school they serve the useful purposes of acquainting students with methods of research that they can understand, of making history "real," of helping the child develop an identification with his community that transcends his personal place in it, and of serving as a bridge from the child's immediate environment to more advanced facility with abstractions of the sort one will need to study larger spans of history and society. These purposes will be served, though, only if these courses are well constructed and purposefully led by an astute teacher. We can organize these courses around study of activities and social relationships with which children are familiar, have the children study local lore and characteristics, and help them learn to generalize and conceptualize on the basis of concrete facts that constitute the substance of the course.

Though the seventh/eight-grade sequence should contain local history, it should not be entirely or even primarily local in focus, if it is to serve both to enlarge the students' vistas and to help them understand their community in more general terms. We begin with a semester, perhaps, of "research" into local patterns, then move into a balanced systematic selection of studies of communities of other sorts, conducted in the "normal" manner of academic studies in which the students examine those activities of other communities that are analogous to the activities of which they have learned first-hand in their own community. The point, we reiterate, is to teach students what history is, and to get them accustomed to learning about past events through a chronological approach that illuminates the present as they experience it—all in a manner that is appropriate for the young adolescent's lack of facility with abstractions.

The high school years should give roughly one year to the study of world history and two years to the study of American history. Less than this simply leaves the student poorly informed. A fourth year of electives in history and social sciences should be available.

In the study of world history, all students should begin with the origins of our Western heritage in the Middle East, then trace its spread through the Mediterranean region into Europe. Study of Asia and Africa would be integrated into the course by taking up the interactions between those cultures and Western cultures as Europeans developed extensive, rather continuous contact with those lands. The point would be to show the student how Western civilization arose and developed and how its development included influencing and being influenced by other cultures. Careful attention should be given to the commercial, economic, cultural, and intellectual conditions that laid the foundations for the emergence, in the seventeenth century, of modern Europe. Study of the seventeenth and eighteenth centuries should focus on the cultural and social changes that attended the rise of modern science, the development of modern states, and the arrival of modern forms of political power and governance, while investigation of the nineteenth and twentieth centuries would be appropriately organized around themes that help us understand the emergence of contemporary political, social, cultural, and economic relationships between countries—and around "missed opportunities" that might have led to different relations.

The two-year American history sequence would place our history in the context provided by the students' knowledge of world history—so that, for instance, students would readily understand the willingness of France to support the American Revolution. In the American history sequence, though, relations with other countries would be seen from a perspective that leads students to understand why, in fact, we acted as we did in this or that instance. Taking "an American perspective" does not mean indulging in self-justification or refusing to deal with evidence that points toward ill-conceived endeavors of unsavory interests. We judge the unsavory aspects of our past as we judge our personal errors—not with self-loathing, but with a desire to understand why they transpired and with the goal of using the resultant self-understanding to improve our decision-making.

The notion of "an American perspective" raises thorny issues that must be faced directly, namely, issues of whose perspective we shall take as *the* American perspective or whether there is any perspective that transcends the special interests of this or that subculture, ethnic group, or social class. I do not offer a simple answer. Identifying the interests that all Americans have in common, distinguishing the different ways that different groups have been served by different governmental policies and social practices at various times in our history, and ascertaining which aspects of a "subculture's" unique past or present characteristics are essential for every citizen to understand, are questions that are to be worked through by serious scholars, dedicated teachers, and informed lay people in thoughtful reflection and earnest debate. What is crucial, though, is that *we not give up the attempt* to forge an understanding of what it is to be an American and an understanding of how the interactions of diverse groups together constitute a culture that we hold in common.

From the facts that not all interests of all Americans are well served all the time, that some interests have at times been horribly violated, and that it is difficult to set forth all the features of the common culture or common interests that would best define an American perspective, it surely does not follow that we ought to succumb to a fragmented view of the past or that there can be no such thing as American history taught and learned from an American perspective. What it means is that we must be much more catholic, subtle, and perspicacious in identifying this history than we have often been in the past. We do not have a responsibility to our students to be infallible, to identify with absolute certitude at a given time everything that our common history should include or can omit. But we do have a responsibility to impart to our students both a sense that we do have a common history, a beginning at understanding large parts of it, and competence to join in the ongoing efforts to define and contribute to our common present and shared future.[8]

At the end of the three-year history sequence, students should have a good general understanding of the broad picture of history. We hope that many students will want more than this, indeed, that a large number will have developed interests that their newly won background in history gives them competence to pursue. In the twelfth grade, students should have access to an array of electives in history and in social sciences and "social studies." These may each be one semester long so that the high school senior can take two different ones. We may envision, for instance, substantive courses in civics, economics, sociology, or political science. We can, as well, envision advanced history courses on particular topics. The senior year is an appropriate time for students to pursue specialized interests, perhaps the history of the family, of civil rights, or of Constitutional interpretation. Moreover, it is a good time for students to study orthodox history topics in greater depth than survey courses allow. A two-semester sequence, for instance, on nineteenth- and twentieth-century Europe would be an asset to any curriculum, as would be a semester on colonialism followed by a semester on totalitarianism.

The precise organization of the curriculum can vary from school to school, of course, so long as students are thoroughly grounded in the facts and forces that have shaped human history. The "social studies" sequence is to be thoroughly historical—the teachings of the social sciences are to be used to illuminate the workings of history, not the other way around. The principal issues to be studied are those that in fact shaped the lives of the peoples under study, not merely those that appear "relevant to us today." The curriculum is to be integrated and intelligible, not a concatenation of discrete, incommensurate subdisciplinary studies. The transcendent obligation is to develop in students an understanding of the movement of history and a sense of historical time and cultural place.

RESPONSIBILITIES FOR REFORM

The sorts of reform necessary to make history teaching what it should be are of many sorts and require the cooperation of people at many levels of the school and in all domains of education.

Teachers can improve their methods and their knowledge by the simple and inexpensive expedients of reading.[9] Curriculum reform is more complicated, but is even more crucial, since in too many schools the history curriculum resembles nothing like a coherent recounting. Schools should—odd though it is to have to say this—be sure that curriculum planners who have jurisdiction over social studies have thorough training and active interest in history, and that teachers are hired and assigned to history courses only if they have studied enough history to know whereof they speak. Too many teachers assigned to history are certified through an "area studies" provision that may allow them to teach history with as little as six hours of college credit in the discipline. Too many social studies curriculum planners have scant knowledge of history and less active interest in it.

Colleges and the disciplinary scholars who inhabit them have major responsibilities, too. For several decades, most professional historians have declined to give attention to the needs of the schools. That schools still teach history is because "ordinary citizens" insist upon it, not because scholars have worked to insure that high school students learn it. This must change, and the change is in the interest of the history profession as much as it is a responsibility that all scholars have. Unless the schools interest people in history and give them enough knowledge to value it and to continue their reading and thinking after their formal schooling is over, there is little reason to believe that a highly mobile culture will continue to know where its roots are—or even that it has any—and to value the historian who traces them. To obviate this state of affairs, scholars should work vigorously to upgrade school programs. Among the many ways that this could be done, two are most readily apparent and easily instituted. Scholars can make themselves available for—and can take the lead in urging schools to develop—inservice training programs for teachers that focus on historical content. In such programs, the scholars must accommodate themselves to the needs of the schools—not by watering down what they have to say, as if teachers were incapable of mature thought, but in understanding the structures of curricula, the lives of teachers, and (most important) the types of history needed by the "ordinary people" who are the schools' constituents. Too often, scholars approach inservice training patronizingly, with predictable results. Second, the history departments in colleges and the scholars who teach there should design courses appropriate for the prospective teacher. Most college history courses are designed either for the nonhistorian or for the nascent research scholar. The prospective teacher is not quite either. The prospective teacher needs guidance in integrating the results of his study of the eight or ten courses that constitute a history major. History departments would do well to offer senior seminars for prospective teachers, in which the scope would be that of a survey course, but the assumption would be that the students already knew a great deal about the subjects to be surveyed. The content of such courses would focus on integrating deeper points of scholarship and learning to form sound judgments as to the "broad sweep" of history. Nowhere in colleges is this sort of course common, but this is what the prospective teacher needs. For his job is precisely to form and evaluate such judgments accurately.

In comparison to the rest of the civilized world, America has little history; we are, after all, only a few hundred years old. But that is no reason for us not to value the teaching of history. That is no reason to think that our students can be handed little or no history, in incoherent forms, by teachers who themselves have too little knowledge of the subject, without the students individually and our society collectively suffering for it. Indeed, in a democratic country most of all, historical understanding is a trait required by—and of—every citizen.

NOTES

1. National History Day is a National Endowment for the Humanities Youth project and has grown from a modest three-state regional event in 1977 to a national contest with students participating from more than forty states.

2. William Carroll, et al., "The Teaching of History in the Public High Schools" (unpublished report, August 1979). Richard S. Kirkendall, "The Status of History in the Schools, *The Journal of American History,* 62 (September 1975), 557–570.

3. Edgar B. Wesley, "Let's Abolish History Courses!", *Phi Delta Kappan* 49 (September 1967), 3. See also S. Samuel Sheris, "Six Myths Which Delude History Teachers," *Phi Delta Kappan* 49 (September 1967), 9–12.

4. Irving Morrissett, Douglas Superka, Sharryl Hawke, "Recommendations for Improving Social Studies in the 1980s," *Social Education* 44 (December 1980), 571–572.

5. Ibid.

6. Fred M. Newman and Donald W. Oliver, *Clarifying Public Controversy: An Approach to Teaching Social Studies* (Boston: Little, Brown, 1970), pp. 242–243.

7. For further development of this idea, see Clair W. Keller, *Involvng Students in the New Social Studies* (Boston: Little, Brown, 1974), pp. 26–27.

8. It might well be advisable for the professional historians' and social studies teachers' organizations to convene a joint committee to identify the essentials of American history—as was done in 1943. Our national need for schools that initiate students into our common culture should outweigh any fears of overcentralized curriculum policymaking.

9. Teachers should also make concerted efforts to "make history come alive" in their classrooms. See my "Using Creative Interviews to Personalize Decision-Making on the American Revolution," *Social Education* 43 (March 1979), 271ff and my "Giving an Alternative to the Traditional Research Paper," *Network News Exchange* (Fall 1982), 6–8. Moreover, it is crucial that teachers become active in professional organizations, which provide ample opportunity for improving one's skills and understanding.

CASE STUDIES

Teaching the Humanities: The Ideal within the Real

Scott Colley

A colleague at my university is fond of claiming he is not a pessimist: "Pessimists are people who believe something dreadful is about to happen. I believe it has already happened." By that definition, the recent report of the National Commission on Excellence in Education is not pessimistic. The title of that report—*A Nation at Risk: The Imperative for Educational Reform*—suggests that the worst has already come about.[1] American education today lies in near ruins as if it were the victim of an act of war. The report states: "For the first time in the history of our country, the educational skills of one generation will not surpass, will not equal, will not even approach, those of their parents." William Bennett, chairman of the National Endowment for the Humanities, has spoken in similar terms about education in the humanities today. Students who have not studied "Aristotle, Aquinas, or Kant are urged to examine ethical dilemmas of their own." We have become a country with a fascination for the "merely contemporary." The humanities lie "shattered."[2]

The education of the young has always been a vexing question, and we can find accounts of frustration and disappointment in chronicles that go back through the history of our civilization. Yet the stakes do seem higher now, and the costs of failure greater than before. Given the evidence, such pessimism may be warranted. On the other hand, there is also evidence that educational reform is possible, and that the quest for excellence is not simply a Utopian dream. The accomplishments of our best students and teachers, and the "pockets of excellence" that exist throughout every school system present us with patterns for greater accomplishment. The ideal school system is, in fact, foreshadowed in the everyday reality of students, teachers, and schools in our own communities.

Two educational models can serve to illustrate the ideal that exists within the real. One model is a special summer program at Vanderbilt University for a small group of gifted and talented high school juniors. The other model—or more properly, the example of three schools that can be taken as a model—reveals how the humanities are being taught and should be taught in secondary schools. A well-funded and highly selective summer program on a university campus can indeed represent appropriate standards for average schools; and the best efforts of our best students and teachers are not too much to ask of the school system as a whole. We have already determined legitimate goals and have met some of these goals in our schools today. The challenge is to move from our small accomplishments into a major educational reform.

A MODEL OF EXCELLENCE: TEACHING THE GIFTED

The Lyndhurst Foundation of Chattanooga approached Vanderbilt University with an invitation to compete for a grant to bring forty Tennessee high school juniors to campus for a month in the summer. The program was to be residential; all of the students' costs were to be paid by the granting agency; and the curriculum was open. We could teach what we wanted to teach. The only two stipulations were that (1) the students had to be among the most intellectually accomplished and enthusiastic in the state, and (2) we were to stimulate the students to recognize the social and moral obligations that accompany their intellectual gifts. The Vanderbilt provost asked me to write a description of such a month-long program, and ultimately the Lyndhurst Foundation awarded Vanderbilt the grant.

In our discussions about a program for talented and gifted high school juniors, we agreed to pursue some goals that are not easily attained in high schools. We wanted to give the students some challenges that would make their summer with us a unique one. We also wanted to bring our students to think about moral issues, and about the special obligation that talented people have to their society, without simply preaching to them. An additional factor was perhaps most significant of all: each of the participants in our program was to be a Tennessean. We wished to include something in our course of study that would take into account the shared geography, if not the shared heritage, of the students who would spend a month together on our campus.

As the course of study developed, it turned out that the uniqueness of the curriculum lay in its balance. Art, literature, and science and technology were equally important elements of the curriculum. The course of study was also more concentrated than is usual in high schools. No single course involved the survey of a single field. Special problems and issues formed the focal points of our approaches. None of the *Summer Challenge* curriculum (that is what we came to call our program) was beyond the capacities of the better teachers and better students in high schools today, although few high schools would have the laboratory facilities and computer capacities from which we benefited. The ways in which young people were challenged in the Vanderbilt summer program suggest analogous ways of shaping the sources of study of many American students. Here is an outline of the Summer Challenge curriculum:

1. The Biological Revolution: From Chromosomes to Moral Complexity

   Students ran an experiment using their own white blood cells in which they isolated and eventually photographed some of their chromosomes. The course afforded occasions to explore moral issues that have been raised by recent biological research.

2. The Computer: Machine or Idol?

   Students learned BASIC, certain programing techniques, and some games that helped them progress beyond a beginner's level on the computer. They also explored how computers function, how they should and should not be used, and their potential for the future. Students considered the implications that the computer revolution has for the ways in which we approach problem solving as well as for the ways in which we define ourselves as persons. (Students who came with some knowledge of computer language were given special instructions and special classwork so that they could build upon what they already knew.)

3. Creativity and Thought in the Arts

   Summer Challenge participants took part in three one-day workshops in music, dance, and theater, and discussed ideas and techniques with a variety of performers and witnessed a number of performances. Performers themselves taught this unit of the summer program, and obliged students to participate in exercises or demonstrations that helped them understand the art form in question better than they had before.

4. Southern Literature and Culture

Students read some of the works of two highly creative groups of poets and essayists who lived and worked at Vanderbilt in the 1920s and 1930s. They also learned about Southern folklore, musical traditions of the South, the importance of Black American culture, and about some recent Southern writers and artists. Students sought to define themselves as Americans by defining themselves as members of a distinct region and a unique state. They were challenged to write a Southern manifesto for the twenty-first century—to determine what sort of society they want to build in their state and in their country.

There was no course in Summer Challenge called "philosophy" or "ethics," although each course was given to serious philosophical and ethical speculation. Questions of value arose daily in the curriculum.

In the brochure that describes our course of study, we listed three points that were central to Summer Challenge: (1) Is one kind of knowledge better than another? (2) Is there a limit to what we can learn? (3) What is the connection between what we know and what we ought to do?

Responses to these points were necessarily complex. Indeed, after four weeks of hard and thoughtful work students only began to form clear answers to the three central questions. The students also began to understand when neat and simple answers fail them, and when ambiguity and paradox must be tolerated for sustained periods of thought and speculation. Students learned that it is possible to know many important things, and that there are well-defined ways of going about obtaining this knowledge. They also learned that some forms of knowing oblige them to live with certain mysteries, puzzles, and uncertainties. Our students were prepared to confront these different types of knowing. The true intellectual continually struggles with difficulty of determining what can and cannot be known.

We insisted that gifted, intelligent people have to consider a number of forms of knowledge, and that art, science, computer technology, and literature are parts of a unified way of understanding the world in which we live. Our students will remember that they ignore certain areas of knowing at their peril; the keys to the future are found in many separate fields. Perhaps our course of study was somewhat utopian in its commitment to the connections between things. All of our Summer Challenge teachers worked to define the complementary character of four courses, and helped the students place their diverse lessons into a coherent viewpoint on human experience.

We wanted our students to perceive the ways in which computer literacy is complemented by cultural literacy, and that good lab techniques complement sound techniques of literacy or aesthetic analysis. The most significant connections we pursued are those that link values to the field in which one has an intellectual interest. Ethics and morality are inherent in everything our students do and everything they study, and we therefore wanted them to pursue the connections between technology and human values, or between art and ethics. In many schools and most academic disciplines, these connections are usually so subtle and complex that most teachers hesitate to speak of them, fearing perhaps that they will oversimplify or distort. The teachers in the Summer Challenge program sought to demonstrate relationships among various fields without ignoring the important distinctions between them. We certainly distinguished the scientific approach from the artistic, and we contrasted computer power with human reason. Such contrasts did not prevent us from showing how knowledge is connected to action, and how the study of academic subjects is connected to the ways in which we assign values in our world.

The Summer Challenge program was, of course, blessed with excellent students, ample resources, and an unusual faculty. The program itself was devoted to the liberal arts, not merely to the humanities. At least half of the students' class time was given to science and technology. But the core of the program was in fact humanistic, dealing with questions of value, obligation, and epistemology. Regular high schools, as well as special programs for the gifted, can offer an education that is primarily humanistic in scope. Reason and the imagination, history and literature, thinking, and the consideration of value should form the curriculum of our schools. Mathematics and science classes, indeed, even health classes, can be occasions when questions of meaning and value arise and are addressed. One of the dangers of any educational system, indeed of any culture, is the habit of separating knowledge into discrete units. Educators err (as citizens err) when they assume that history and physics are fields that never touch; or when they suppose that discussions of meaning and interpretation belong only in English classes, not in biology or chemistry. The greatest danger to education as well as to the humanities is the popular assumption that the humanistic fields have little or nothing to do with real life. Among the important goals of every school should be (1) respecting the academic integrity of each subject while (2) showing how that subject assists persons as they go about the everyday business of their lives. No educator can pretend, for instance, that every history lesson has automatic relevance to whatever may be in the newspaper; yet, no educator should separate textbook lessons from the many examples and lessons afforded by daily life.

MODELS OF EXCELLENCE IN ORDINARY HIGH SCHOOLS

A special summer program can supply some useful goals for regular academic-year courses of study. But special programs illustrate ideals more clearly than they represent the difficulties that teachers and students face in regular schools during ordinary periods of the year. In order to balance the ideal with the real, I visited three Tennessee high schools to discover how they approached instruction in the humanities—primarily English—as well as to learn how closely the educational approaches of the schools resembled the education goals of Summer Challenge. Three high schools can hardly represent the range of experiences one might encounter in the 480 high schools of Tennessee; a sample of at least a dozen schools would produce much more accurate information about the teaching of the humanities in the state. Tennessee, it may be noted, is hardly characteristic of national approaches to secondary education, ranking as it does at the bottom of per pupil expenditures, and reflecting perhaps a more conservative, rural population than other areas that might have served as samples. Some of the triumphs and some of the problems in Tennessee are local ones. Yet educators will recognize in these schools certain patterns and personality types that can throw light on what is going on even in very different parts of the country. (The names of the schools have been changed.)

Before visiting the schools, I outlined some goals of a humanistic education, and I later discussed these goals with many of the teachers whose classes I had visited. The following seven points represent some ideals about which we could easily agree:

1. Students should learn to write with critical facility and to speak with some articulateness.
2. They should learn to read with critical insight.
3. They should learn to think critically.
4. They should recognize the relationships between reason and imagination, between intellectual and artistic (or poetic) ways of knowing about human experience.
5. They should learn about their history and culture.
6. They should learn about histories and cultures that have influenced their own.
7. They should explore the connections between knowledge and ac-

tion; that is, they should know how to use what they learn in school in their lives as moral, responsible people.

These goals are founded upon some assumptions about the connection between knowledge and morality. Knowledge is empty unless we can act upon it, and our actions have to be based upon a moral system. Our students cannot consider knowledge simply as the subject matter of books, but rather must see it as a guide to what they should do. They should recognize the value of clear speaking, and critical writing, reading, and thinking in day-to-day life. Certainly our students should recognize that the uses of the imagination are as significant as the uses of the intellect, and vice versa, and that reason and feeling should work in harmony. Students need to learn how they have been formed from their history and culture, and how they are now forming that history and culture: they are the products of past time, and are contributors to time that is yet to be. Ideals or goals are important because they remind us what we should strive for, although we must realize that no teacher or student can expect to meet every one. Perhaps these are best understood as goals for twelve years of education. In my visits, I sought to discover how well these ideals are met within the reality of three very different Tennessee high schools.

English at Comprehensive High

There has been a public high school in this small city in Tennessee for well over one hundred years. The present principal graduated from Comprehensive High over thirty years ago. It has been a good school for many years, and certainly one element in its success today is its habit of success. In the past few years, Comprehensive High School has produced a Rhodes Scholar, eight honor scholars at Vanderbilt University (only a dozen or so honor scholarships of the type are awarded each year), a dozen or more National Merit Scholarship semifinalists, and many winners in nationwide mathematics and language competitions. Comprehensive High School also produced six of the top sixty finalists in the competition for places in the Summer Challenge program. It was this last remarkable accomplishment that drew me to visit this school to talk to students, teachers, and administrators, and to sit in on classes.

English is required each year of high school; Comprehensive offers these classes on three levels: basic, average, and advanced. Basic English is designed for students who enter the ninth grade with poor achievement scores, or who fail to pass the Tennessee proficiency examination during their freshman year. Basic English is offered each year thereafter for students who continue to fail the examination. (Students have five chances to pass this ninth-grade-level examination, including two opportunities in their senior year. Students who cannot pass the examination do not receive a high school diploma. The test covers mathematics, reading, and spelling.) Average English involves the majority of the high school students, and a small percentage (about 15 percent) enroll in advanced classes. The small number of Comprehensive students who complete four years of advanced English are probably as well-educated in that subject as any public high school students anywhere.

After five tries at the proficiency examination in English, about twelve students in a graduating class of three hundred will fail to earn their high school diplomas. A number of others will pass the examination only because they devote the best part of their school years preparing for it. The average and advanced English classes profit in paradoxical ways from the failure of a quarter or more students to pass the proficiency examination easily. The D and F students are grouped in basic English; the A students are in advanced English. It is clear to see who remains in the middle.

While students in average and advanced ninth-grade English are reading *The Odyssey, Great Expectations,* and *Romeo and Juliet,* students in basic courses are laboring through assignments in *Read Magazine* and *Scope Magazine.* Advanced ninth-graders read more than the average ones, and do extra work in essay writing and composition. The pattern of ninth-grade English is repeated thereafter: basic students continue to work on simple problems of grammar, usage, and reading, while the advanced students continue to work somewhat harder than average students. The tenth grade is devoted to a survey of literary genres (poetry, fiction, and drama), eleventh grade is a survey of American literature, and the twelfth grade is a survey of British literature. The curriculum for average and advanced English is similar to what it was twenty-five years ago.

The school may also benefit in a paradoxical way from an unfortunate architectural design. The present building opened in 1968, and is given to an open classroom arrangement. It is made up of a series of enormous circular rooms, each one the size of a gymnasium. Wedge-shaped classrooms, separated only by temporary partitions, are grouped in these enormous circles, with the result that students can overhear classes in English, history, and Spanish simultaneously. The struggle to hear one's own teacher certainly could in fact force some students to concentrate, although the din must prevent some students from learning all that they might in a quieter classroom.

Students at Comprehensive High do more essay writing than in most other schools. Students in advanced classes write as many as eighty notebook pages each term, which comes out to just about a page of writing for every day in class. Even students in basic English write about thirty notebook pages a term; many of these pages are daily journal entries composed during the opening minutes of class time. One teacher started her students in free writing assignments for two minutes a day; after a month she doubled that time; then there was a two- or three-month period of six-minute free writing assignments; only after seven months of classes did they move into ten-minute free writing exercises. These assignments are checked, but not marked. The teachers simply try to bring their students to write something during such moments. Corrections and revisions take place during other exercises.

During an average week, about three days of average and advanced English courses are given to reading and literary analysis; one day is given to grammar and usage; and another to composition and rhetoric. Senior advanced English might devote somewhat more time to literary analysis. It is clear that Comprehensive teachers are content to accomplish only a little at a time, counting upon the accumulation of knowledge over a long period rather than upon sudden and dramatic accomplishments at any given moment. Besides the obvious distractions of neighboring classes, there are constant interruptions from the public address system, and frequent delays and absences occasioned by field trips, contests, athletic meets, and extracurricular events that take place during school hours rather than after. Every teacher spoke of these interruptions, and all teachers mentioned how difficult it is to cover their material in the 160 school days that are available to them during an academic year. Students at the school are encouraged to take part in a number of out-of-class activities, and while such activity complements their classroom performance, the constant coming and going, background noise, school announcements, and visits from the occasional university dean make an average day an untidy affair. A 50-minute period becomes considerably shorter due to all of the intrusions that accompany a typical day at an active and energetic school.

Most English teachers at Comprehensive High agree that, rather than simply teaching English, they are teaching students to open their minds, to think, to develop curiosity, to look to the future rather than only at the present, indeed, to look deep into themselves rather than to live on the surface of things. Teachers also agreed that they want their students to use both reason and imagination; they want them to be more articulate in speech and more fluid in writing; and they want their students to understand human experience by analogy to the experiences that are recorded in poems, plays, and novels. One teacher of advanced ninth-graders told me that her secret triumph of the year so far came when some of the boys in her class saw themselves as sharing certain human problems with the female protagonist of *A Tree Grows in Brooklyn*. That critical detachment is one of the special goals of all teachers who spoke to me about their classes. Not a single teacher mentioned the mastery of English and American literature as a notable goal although several mentioned that they wished to prepare their college-bound students for college life.

Comprehensive High School functions well because of its core of experienced and skilled teachers, and because of the good leadership it receives from the principal. The principal, the guidance counselor, and the teachers also reflect a trait that must account for much of their success: they all refer to students as individuals and not merely as members of groups. In every conversation, students come up by name, by background, by family circumstances, by the needs they have to learn this lesson or that subject. In a settled community like this one, in which many of the high school teachers have resided all their lives, it is possible to maintain that wonderful sense of the individual. Both the principal and her teachers will telephone parents when the students are having problems in the classroom, and parent-teacher meetings are an important part of life at the school.

Possibly the most dramatic reason that Comprehensive High is a good school is the principal's acceptance of competition and awards as a motivating factor in learning. Over 85 percent of the students who study foreign languages take part in countywide foreign language fairs and contests; math bowls, regional science fairs, contests for business students, essay contests, choir trips, and a host of other activities fill the days of the school. The principal values publicity for her teachers and students, and sees that the local newspapers, the school's own paper, and the public address system keep everyone informed of the latest triumph.

Many of the students in the high school develop a love for such competition, and carry the habit from one activity to another, competing in Latin and science, drama and music. The school sponsors trips to Nashville to attend plays at the Tennessee Performing Arts Center, and also organizes and runs European tours for the choir and for groups of foreign language students. The library and school office keep a number of student volunteers busy, and many students donate their study hour to such volunteer efforts. Comprehensive High is in constant motion. Some students certainly enjoy the many competitions as opportunities to miss classes, and of course, teachers are aware of the drawbacks of so many interrupted class periods. But the overall effect seems to be a healthy one, as the best students think of their high school as a place that demands energy and imagination. These students learn that education is only partly a matter of textbooks and classrooms.

A visit to most schools will elicit more attention to accomplishments than to failures, and it seems clear that while Comprehensive is a remarkable place, it is not without some areas of concern. There is only one teacher for Latin, one for French, and one for Spanish. The Spanish teacher advises the yearbook staff and teaches a journalism class that in fact produced the annual. She also teaches first- through fourth-year Spanish, doubling the third- and fourth-year students in the same class. Because of scheduling problems, students who need Advanced Placement English or another special course will often face a conflict with Spanish class, and will therefore drop the Spanish before completing the third year. About 20–25 percent of Comprehensive's students will graduate with at least two years of a foreign language, but only 10 percent will have completed the third-year course. Beyond English and the foreign languages, the humanities curriculum is modest. Besides the required junior-level American history, students can elect only one other history course, world history, although the school does offer music theory and a course in art. The guidance counselor noted that the administration is under pressure to cease offering some low-enrollment courses, and that these include the higher levels of the languages. There are no times for staff meetings during the school day, and teachers rarely gather to talk about the problems of teaching English, much less the problems of interpreting the humanities to high school students.

Teaching English and History at Rural High School

Rural High serves 400 students in the southern part of Wayne County, an area in which 70 percent of the adult residents have not completed high school. Many of the students will drop out of school before graduating, as did their parents before them. A number of young teen-agers get married, and others drift away to find a job to keep their automobiles in operation. Many of the students who remain in school are engaged in vocational training, and are bused each day to another county high school to take such courses. Each year the high school offers one college-preparatory English class, which is taken by about 13 members of a senior class of about 85 students. Beyond this one special class, English instruction is divided between regular and "leveled" classes. About a third of the students in the school are in leveled English, which is little more than a preparation for the state proficiency examination in reading and spelling. Many students fail the proficiency examination; one English teacher assured me that over half of her sophomores in leveled English were incapable of identifying a verb after three semesters of high school instruction. The principal and guidance counselor are in their first year at Rural, and could not predict how many seniors would not receive a diploma because of repeated failure of the state examination.

It was at Rural High that I witnessed the greatest extremes in the abilities and interests of the students and in the imagination and techniques of the teachers. In tenth-grade leveled English the students spent a period reading aloud *The Miracle Worker*. The play is not a regular part of the tenth-grade leveled curriculum, but the teacher had the students read it to break the monotony of constant practice and drill in grammar and spelling. Indeed, the Tennessee proficiency examination had taken place some days before, and this foray into literature was both a diversion and a reward. *The Miracle Worker* is set in Tuscumbia, Alabama, which is only forty miles south of Rural, and the play is performed in Tuscumbia every summer. The teacher obviously hoped that some of her students would want to attend one of the performances there. Students took turns reading the parts, and seemed quite interested in the violence of the breakfast scene in which Helen Keller is convinced by Miss Sullivan to sit at the table and eat with her knife and fork. The teacher seemed to understand very well what sort of task the miracle worker faced.

Students tripped over a number of words, including "accustomed," "heroic," "tyrant," and "whims," although they seemed to know the meaning of these words when their teacher helped them with pronunciation. They also had difficulty with figurative language, and were particularly puzzled by the expression "when you are under the strawberries." Only when the teacher demanded to know what anyone would do under strawberries did someone eventually volunteer that the phrase means "dead and buried." Few of the students could distinguish between dialogue and stage directions, and they simply read all of the words they came to. The teacher showed great patience and yet was firm in her conduct of the class. She corrected misread words, repeated warnings about stage directions, and continually interrupted the reading to ask students what the scene looked like, or what was happening beneath the surface of the dialogue. She asked students to think about the role of women in family life nearly a century ago, and encouraged the students to imagine social customs in rural Alabama of the 1880s. The teacher stressed time and again the nuances of word and feeling that occur in the text as well as in human life, and sought to bring the students to imagine moments in their own experience that were similar to those witnessed in the drama. The class as a group was quiet, attentive, but sluggish; the teacher seemed to drag them from line to line, from point to point. The students came to life at intervals when the teacher made a joke or challenged one of them to say what he would do if Helen Keller had hit him in the face with her fist. ("I'd hit her back," which is what the character Miss Sullivan does as well.) A livelier interest surfaced when the teacher ended the class ten minutes early to take care of orders for class T-shirts, another of the responsibilities of English teachers at this school.

Another class in average English provided a sobering example of poor teaching. A teacher spent the first twenty-five minutes of the class going from desk to desk to see that her students had done their homework, leaving the others to chat and idle. Then she devoted fully thirty-five minutes to reading aloud a section of Warriner's English grammar handbook which covered the substance of the homework assignment. Her method was to read several lines of Warriner and then to ask very simple questions to the students, such as "Where do you put the closing of a business letter?" or "Where do you put the greeting?"—points that were fully covered in the book the students had open in front of them. The class was subject to several digressions, including a brief contention about college basketball teams and the question of whether Woodlawn, Tennessee, has its own ZIP code. No one had yet written a business letter as a part of the class assignment; the class drill and the homework were devoted simply to the rules for writing one. Indeed, when one of the students volunteered that he had recently written several business letters to inquire about athletic trophies, the teacher let the comment slide by, and made no attempt to take advantage of a student's actual experience with the subject under discussion. The teacher later was quite vague about how much her students do write, and doubted it came to more than the equivalent of a notebook page a week. She complained that she had many students, and opined that they learned better when she went over lessons carefully. She seemed surprised when I suggested that even ninth-graders could profit from ambitious writing exercises.

On the other hand, one of the most exciting high school classes I can remember attending took place at Rural High. A teacher of American history gathered her students in groups of five or six, and allowed the groups to reach conclusions about questions she was asking. No single student was vulnerable; indeed, everyone seemed to feel there was safety in numbers. For that reason, perhaps, discussion was open, and the mood of the class was alert, even bold. The teacher earlier had circulated copies of letters that three brothers in the Confederate army had sent to their parents in Texas during the Civil War. The copies were typed but maintained the writers' spelling and habits of abbreviation. The study groups had discussed among themselves certain questions, and afterwards there was a large group discussion led by the teacher. It was remarkable to see how she involved her students in the consideration of these primary documents: she emphasized that such letters are the raw materials of much historical writing, and showed the students how they could interpret subtle clues to discover much about the letter writers and the military and political circumstances of which they were a part. The students had studied the Civil War in their textbook, and were able to draw upon these lessons in their analysis of the letters. The teacher had taken them all to a Civil War battlefield earlier in the year, and therefore some of the geography mentioned in the textbook and the letters was familiar to them. The hour was a dazzling experience. The students voiced good insights, and the teacher marched them through a good deal of material in a very short time. Not a moment of class time was wasted. There was a sort of electricity in the classroom, an electricity due in large part to the teacher's personality, but also due in some part to the quality and content of the letters the students had read. At least one of the writers was their age, and many of the concerns voiced in the correspondence seemed familiar and pressing to the students.

The senior college-preparatory English class was not the tour de force that the American history class was, but it was yet another in a series of classes that inspire confidence in the imagination and skill of many of our high school English teachers. The class hour began with a short spelling test; spelling and vocabulary are important parts of the precollege curriculum. There followed a forty-five-minute period of discussion and exercises in study skills in which the students considered outlining techniques and practiced outlining short lectures that the teacher read to them. The pattern of the class was simple: the students were introduced to a principle; they worked on a written exercise that tested or illustrated the principle; and then they discussed their results. The class, a small one, was well disciplined and apparently had long maintained an attentive and serious approach to learning. Everyone fell to work quickly, and worked steadily through the hour. The teacher used her time well, and had calculated almost to the minute how to fill the class hour with exercises and with discussion of study skills. The lessons were based upon a workbook that the school was not able to afford to buy in adequate numbers; therefore the teacher had xeroxed various pages for her students to use in their class work.

The Humanities at the Private School of Nashville

The Private School of Nashville, or PSN as everyone calls it, exists in another world from Rural High. Many of the parents of PSN students have advanced degrees: there are a number of lawyers, doctors, educators, and other professionals among the parents who send their children to the school. Many students come originally from other states, even other countries. Unlike Comprehensive or Rural High, PSN students fan out across America when they go to college, attending some of the best universities in the country as well as many good colleges and universities in Tennessee. Tuition is high by local standards—about $3,000 a year—so the students represent much less of the cross-section one would encounter at almost any public high school. Students do not wear school uniforms or the obligatory coats and ties that are often required at the elite prep schools in the city. Indeed, regulation dress is decidedly sloppy, and students enjoy appearing unorthodox in both appearance and in superficial manner. Many of the students are quite bright. Academic standards are high, and students will be asked to leave the school if they do not keep up the level of their work. The school runs from kindergarten through twelfth grade, and the high school is rather small, with a graduating class of about sixty.

The head of the English Department at PSN holds a Ph.D. and had taught in a university for a while before entering high school teaching. Several of the other English teachers hold master's degrees, and all have a good deal of classroom experience. PSN students keep a year ahead of most public high schools in their English classes, using a tenth-grade textbook in the ninth grade, covering British literature in the tenth grade, American literature in the eleventh, and, finally, Shakespeare and advanced composition in the senior year. The ninth-graders read *Oedipus Rex, Brave New World, Julius Caesar, Richard III, One Day in the Life of Ivan Denisovich,* and *A Separate Peace,* as well as quite a lot of poetry and short fiction. Most English classes spend three days a week on literature, one day on grammar and usage, and a day on vocabulary, although the pattern varies from week to week. The school uses a series of graded vocabulary workbooks that carry the students from middle school up to their senior year. Seniors write a good deal, and seem to do quite well when they eventually take college English, but younger students submit only about twenty pages a term, a surprisingly modest total.

The teachers at PSN prepare their students for the self-reliance and independence that are required in college life. There are no hall passes; students are allowed to wander around or go outside during free periods; homework is not checked every day, and many assignments are given well in advance, with the students expected to keep the due date in mind without constant reminders. One English teacher commented that literary analysis may be the least important of her goals for ninth- and tenth-graders in the school. What she most wants to teach is thinking. Students too frequently fail to discriminate between fact and judgment, she claims, and it is her task to teach them the relationship between the two. One popular assignment demands that students record what happened to them on the way to school without making judgments. The teacher obliged them to discover how difficult it is simply to report facts. Another exercise asks students to study a political cartoon, do research into the circumstances that occasioned the cartoon, and to comment upon the ways in which the cartoonist blends fact and judgment in an exaggerated analysis of a news event. Students are also encouraged to write satires, parodies, or burlesques of great works they are studying, rather than simply writing literary critiques. The teacher believes that students do better when they determine how to approach a literary work, at least in the early years of high school; the juniors and seniors engage in much more formal analysis of the works they read.

Despite superficial appearances, instruction in English at PSN can be quite traditional and formal. Students do work on grammar, and learn also a deal of critical terminology, mentioning point of view, irony, tone, and the like during class discussions. Writing is considered by PSN teachers as a form of problem solving, and literary terms are thought of as devices to make discussion easier. The teachers emphasize the concepts that lie beneath terminology, and emphasize the thought processes that result in the written word. Teachers at the school were quite aware that English is more than a college preparatory course, and is rather a preparation as well as a guide to the conduct of one's own existence. PSN students seem to thrive in their English classes, although transfer students often have difficulty adjusting to the way English is taught at the school. One teacher says that many transfer students persist in reading only on a literal level, and are not nearly as responsive to nuance and tone as are students who have been at PSN for some time. PSN students think for themselves, and respond quickly to subtle qualities of literary works, although at their worst, PSN students occasionally say something that sounds clever rather than something that is accurate.

What Do These Schools Reveal to Us?

Avoiding Problems: The Dangers of Tracking

Teachers, if not their students, avoid certain problems by way of tracking systems. The tracking at PSN is accomplished by social and financial tests while tracking at public high schools is encouraged by the Tennessee proficiency examination, by the appeal of vocational training, and by the low self-esteem with which many students enter English classes. Many high school students think they are incapable of performing well in English, and prefer to duck low in their desks, keep quiet, and become invisible rather than enter into the spirit of education. These mute students fail to learn much and are found among the tenth- and eleventh-graders who cannot recognize the word "whim" or cannot pick a verb from a paragraph in their textbook. Many capable students try to fall back into basic or leveled English, remaining content to sit quietly through 160 hours a year of grammar lessons that can be largely ignored. Basic English is the same, year after year; it is boring, but it is not surprising. Hence a number of students choose the boredom of something that is predictable, rather than risk the ambiguities and mysteries they fear are lurking at the heart of a regular English class. Such tracking, while it may provide for good discipline and an efficient management of students' course loads, is the despair of thoughtful teachers and is one of the worst consequences of the proficiency examination. Few students in basic or leveled English in grades ten to twelve encounter the humanities. Occasionally their teachers will attempt to force such an encounter, but halting answers and silence protect the unwilling students from the dreaded lesson.

The Complexity of Teaching English

An English class is not merely a place where students read the classics of British and American literature or study grammar. English class is where students receive lessons in reading, writing, elementary logic, common sense, interpretation, literary analysis, rhetoric, research and study skills, cultural history, aesthetics, the uses of reason and the imagination, and historical consciousness. High school English is the place where most students are introduced to the humanities. No teacher complained about the complexity of high school English, but most wished they could have help in one or more dimensions of their subject. Several would delight in an extended summer workshop or seminar in American studies in which music, art, literature and history are considered together (or a similar approach to British literature). One teacher firmly declared that she needed help in teaching basic English, observing that her students persistently fail to learn enough to pass the proficiency examination, and wondering whether she was presenting the material with enough skill and intelligence. Because of the complexity of teaching English, many instructors voice similar concerns. Outsiders, and even educators, should remember that teaching English involves a variety of intellectual and imaginative powers, and that simple formulas or solutions may be appropriate to some aspects of teaching English but will be inappropriate to many other aspects of the field. One case in point: the "back to the basics" movement has resulted in an improvement in basic skills, but other test scores that evaluate high school performance have gone down in recent years. Certain goals may be reached at the expense of other equally important goals.[3]

Learning from the Best Teachers and Students

A history teacher at Rural High demonstrated that excellent teaching and learning can take place in a required course that is offered to a cross-section of a rural student body. The faculty at Comprehensive High School affirms that all students can be given many written assignments, and that a majority of the student body can achieve on a high level in many areas of study. The difference between the two public schools is a matter of degree: Comprehensive High accomplishes more because the principal and teachers there are convinced that certain accomplishments are possible. If the principal and teachers at Rural High were equally convinced about the potential of their students to learn certain lessons, the students would indeed learn more. The same students who stumble through boring and repetitive classes at Rural High also sparkle on occasion in the very good classes. Naturally, no outsider should oversimplify the difficulties that teachers face in school systems in which there is a lack of parental support and a high dropout rate. Yet a detached observer cannot help noticing very good classes in modest schools, and cannot help wondering why some other teachers do not seek the standards that the very good ones do.

The privileged students at Private School of Nashville and the gifted students in Vanderbilt's Summer Challenge suggest what can happen if all students are expected to perform at a high level in all aspects of a liberal arts curriculum. Enthusiasm and good performance are contagious under the proper circumstances. Is it too risky to attempt to stimulate enthusiasm and good performance when the circumstances are not ideal? The best students in the best schools recognize that learning is an integral part of their growth and development, and that the lessons they encounter in books are lessons that count in their lives. Listless, mute students apparently do not see such connections. Part of the lesson these poor students should receive is a lesson in the power of a liberal education. Thinking, problem solving, and critical analysis are skills that the best students possess. These skills are no less important to students who have no ambitions to go on to college, or indeed, might have no ambitions to complete their high school studies. In many ways, the three questions posed to the Vanderbilt Summer Challenge students are questions that, in one form or another, should be posed in English and history courses in every high school.

The Habit of Connecting: A Conclusion

High school English is already a multidisciplinary approach to learning. The English curriculum is made up of at least a dozen distinguishable elements. Grammar and literature are only two of these. For years English teachers have been obliged to forge connections among the many facets of their subject, and for years, certain students have been able to recognize these connections. The model of high school English, as taught well, is a model for the excellent school of tomorrow. Reading, writing, analysis, logic, common sense, a sense of history, a sense of aesthetics, and recognition of our shared culture are some of the laudable goals for the education of our young. We meet these goals now, in bits and pieces, here and there. If we were to teach these lessons more systematically to more students, the problem of low scores and the problem of functionally illiterate young adults would be eased. The Summer Challenge students studied computer languages and molecular biology as if these subjects were somehow connected to an English class. The students did not simply study the subject in a vacuum, but thought of subjects as parts of an approach to a cultural and moral understanding of the world we all inhabit. Good students at Comprehensive High School excel in their courses because they seek connections between their day-to-day lives and the subject matter of their textbooks (even if some of these connections simply involve entering a countywide contest in Latin grammar and vocabulary). We should ask no less of other students across the country who now evade the responsibility of their own educations. A quest for excellence is not simply a quest for perfect teachers or perfect students. It is a quest that involves a clear definition of what there is to be learned.

Any account of secondary education must take into account contradictory facts and figures. The Commission on Excellence in Education reported a serious shortage of mathematics and science teachers in all fifty states; furthermore, since 1969, the amount of time graduates spend on academic courses declined from 70 percent to 62 percent while the time given to nonacademic subjects such as driver training grew from 8 to 13 percent. In thirty-five states, only one year of mathematics and one year of science are required for a high school diploma; about 13 percent of all seventeen-year-olds in the country are functionally illiterate, and the figure might be as high as 40 percent among minority youth. Across the country, nearly 28 percent of the students in the seventh grade will fail to graduate from high school five years later. In Tennessee the figure is more alarming: 33 percent of Tennessee seventh-graders fail ultimately to graduate.

Yet there are other signs that the decline of three decades has ceased and that further improvements will come about in high schools. The National Commission on Excellence has put forward proposals that will support the efforts of educational reformers across the country. The state of Tennessee already has begun to require an additional course in mathematics and science for the high school diploma, the governor has urged higher salaries and a master teacher plan for the state. The number of summer programs for gifted and talented students is growing, not only in Tennessee, but in many other states as well. Indeed, the informal and anecdotal evidence afforded by visits to three high schools, and a month with forty high school juniors, convinces me of the presence of many hard-working teachers and students in the high schools who are reaching standards that are not well reflected in aggregate national statistics. The facts and figures do illustrate an unquestionable pattern of decline, yet observation and experience not only offer hope but supply examples of excellence that should and can be duplicated elsewhere.

NOTES

1. Washington, D.C.: U.S. Department of Education, 1983.
2. From an address to the National Council of Teachers of English, December 1982.
3. Edward B. Fiske, "Students Gain in Basic Skills but High School Scores Fall," *New York Times,* 10 April 1983, 1.

The Diminished Past: Conditions and Ideals in the Social Studies

Gilbert T. Sewall

During the last sixty years, but more speedily in the last fifteen, the classic high school history program erected toward the end of the nineteenth century has been displaced. History labels may remain, as in the case of world history or American history courses. But traditional narrative history—especially that focusing on the record and ideals of Western civilization—has often been supplanted by significantly different subject matter and methods, usually traveling under the rubric of the social studies.

This development reflects in part the inroads of the social sciences in providing authoritative explanations of mankind's origins and intercommunications. Economics, sociology, anthropology, and psychology have all left deep (though often unconscious) impressions in the thinking of broadly educated people, including teachers. The stature of these relatively new disciplines reflects a contemporary scene trying to make sense of social complexity and contradiction through rational, scientific analysis. Not surprisingly, curriculum planners in the social studies have tried to respond to the perplexities of the present. Unfortunately, some have endorsed a style of social studies emphasizing the study of nonhistorical themes and current events and claiming to be more *engagé* and valuable than the narration of earlier centuries.

THE DECLINE OF HISTORY?

I will first assume what I cannot exactly prove: that people living in a working democracy need to know some history and, above all, the history of their own nation and culture; that schools are where they should learn these fundamentals; and that in many schools the substance of history in the curriculum has been reduced.

I base these assumptions partly on experience. Between 1970 and 1978 I taught honors courses in history and economics at Phillips Academy. During this time I witnessed fairly subtle, rather profound, but not unique, changes in the single required "departmental" course, American history. I have since discovered that similar changes occurred during the 1970s in other precollegiate schools across the country.

In 1970, American history was by common agreement the school's most "difficult" course. Based on a brilliant syllabus evolved from the 1920s, the course had become something of a rite of passage for the student body. During my tenure this stated diploma requirement remained on the books. (In fact, the state diploma requirement in "history and the social sciences" increased, as about two dozen elective courses of varying quality were introduced.)

What declined was the content in this required course; during the 1970s the department's standard expectations for students in American history—and many other social studies courses—fell. In 1970, to graduate, *all* students had to master difficult points in American history, from intricate rulings of the Supreme Court on the commerce clause to the subtleties of New Deal farm policy. They were expected to comprehend the congressional debate over slavery in the territories during the nineteenth century and over isolationism during the twentieth. Toward the end of the year each student was required to complete a thirty-page research paper based on primary materials. There were many problems with the course: some of the readings were stale, and the syllabus's love of detail was positively antiquarian. But standard complaints (among some students and faculty members) revolved around the course's "narrow" focus (constitutional, political, economic) and excessive "coverage" (too much, too fast).

To correct real and perceived shortcomings, this American history course has been revised three times in fifteen years. All to the good, livelier paperback readings have been introduced. Methods of historical inquiry have received additional attention. The study of the eighteenth and nineteenth century has been compressed to make room for more twentieth-century history. But also, class meetings per week have fallen from five to four. Each time a revision has taken place, common syllabus content and departmental tests have become simpler. Significantly, Andover students still complain loudly about the rote memorization of names and dates, invoking their higher sensibility. ("I'm a concept person, not a fact person," some of them say, employing the crude and incoherent dualism that teachers at Andover and elsewhere have tended to tolerate.) These students remain blissfully unaware how much larger a factual base of national historical reasoning had been required of students no brighter than themselves, say, ten years earlier.

During the 1970s, at Andover, what had been a consistently high departmental standard began to break apart. Some new and younger instructors required a minimal amount of work from students, while others hewed to the stiffer standards of the past. Pupils increasingly tracked themselves, primarily through the device of area scheduling and student course selection, the less able or interested selecting American history and elective sections with less exacting requirements. A sterling regimen in American history remained only for those students who sought it. Toward the end of the decade, veteran teachers who had taught from the pre-1970 syllabus began to retire. With them began to go direct knowledge of some lapsed demands and rigor in the school's history requirements. To be fair, this American history course remains a demanding—even model—introductory survey. Relatively speaking, the Andover case simply seems to reflect the trend of the 1970s, in bellwether and marginal schools alike, to reduce content and relax standards in the social studies curriculum and academic program.[1]

To look at scores on the College Board achievement test in American history and social studies, the reverse might seem true. Between 1966 and 1982 median scores dropped a negligible 512 to 505, suggesting constancy in achievement for college-bound seniors. But on closer inspection, other facts emerge: (1) that during these 16 years, the number of students taking the test dropped from 124,000 to 55,000, resulting in a *much* more select population of test-takers; (2) that actually the published median was much lower in years before several "rescalings" took place to make achievement scores consistent with declining Scholastic Aptitude Test scores.[2]

These rescalings obscured what appeared to be a long-term slide in history and social studies achievement among the most selective high school student population.

Was this just scattered softening at the top? Maybe not. National Assessment of Educational Progress data from the 1970s indicate that student knowledge of the structure and function of government declined sharply during the decade. In 1976, for instance, only 42 percent of eighth-graders could explain the basic meaning of democracy; 36 percent of twelfth-graders understood how presidential candidates are selected. Four years earlier more than half of each group taking the test could answer the same questions correctly.[3] Even civics lessons (an indispensable responsibility of high school social studies departments) seem to escape an unacceptably large fraction of contemporary youth.

In the last three years I have visited a score of high schools, located in various parts of the country and serving children of different classes, backgrounds, and capabilities. On such expeditions I have made a special point of observing social studies departments and monitoring history classes. I have sat through zero-substance classes (bull sessions and video shows), rote classes (fill in the ditto sheets provided by the teacher's guide), and trendy classes (let's talk about parenting and child abuse). I have heard curriculum planners in these schools advocate questionable topics and approaches, supposedly to make the social studies more "humanistic" or "socially responsive."

What I have not seen are a sufficient number of challenging courses taught by teachers who conceive of the past as a means to empower and liberate their students. I can't count how many times I have heard effective social studies teachers complain about ahistoricism and intellectual sloth among their colleagues. According to these teachers ill-advised changes in subject matter and pedagogy have allowed unmotivated teachers and students to evade the (sometimes tedious or complicated) fundamentals of historical discipline.

IDEALS IN THE SOCIAL STUDIES

Properly taught and learned, the social studies help to produce activated, informed, realistic citizens who have functional understanding of their time and place. By exploring the special opportunities, issues, and threats in other historical ages, we contemplate and help to delineate those of our own. The study of the achievements and ideals and policies of other times makes us less the slaves of the present's supposed imperatives.

The social studies—grounded in the synthesizing discipline of history—can give examples of social concord and crisis in the past, making current problems seem less unique, insoluble, or apocalyptic. They can teach that not every difficulty is a crisis, that change is rarely simple, that adversaries are rarely pitted in a Manichaean contest, and that utopia is not just around the corner. They can give evidence of a world much larger, older, and more complicated than any single individual, thus giving emerging adults in high school a sense of modesty and perspective. The social studies, employing the tools of historical analysis, can show them how other cultures have tried to transform or redeem themselves, with intended and unintended results. Gradually students might become attuned to the sensibility so nicely conveyed in the philosopher William Barrett's epigram: "Today is always and for all men the digging of one's way out of the ruins of yesterday."[4]

In a citizen-propelled polity such as ours, learning history also gives emerging adults the foundations to analyze and judge contemporary events and trends. In charting this or that initiative to transform or redeem some present situation, political and interest groups often base their arguments on historical claims. Lawyers and justices speak of precedents. Journalists seek to give "context" to their reports, providing background and statistical evidence to validate their conclusions. A sound, historically based social studies curriculum provides the best sort of citizenship training: it teaches the skills and modes of thought that enable students to understand and evaluate reigning opinion makers and leaders, both in outlook and ultimate aims.[5]

Whatever the curriculum, an effective social studies program depends on teachers who understand their subjects and who have the personal qualities to convey them vitally and sensitively. Such teachers, then, should have a strong background in history and other liberal subjects before entering the classroom; if not, they must teach themselves on the job. Such teachers should be self-confident in their mastery of their material, have some elocutionary skill, and be able to conduct directed discussions with their students. Ideally, they should be adept at *supplementing* (not replacing) "chalk and talk" with *imaginative* (not pro forma) audio-visual displays. They should be able to create challenging tests and writing assignments—and grade them discerningly. It must go without saying that this kind of social-studies teaching is hard to do—and that there are far too few instructors able to excel here in substance and style.

The teachers are the key. There is no inherently perfect social studies curriculum. Published and mandated social studies curricula—state, local, and school-level—bear only vague resemblance to what is taught, tested, and learned in class. Still, sketching a curriculum indicates what in my view is proper subject matter for ordinary high school social studies programs.

Thus, what follows is a curriculum that I could be proud of, either as a department chairman, a principal, or an assistant superintendent for curriculum. It would be a four-tier (ninth through twelfth grades) required program with similar fundamentals for students of all abilities.

Stage One:	Classical Mythology (one semester)
	Geography (one semester)
Stage Two:	American History (one year)
Stage Three:	Western Civilization since Ancient Greece (one year)
Stage Four:	Area Studies: Asia, Latin America, *or* the Middle East and Africa (one semester)
	and
	U.S. Constitutional Law, Economics, Statistics and Demography, Ancient History, Twentieth-Century Diplomatic History, *or* History of Science since Galileo (one semester)

This curriculum would attempt to fuse classical studies with a demanding, comprehensive set of modern topics; to stress the humanistic aspects of history; to downplay the merely contemporary; to put emphasis on international education; and to consign all "personal service" courses that currently fulfill social studies requirements to the dustbin of history.

To engage reluctant, complacent, or limited students in the conversation of the humanities, by the way, I have found materials from art history very stimulating. Kenneth Clark made the point that cultures leave their record in the form of deeds, words, and art—and that the deeds and words of the past may be best understood by the trustworthy evidence of art.[6] At least in the beginning, art history examines *things,* not abstract concepts. It does so pictorially, at once revealing radically different forms and symbols which nonetheless in the course of time repeat the most basic human themes. With objects (evidence) in front of them, students can be asked to identify (or compare) aesthetic ideals and cultural objectives. They can be asked to analyze form—the manipulation of color, line, space, and medium to achieve a composed design. An art history class might dwell one day on the purposes of Roman architecture and urban planning. Some months later it might explore different outlooks toward nature as expressed by the French and English garden. Through such exercises, students began to sense how other eras have tried to reify their ideals, in both sacred and secular realms, giving us indispensable keys to understanding the past.

In my Western civilization course, much time would be spent on art history topics, using them, where possible, to introduce the political, economic, and intellectual histories of other eras and to build a sense of chronology. I wonder why so few "Pyramids to Picasso" courses exist in secondary schools. More than any discipline that I know, art history catches student interest, while acting as a synthesizing vehicle for the record of the humanities.

THREE CALIFORNIA SCHOOLS

I am familiar with many metropolitan U.S. high schools located east of the Mississippi River and in California. I have less firsthand experience with the band of smaller school districts and social-studies programs in the Mississippi Valley and Mountain states, where a large number of complaints still are lodged over the presence of outdated textbooks, fill-in-the-blank courses, uncommitted coach-teachers, and narrow curricula. In highly secularized parts of the nation, as the Eastern seaboard and California, the problems tend not to be the old social studies. For a number of years the accent has been on new approaches.

Between 1981 and 1983 I made many visits to California schools, including the three that follow, represented here because of their relatively diverse student bodies. These questions (and others) were on my mind: What is the content of the social studies syllabus and of lessons? What are considered new and exciting courses and methods? What are the differences in the program offered to college-bound students and to less able pupils?

Glorygone was for generations a flagship school in a prosperous suburb.[7] More recently, the town evolved into a secondary metropolitan center. Since the late 1960s it faced new social and educational problems usually associated with inner cities. The district has long had a sizable nonwhite population. But until the 1960s virtually all poor black and Hispanic teen-agers either dropped out of school before eleventh grade or attended another high school.

Then, in 1969, a desegregation order precipitated a sudden, middle-class withdrawal from the district: by 1980, the white population in the student population of the public schools had dropped from an average of 70 to 32 percent. An estimated 65 percent of the district's white school-age children were attending private schools. Some middle-class families send their children to public high school. Glorygone sends the top tenth of its graduating class to competitive California or out-of-state colleges, mainly through the efforts of the ambitious parents of all classes and a handful of teachers. The naturally ambitious or family propelled student will, with luck and pluck, receive a satisfactory education here.

The published curriculum is a required Geography/World History/American History/Civics sequence overlaid with electives: The Student and the Law, Urban Problems, Child Growth and Development, Current Affairs, Early Childhood Education, Marriage and the Family, Mexican-American Studies. To make room for a new required course in Emerging Nations, the World History course is now truncated to one semester. What is most interesting, though, is that, at least in required "departmental" courses, published titles mean next to nothing.

I step into Mr. Adams's geography class, filled with pleasant black teen-agers, few of whom had brought either notebooks or textbooks to class. "This is not your Harvard Phi Beta class," Mr. Adams says, signaling to me (and his students) that this was a "slow" class. It takes no time to realize: Mr. Adams and his students are in league, teacher and taught in tacit contract to do as little geography as possible. Mr. Adams talks affably but pointlessly about a proposed federal tax on gasoline. The students half listen. During the period, the mandated subject, geography, never comes up.

Two periods later, in an honors section of American history, Mr. Adams assigns a chapter on the advent of the Civil War and lists on the blackboard "things you should remember for the test," e.g., abolitionism. That completed, he begins another off-the-cuff monologue, as most students drift into twilight consciousness for the remainder of the period. Again, Mr. Adams and his students have struck a tacit agreement to teach and learn the minimum. A colleague of Mr. Adams later tells me with some resignation that Mr. Adams's students "approved of" the instructor and therefore remained docile in class, thus making Mr. Adams a "better" teacher than some other department members.

I attend a special history class for Hispanic students, ninth through twelfth grade, called "bilingual" but conducted in English. The day's lesson is famous Americans. The teacher, Miss Botero, begins with Susan B. Anthony. "How many of you believe that men and women should be equal?" the teacher asks the class. No response. The classroom buzzes in Spanish. The girls apply nail polish and comb their hair ostentatiously. "Who would rather have babies than go out to work as a doctor or dentist?" Suddenly, Miss Botero's lesson switches to Neil Armstrong, and then to Crispus Attucks, and then to Davey Crockett. In treating Davey Crockett at the Alamo, it is darkly hinted that Mexico still has valid claims to the land ceded to the United States in 1848. On Thomas Edison, Miss Botero exclaims, "Just think, if there were no Edison, you wouldn't have to come to school." The girls continue to apply nail polish.

Mr. Adams's and Miss Botero's classes satisfy Glorygone's diploma requirements in American history. Mr. Cummings's class in American history meets exactly the same requirement. Like Mr. Adams, Mr. Cummings has a contract with his students. Unlike Mr. Adams, his contract is based on high expectations of achievement: students who choose to take his classes know that they will have to work hard, mastering facts, collecting facts into evidence to back up generalizations about the past, and articulating their conclusions in speech and writing. They also know that Mr. Cummings will deliver the kind of course and counsel to steer ambitious students like themselves toward a world of wider opportunities. They find Mr. Cummings "interesting" and "classy," and probably most of all, "smart."

The subject is the advent of Reconstruction at the end of the Civil War. Mr. Cummings first makes the case of Northern congressmen who felt, unlike Lincoln, that severe punishment of a rebellious section was sound political and economic policy. Then, he switches to the story behind Andrew Johnson's vice-presidency. (During the Civil War a loyal Tennessee senator and Democrat made a good ticket-balancer for an Illinois Republican.) Suddenly, several enlargements of nineteenth-century photographs appear from a closet: the class together pictorially traces the progress of the Lincoln assassination at Ford's Theater in April 1865. Then Mr. Cummings turns back to his first topic, to make the point that President Johnson, a Southerner, was up against much as he tried to lead the postbellum nation.

The class is exhausting and exhilarating. At the end of fifty minutes all but a few students remain fully attentive and engaged. Several students crowd around Mr. Cummings's desk to ask follow-up questions, notably about the assassination.

Like most good teachers, Mr. Cummings is theatrical. He enjoys his daily performances and has the stamina to keep them up after a decade of high school teaching, broken by graduate work in history and education at Stanford University. But the dramatics hide painstaking effort on his part to conjoin academic content and student interest. Out of personal respect for the substance of the past, Mr. Cummings compels his students to be interested along with him. The classroom's atmosphere is at once formal and affectionate, serious and chatty: to meet the terms of the contract, teacher and students alike are trying very hard to please each other. Both parties in the educational process are working hard.

Mountain is two hundred miles away from Mr. Cummings's classroom, a regional high school nestled in the eastern valleys of the Sierra Nevada. At first glance the school would appear to be the embodiment of the no-nonsense "backward" rural school, situated in the midst of a park on the main street of a scrubbed, scenic town, its two-story whitewashed adobe main building shaded by cottonwood trees.

It is surprising, then, to hear the faculty complain that the students are increasingly indifferent to learning as is the community. This lack of interest, they say with a mixture of despair and defensiveness, cannot be controlled. The administration and teachers have tried all the standard remedies: more elective courses, more entertaining methods, "alternative" classes geared toward slow or alienated pupils. They have not worked.

Mountain serves about 130 square miles of beautiful, rugged, isolated land, where some families have money (from ranching, real estate, tourism) and others do not (day labor, drifters, trailer people). About 40 percent of the eleventh- and twelfth-grade boys work 20 or more hours per week at motels, restaurants, and gas stations; many of them have to maintain very expensive four-wheel-drive vehicles and pay for season ski tickets. To work or ski or, during warmer weather, to party, some students simply leave school after morning classes. After graduation, many of them will go to school or work in the beach cities of Los Angeles or Orange County.

I am sitting in the classroom of the social studies "senior teacher." Mr. Deeder is a gentle man who came to Mountain from teaching in a middle-class Los Angeles suburb fifteen years ago to lead the outdoors life. He is the single American history teacher and full-time social studies instructor at Mountain.

I attend an eleventh-grade American history class. It is early afternoon, and a false fire alarm during the previous period was an excuse for many boys to leave campus. The class is mainly girls, but students of both sexes appear sluggish and apathetic. Gradually, it becomes clear that Mr. Deeder is conducting what he later calls a "minicourse" on the period from the Nazi-Soviet Pact of 1939 to the Czechoslovakia coup of 1948. Bereft of chronology, the minilecture is hard to follow. Mr. Deeder punctuates his narrative with questions, which he asks nervously, by his manner indicating to his students his apologies for the "boring" material being covered. He agrees earnestly with student responses, no matter what pupils say, unable or unwilling to acknowledge the quality of their commentary.

Then, Mr. Deeder turns to the next unit, describing his plans for classes during the last month of school. Students will conduct panels "equivalent to a test grade," he says. He asks for volunteers to "get into the issues" on the Nisei internment[8] and the atom bomb. In a voice redolent of television advertising, he says that the class will relive the Nuremburg trials. The girls do not want to volunteer. The afternoon is hot. Mr. Deeder is desperate to engage the class, conscious too that these methods are supposed to excite student interest and create purposeful classrooms. Mr. Deeder takes another shot at countering the air of boredom hanging heavily over the class: "Last year," he declares, "we put Harry Truman on trial for his war crimes."

Mr. Deeder is a self-declared progressive who attends at least one conference each year to learn about vanguard thinking in the social studies. He seems to have full trust in the prescriptions of the experts designated by the California Council of Teachers of Social Studies: in sessions with them, Mr. Deeder has given pep talks about trendy curriculum content, inquiry methods, role playing, game theory, and computer-assisted learning. Fundamentally innocent, he takes on faith the proposition that any up-to-date social studies instructor must teach as he himself has learned to do. In order to stimulate "critical thinking," he says, the American past should be presented "with all the warts." Students "must be involved in the learning process," he adds. As we talk, I have the distinct impression that Mr. Deeder is merely parroting what others have told him, that his lack of internal standards and self-confidence leave him susceptible to curricular humbug, methodological gimmickry, and mindless anti-Americanism.

Collegiate operates in a different scholastic universe. Located on the edge of a large urban district, it is a public high school that admits students selectively by districtwide competition. The school's demonstrated academic effectiveness (a large number of Collegiate's graduates matriculate at the University of California and other prestigious schools) make it appealing to families of all races and income levels: still, Collegiate functions primarily as a springboard for able, disadvantaged children—many of them Asian—who would otherwise be deprived of exceptional academic courses in "regular" city high schools.

Collegiate interests me chiefly because its taught and tested program is nearly identical to several other private and public schools that I have visited in the state, also "collegiate" in outlook and interests. These schools vary greatly in terms of locations, ethos, student backgrounds, and physical plants. What they share is intense interest in promoting the highest possible academic outcomes for all their students.

Collegiate and schools like it have demanding curricula. Collegiate requires two years of social science for graduation: a year of American history, a semester of civics, and another free-for-all semestor of electives. Electives of merit include: economics, ecology/Bay area, history of political thought, history of Communist China, English history, Latin-American studies. Many Collegiate students take three full years of social studies, since they are urged to take tenth-grade world history. Also, to graduate, Collegiate students are required to major in one area of the curriculum (e.g., English, social science, mathematics). To major in social science, students must take eight semesters of course work in the area. (Collegiate is a six-semester school, that is, it runs from tenth through twelfth grade.)

Walking down the corridor at Collegiate, I am struck by the fact that in classroom after classroom, I can observe *several* classes where teachers are conducting interesting, energetic lessons. Fewer teachers stick out as exceptionally able or inept than in schools with lesser academic aims. No single social science teacher at Collegiate appears to be as brilliant as Mr. Cummings; all of them seem more serious than Mr. Adams, Miss Botero, or Mr. Deeder. The social science department, excluding differences in quality tolerated among the elective offerings, shares a fairly definite consensus on academic aims. Master teachers at the school are well grounded in their academic subjects: historical scholarship is respected by colleagues and students alike. Many of the less able, less secure, and less experienced teachers in the department try to emulate senior teachers' standards and classroom strategies.

One additional strength in Collegiate's program is the overarching presence of an Advanced Placement program in United States and European history. Collegiate believes in strenuous testing. It considers, correctly, the Advanced Placement history curricula and tests to be excellent models on which to build a sound historically grounded social studies program. In American history, then, Collegiate puts special emphasis on topics such as the substance of the Constitution, the settlement of the trans-Appalachian continent, slavery and the Civil War, the development of an industrial market economy, the reform movements of the last century, and the emergence of the country as a global power. Over the last few years, it has shown new interest in documentary sources and literary works to round out more traditional textbooks and topics.

Advanced Placement is customarily lauded for linking secondary school opportunities to college work. And it is true, taking a battery of these tests might lead to sophomore standing or the waiver of prerequisites. But more important, Advanced Placement courses tend to inform the content and aims of an entire social studies program. While a small number of students benefit directly from taking Advanced Placement courses, advised skills and knowledge for "advanced" students tend to become an ideal standard for others: the adroit manipulation of facts to describe and make judgments about past events and trends; the comprehension of cause and effect; the tricks of clear expository writing; the imaginative evaluations of primary sources; facility with chronology, map reading, charts and political cartoons.

Going to classes in a department with high aims, students advance through required classes taught by teachers aware of (some of them, quite driven by) what college-bound students need intellectually to succeed in higher education. Not just the fortunate few in special classes benefit from instructors who feel that their mission is to send as many graduates as possible off with minds well-furnished with historical information. At Collegiate, all students are beneficiaries of high, single-tracked standards.

AN OUTLOOK FOR THE SOCIAL STUDIES

The "old social studies" had—and have—their share of problems. Everyone remembers a traditional names-and-dates history course that seemed mechanical and monochromatic—too often the first or last history course taken. Rote fill-in-drills, endless lists, and the absence of inspiring presentations still plague many social studies courses, making for bad methods and little learning. The standards of history vary widely. A Mr. Adams coasts, combining the worst features of the old social studies with the absence of serious instruction. A Mr. Cummings takes the old social studies and spices them up, constantly integrating new lessons (slave songs and Civil War ballads, mock debates between Alexander Hamilton and Thomas Jefferson) and gradually dropping lessons that don't work. There are many more Mr. Adamses than Mr. Cummingses.

New initiatives in the social studies have mucked the waters, resulting in the evasion or trivialization of important history lessons. An alternative view of the curriculum grew up in the 1960s and 1970s, self-consciously modern and intolerant of history-based social studies. To be sure, the view is more common among interested social-studies consultants, trade associations, university professors, foundation executives, and textbook publishers than among classroom teachers. But, this notion informs the dominant lines of thinking among those who are in the curriculum business, receiving salaries, fees, and profits to disseminate billions of dollars of social studies advice and materials.

Despite the old lessons of the past, it is said, peace and human tranquility have proven elusive. Nuclear warfare's destructive capacity constitutes our era's unique—and potentially catastrophic—problem. Since Vietnam, tired myths of American innocence have been roundly discredited. It is depressing, though, that so many eager curriculum planners and teachers have emphasized, as innovation, social studies topics that stress numinous self-awareness, group consciousness, and a defeatist interpretation of their own society's past and future. It is depressing that these educators have preferred to organize the social studies around fuzzy global universals such as "global interdependence" or "human rights" instead of particular historical facts and trends.

The answer is not to trick up lesson plans on state-of-the-planet awareness, or even to do what the New York State Education Department tried to do last year.[9] A new published state social studies curriculum was to be organized by themes, deemphasizing American and European history, and virtually ignoring chronology. The ninth- and tenth-grade curriculum was to concentrate on six concepts, illustrated mostly through episodes plucked from the Third World. The concepts: ecology, human needs, human rights, cultural interaction, the global system of economic interdependence, and the future. American history was to be reduced to a one-semester course. (The State Education Department later backed off, amid public outcries.)

The answer to poor social studies teaching is not to dispense with history. The answer is to teach it better. We are not improving matters at all when we bypass the basics of geography, history, economics, or government, yet ask students to grapple with complicated methods and abstract concepts that they are intellectually unable to manage, e.g., asking students who have studied neither the events leading to the creation of Israel nor the idea of political sovereignty to debate the rights of Arabs and Jews to the West Bank of the Jordan or asking students what they would have said to Nixon if they had been his aides in the winter of 1973—before they have ever studied the Constitution.

No one wants to return to the history lesson as catechismic drill. Still, in the most effective social studies programs that I have observed, a strong narrative American and European history program anchors the curriculum. Teachers in multiple-section required courses are backed up by a departmentally prepared syllabus or workbook. Department heads and master teachers seek to minimize inconsistencies among different teachers in subject content, paying more attention to standards than methods. Students are tested, sometimes taking lengthy essay-type final examinations. These schools test only rarely by easy-to-grade, fill-in-the-blank, and multiple choice instruments. In social studies and other courses, students write regularly, taking at least a crack at a documented research paper before graduation.

At best, whole departments of teachers work together with different views but mutual respect for the significance of past achievements, both national and global. Social studies teachers are usually most capable when they are sympathetic scholars of history and social science, intent on helping the untutored dig out of the ruins of yesterday. They do this best by respecting—and being familiar with—the terrain themselves. And to do it, social studies teachers need to have internalized standards of judgment and scholarship, not least in order to test the ongoing claims of educational novelty. Meanwhile, when one is playing to a rough audience in class, touches of the storyteller, the show-off, and the reasoned patriot do not hurt.

NOTES

1. This perception of across-the-board curriculum dilution is bolstered by National Institute for Education analyst Clifford Adelman's study of high school transcripts, 1964–1981, undertaken for the National Commission on Excellence in Education.

2. These findings are derived from "Summary Statistics for the American History and Social Studies Test 1965–66 through 1981–82," published by the Educational Testing Service in 1983.

3. Trends in civic and political understanding were reported in the February 1977 newsletter of the National Assessment of Education Progress, published by the Educational Commission of the States.

4. William Barrett, *Irrational Man* (Garden City, N.Y.: Doubleday, 1958), p. 271.

5. The special mission of the social studies (and humanities) in a self-governing nation is a point that has been made repeatedly since the time of Thomas Jefferson. For background, see Lawrence A. Cremin, *American Education: The National Experience, 1783–1876* (New York: Harper and Row, 1980), pp. 107–114. The case for sound mass education in a democracy has been recently made in Steven M. Cahn, *Education and the Democratic Ideal* (Chicago: Nelson-Hall, 1979).

6. Quoting John Ruskin on this point, Kenneth Clark opened his heralded *Civilization* series with this observation.

7. In the case of the three California schools, I have changed the names of the institutions and the teachers portrayed.

8. Since one of the internment camps, Manzanar, was located near Mountain, this is an issue of local guilt and concern. Mr. Deeder does not mention this interesting point to his class.

9. The "Proposed Framework for the New York State Secondary Social Studies Curriculum," March 8, 1983, prepared by state official Donald H. Bragaw. The reaction was reported on the front page of the *New York Times,* April 19, 1983.

THE EDUCATIONS OF TEACHERS

On a Background for Teachers

Peter R. Pouncey

High school teachers should certainly receive first-rate education in the field, or fields, that they will teach, and they should know the best that is known in the emerging sciences of pedagogy. This, though, is not enough. Teachers should be fully educated persons in the broadest sense; not simply because it is good to be fully educated, though indeed it is, but because teachers especially—and paradoxically—must be generally educated if they are to perform their specific professional tasks well. The reasons for this follow from the fact that the high school teacher is the first to teach all Americans as each person emerges from childhood and the last to teach *all* of America—those who will go to college and those who will go to work, or look for work and fail to find it, or get married straight-away and raise a family.

There is no more diverse constituency in American education, in terms of talent, motivation, and background, than the high school popula-tion, and its complexity is compounded by the anxieties and energies of adolescence. To all of this the good high school teacher brings a special kind of social sympathy, intent on giving every child a sense of purpose and personal worth. But intellectually and academically, as things now stand, high school teachers confront their classes as specialists, as English teachers or social studies teachers. Why is this regrettable? One could argue that the breadth of the high school teacher's constituency demands an equal breadth of intellectual vision and amplitude of preparation—an ability to appreciate different facets of a culture and different methodologies, so that one has the mental versatility to appreciate the different points of view that are expressed in the classroom.

This argument has some validity as it stands, but it can be made stronger. One wants to stress not so much the *multiple* demands upon the teacher's education—which might seem to call for a hydra-headed, hodge-podge background—as the essential need for unity to a broad background. The goal is to integrate the achievement of many disciplines into a synthesis that comes as close as possible to a whole culture—something more comprehensive, multifaceted, real. To achieve this, or even to approximate it, is a large pedagogic, as well as intellectual, gain. A discipline, treated in virtual isolation, is open to rejection by the diffident or skeptical as two-dimensional and irrelevant to other concerns. But when its contributions are seen as part of a culture, especially one that is historically continuous with one's own, rejection is harder. A culture is the sum of a people's achievements—how they lived, what they did, what sense they made of their world. Clearly, no single line of vision can do justice to such variety, but when the point of view is itself varied, the characters can be made, as it were, to step off the page, and allow themselves to be seen in the round.

There is one further substantial point to be made. A large part of education (as "progressives" in this century have often complained) is retrospective: students are forced to deal with the experience of the past, with a *tradition.* There is good reason for this, quite apart from the fact that there is no syllabus on the *future;* but resistance to the lessons of the past, and fear that they will stifle any originality that we have, run deep in all of us, nonetheless. There is a tension in all of us between the legacy of the past and the urge to escape from it into some fresher future that we define for ourselves. On the one hand, we build seasonal rituals and ceremonies and habitual values into our lives to give life dignity and the poise of continuity; on the other, we seek to refresh ourselves with new sensations, ideas, and experiences, to break out of the rut and to shatter the mold. This tension in us between the time-honored and the time-worn, between the tradition that dignifies and the habit that dulls, is a crucial factor in everyone's education; humanities teachers need to carry their students past this kind of ambivalence. To succeed, though, they must come to terms with the tradition themselves, separating out what is still vital from what is moribund, and allowing its more life-giving roots to offer enrichment and stability to their own lives. To do this well and with conviction, they must venture beyond the comfortable limits of their major and minor fields to explore the further reaches of the tradition. In short, if the teachers are to humanize their classes, they must first fully humanize themselves.

Teachers, then, must themselves have acquired an education in the fullest sense, beyond merely a major, some pedagogy, and an assortment of "distribution requirements." I propose that every teacher needs a unified "core curriculum" in his or her own preparation to teach. My task here is to assay what such a core curriculum might be.[1]

AN ACTIVE CARE FOR LANGUAGE

Paramount over all other things that a teacher must acquire is *an active care for language,* especially one's own. To know what words mean and to use them exactly is fundamental to any self-knowledge, to any critical sense, and therefore to any education properly defined. Twenty-five years ago this point would have been regarded as so elementary that one would have been embarrassed to make it. But one hears now of prestigious law firms employing remedial writing instructors for their highly educated young associates—not to hone existing skills in the hope that the law firm will be graced with a new Burke or Holmes, but in the hope that the young lawyer may finally and dependably be able to produce a grammatical sentence and a properly constructed paragraph, accurately conveying a sense that does not mislead the court or the client. This is a fairly low level of aspiration, but it is easy to see why it is so necessary. For the last fifteen years we have listened to arguments about "students' rights to their own language" (and we are not talking about a *foreign* language here) as though language were not a means of communication, but a kind of private property, or a personal right, entitling the individual, like some lonely Adam in the Garden of Eden, to give the flora his own names. It is significant that on the whole students are not encouraged to invent their own number systems. There are severe disadvantages to counting incorrectly, whether one is making money or a phone call. But what folly not to realize that language should have equal precision, and that its loss is attended with equally unfortunate consequences! The basic laws of syntax operate to render meaning clearly, no less than the simple operations of arithmetic work to make totals, and we would be correct in assuming that both can, and should, be learnt by everyone once and for all in elementary school. (Though one should keep attending to them: Carl Sandburg wrote, when he was seventy-two: "I am still studying verbs and the mystery of how they connect nouns. I am more suspicious of adjectives than at any time in all my born days." It is a fine, activist, American view of language, and he was, of course, right—one can go a long way with nouns and verbs, with people doing things.)

In my experience, current bad writing by college freshmen proceeds for the most part not from any desire to democratize or simplify prose, but from the opposite—from a kind of pretentiousness. Their papers are full of pompous abstractions, which escape from their authors' control into the wildest non sequiturs; and the students seem to hope the whole melange will strike the reader as, if not profound, at least formidably academic. What it *is* is infuriating, and also saddening—because effectively it reduces education to a kind of stultification, which saps individuality in two ways. First, by fooling themselves that this kind of derivative academese is what constitutes writing, students distance themselves from the immediacy of their own experience. To manipulate abstracted language in this way is to repel direct feeling and sensation and to live on borrowed thoughts and (at best) second impressions. It also affects students' ability to read a text with any accuracy or intensity. Just as they do not seem prepared to think out exactly what they mean and then to say it simply and directly in their own words, so they seem reluctant to live with "the words on the page," in Leavis's famous slogan, to extract the full and precise meaning from just those words. Instead, there is a quick escape to large and usually insupportable generalizations.

We must insist on the first and most indispensable stipulation in what I have called "an active care for language"—precision of the sort that troubles with the meaning of words and with the ways words are combined, so that meaning is clear and the words convey the writer's thought exactly. This is the first and most important element of an individual prose style. The teacher should take care to practice it and should insist on it in everything students write—whether they are describing a conversation with their grandmother, a ball game, a friend, a book or a movie enjoyed or hated. Students must be led to *say exactly what they mean*. We would hope that this would be said in clear, strong, vivid prose, with sharp perceptions shown by sharp phrases and words with full flavor. Where a regional vocabulary has a word that is closer to some particular experience than a blander, common synonym, it should be used, but the clarity of the whole should never be impaired by loose or contorted syntax.

This elementary level of precision in writing is indispensable to all teaching and to all learning, and anyone who is prepared to dispense with it should not be a teacher. But an active care for language should carry a teacher far beyond this, into an appreciation of the extraordinary power of words. By their sound and rhythm and by the depth of associations of feeling and imagination that they awaken in the listener or reader, words go beyond the prosaic communication of sense to poetry and to music. Teachers should move freely in this powerful realm. Expecting this is not reaching for any impossible height. By any standards I care for, the world has never known an orator to excel the grace and power of Abraham Lincoln. He had comparatively little schooling but the good fortune to have absorbed into his very bones the rhythms and the strong language of Shakespeare and the King James Bible. I think Lincoln was so soaked in these rhythms that they became second nature to him, so that he could call on their music for his own rhetoric quite naturally, without any contrivance or awkward impression of derivativeness. The style had become entirely his own. (We note, then, that even though a speaker presses for "innovation," his thought and language are soaked in the traditions of the past.)

For all the current resources of education, how many teachers are there, and how many students have they taught, who have read *any* text with the attention and intensity necessary to claim its music for themselves, in the same confident way as Lincoln, who largely taught himself? The fact is that too often we write carelessly, and we read carelessly, and our whole society is the poorer for it.

FOREIGN LANGUAGE

If ever a country was linguistically deprived it is America. The final reductio ad absurdum was reached when colleges, under pressure in the late 1960s, allowed the language requirement to be satisfied in translation. After a while, some colleges became embarrassed with this absurdity, and the course title was changed to "foreign *literature*." In any case, the students and the country again are the poorer for these changes. The greatest problem with ignorance of foreign languages is not merely a matter of the cultural arrogance or political precariousness of forcing foreigners to meet you on your own terms. The most important impact of a foreign language is to force the student to reflect on how idiom conveys thought, on what cultural assumptions lie behind what usages, and more generally, on the structure of language itself: the result should be that one has a sharper eye for one's native language. It is this that is lost when one remains ignorant of other languages.

We are not talking about anything particularly advanced or esoteric. An example will make it clear. On the very first day of learning Greek, the student discovers that the Greeks invented a definite article, with masculine, feminine, and neuter forms in singular and plural through various cases. This may seem a little daunting, and the student may be aggrieved when he is told on the same day that Latin has no article at all. But the contrast between the two practices should eventually enforce reflections on what exact function the article serves in the language, and how another language can ever be as *specific* without it. Or the student may reflect on all the inflections of gender and case that are starting to saturate the memory, and finally realize that by flagging the function of every word in the sentence by its endings in this way, the language gains enormous flexibility in word order: you can juggle the word order to achieve any emphasis you want, and the object will always remain the object, and visibly so, by its ending, wherever you put it. And this makes one consider what devices are available to show emphasis in English, which has comparatively few inflections. And so on. This elementary kind of comparative linguistics is, I think, a salutary check against the sloppiness to which we are all prone with our vernacular. It is quite possible that the widely noted decline in writing skills is due, not merely to a general laissez-faire climate, but, at least in part, to the rejection of foreign language studies over the same period.

HISTORY—AND WHAT CONSTITUTES IT

"Fellow-citizens," said Lincoln, "we cannot escape history." He was speaking, of course, of a particular crisis, when his government would have to take a stand, and its stand would be judged by posterity. But the maxim is true for all of us; genetically and culturally, we cannot escape history. The problem is to know what sort of study of history is most useful for the high school teacher of humanities.

The large sweep of national movements is not the first requirement for a teacher's knowledge of history. The humanities teacher should absorb the history of his own locality first, whether urban or rural. The emphasis will differ according to the place, but even urban areas allow some scope for natural history—right down to the geological conformation of the land. Of any city it is always relevant to ask, "What was here before?" One can then build the records of first settlements and follow the movements of people and tribes, the migrations and displacements. What heroes emerge, if any? What exploiters and villains, what eccentrics, what black sheep? A true historian should attend not merely to the official or serious documents, but to the folklore and the tales of oral tradition, both tall and true; and he should follow the patterns of work, from early crafts to present industry, and of play, of belief, and of politics. He should see how the locality has been touched or shaped by the larger national issues. And what about the present? How does the local climate work on the current political, educational, cultural trends and obsessions? Having absorbed all this, the teacher is properly at home in the neighborhood, and more particularly at home with and for the students, who share this background.

But to gain this kind of frame of reference, when one has felt one's way into the history of a place, is really only to have begun. The very act of exploration raises the most fundamental questions of history—for example, what is the proper stuff of history, and who or what makes it? And beyond these, there are all the questions of distortion, which we are aware of from considering the way our own memory works on the past to present us with a record that we will live with. One can see the same work of transformation shaping a town's or a state's sense of itself. Clearly, the borderline between history and myth is always ambiguous.

I believe a teacher of the humanities should ponder these questions deeply. I suggest a short reading list in which they could not be avoided. The first book on the list is Herodotus' *Histories,* the first complete work of history to survive in the West. It is a marvelously jaunty book, full of casual excursions into bizarre ethnic customs and rituals all over the known world, as well as a dramatic account of the conflict between Persia and the Greeks. The text is a crucial document, because it implants in the Western mind firmly, and perhaps ineradicably for all time, the notion of a great divide between East and West. And it is not as loosely structured as it may seem: the connections between Herodotus' anthropology and geography on the one side and his history on the other are anything but haphazard.

But what is more important at the moment is the inescapable fact, evident on a first reading, that the author's view of history is very close to an epic one. He is doing something different from the epic writer, of course—he is writing in prose and not verse, for one thing. But in his insistence, declared at the outset, that he is writing "so that the great and wonderful deeds . . . should not go uncelebrated," he is very close to the epic poets. Clio, whose name means "fame" and "celebrity," is the common muse of epic and history. Herodotus stands, apparently quite comfortably, at the moment when the two genres begin to diverge, but his basic historical assumptions are still close to epic. Above all, he still thinks of individual exploits as the principal substance of history. In his record of battles, for example, which are the scenes of the greatest collective action, he will still, as a point of honor, provide us with a list of names of those who fought best, whose *aristeia,* in Homeric terms, deserve the rewards of *kleos* (fame). In his great poetic set piece on the battle of Thermopylae, he will pay his tribute to the Spartans by giving Simonides' three separate epitaphs in elegiac couplets—for the whole army, for the King Leonidas who commanded it, and for the seer Megistias, who saw the final doom approaching and stayed to die.

When we turn to Thucydides' *Peloponnesian War,* just one generation later, it is like turning to a different world. Hume says somewhere that the first page of Thucydides is the first page of modern history. Thucydides himself apologizes for the fact that romance, or what he calls "the mythical element," may be found missing from his account. It certainly is missing, but in its place we have a great concentration on the most important factors that build power and make war—money reserves, manpower, and the constant drives in human nature of fear and self-interest. History, then, is not a matter of individual exploits, but of collective action and of the movement of great resources. If anything, the individual part plays a negative role, breaking up collective action by his divisive self-seeking. Clearly the individual cannot be banished from the historical process altogether—politicians must propose policies, and generals form strategies, but their role is different under Thucydides' conception. Instead of performing heroic exploits on the field, like an Achilles, who can terrify a whole army with a shout, or a Leonidas, who can lead 300 men against millions and hold his own for three days, one has a Pericles, who somehow selflessly embodies the national interest, or Cleon, who unquestionably, in Thucydides' mind, embodies the kind of selfishness that destroys it. It is indeed a sombre account; but I know of no history written since in any language that approaches its concentrated power and intelligence. It is incredible that a man could make such far-reaching sense of such complicated events while he was still experiencing them. Thucydides' work, as he predicted—and he was never wrong—is "a possession for all time," the world's first self-postulated classic.

As a long but natural third step in the progression I am following, I would recommend that teachers read a work by Fernand Braudel, the contemporary French historian—either his *Mediterranean World in the Ages of Philip II,* or his *Capitalism and Material Life,* now updated as the first volume of *The Structures of Everyday Life.* Braudel is not, in these works, so interested in individual exploits, like Herodotus, nor in largely anonymous empire building, like Thucydides, but in the multifarious factors that combine to shape the life of the common man and help to get him through the day. What he eats and what he wears, what he works at and with what tools, what his wife does and at what age she marries him, what grows in their part of the world, what kind of transportation exists, what climate, what diseases—there is no detail that seems irrelevant to the general substratum of the economy, which regulates the patterns of human life often for centuries on end, impervious to the alarums and excursions of so-called world events.

We can now see how the progression develops: from the epic hero, who stands center stage and performs great deeds for the historian to record, we moved in a generation to anonymous collective activity, but still in the realm of *public* events; now, with Braudel, we seem to have reached a view of history that retains the anonymity but turns to the very subtle, humdrum details of the domestic lives of the bulk of the population. One could certainly insert at various points along this spectrum intermediate or alternative views, but this is a large enough sweep to set anyone thinking about the range, purposes, and methods of history.

At this point the teacher should read Tolstoy's *War and Peace,* including the brilliant second Epilogue on the nature of historical explanation, which everyone avoids. He should encounter Tolstoy's scathing skepticism directed at the artificiality and delusion of all historical constructions, and consider his view that we are all the victims of historical process and that the most deluded among us are those who imagine they can explain it or that their actions have some influence on it. After this, the future teacher is entitled to read something short and brilliant, which directly addresses (with great sympathy) Tolstoy's theory of history, but also the other questions we have been considering—Isaiah Berlin's great essay, *The Hedgehog and the Fox.*

Finally, every teacher in America should read Richard Hofstadter's *Anti-Intellectualism in American Life.* It is an extraordinarily humane view of all the various strands of ideology, attitude, and historical circumstance which agitate this perplexing question of how we should educate our children. Hofstadter has symphathy, but he also has sufficient amplitude and confidence to make sharp judgments. In my view, there has been no other American historian of his quality in this century.

Literature

The literature that every teacher should master consists largely of texts that already seem familiar to us. Thus, the task of recommending a background in literature faces one of the challenges of the teacher himself—to keep the freshness of the printed word alive for himself and for his students, however many readings it receives.

One of the worst features about many recent trends of modern criticism, or hermeneutics as it sometimes likes to be called, is that with its intrusive metaphysics and its clutter of jargon, it kills the immediacy of the text. I shall, then, avoid the imposition of critical models, and confront a few books simply as autonomous works of genius that deserve intensely personal readings from everyone, whether they read for themselves or are preparing them for exposition to a class. I make no effort to be exhaustive here, but the works I suggest are ones that should be included in any list. I offer suggestions on how works can be grouped to sharpen our perceptions of each, by their contrasts or complementariness.

The Odyssey and *Huckleberry Finn*. These works are often taken together, I have discovered, in eighth or ninth grade; my son, having changed schools between the two grades, has been reading both of them for the second time. Each story seems to be an adventure involving a voyage, with a series of terrifying adventures ashore. But the voyage is in fact a *nostos,* a home-coming, a journey back to the beginning and to the proper reestablishment of the hero's identity. The force of the image of traveling far to find oneself is one of the strongest in literature. At the outset, both heroes are anonymous, and their travels seem to be aimless; the sea carries Odysseus where it wills, from one near disaster to another, and the great river carries Huck relentlessly downstream at its pleasure, away from one tight corner after another. In both books deception and guile are cardinal features of the story; Odysseus himself, with his elaborate lying tales about himself, is the greatest deceiver, while Huck seems more open: but Huck is surrounded by deception and must often try his hand at it as well. The assumption of both books is that the world is strange and hostile. The heroes "come in out of the dark"—but in spite of this both books end, interestingly, with the prospect of new journeys.

We should make the differences between the two works more clear, though. Odysseus is an epic hero—he will proceed through a series of recognition scenes, involving the Phaeacians, his swineherd, his dog, his nurse, his son, his wife, and ultimately his father, to reclaim his full status. He will stand up as a beggar in his hall—and one should have a firm sense of the outrage to ancient sensibility of an epic king singing for his supper in rags in his own hall. He will stand up, string the bow that only he can bend, and he will take his vengeance; and the suitors, who have been squandering his substance, before their end will know him for what he is. Odysseus is an epic hero, but the poet has also made him *human,* in the straight-forwardness of his obsession to reach home and his wife, passing up all manner of fancy places and fancy women on the way—Circe, Calypso, Nausicaa. (Samuel Butler thought the *Odyssey* was written by a woman.) In the case of Nausicaa, Homer plays delightfully with the reader's expectations, frustrating the conventions of a fairy-story: the hero is washed ashore, shaggy and penniless; he is discovered by a golden princess, highly nubile and with marriage on her mind; she takes this stranger home; no one knows who he is; the stranger enters athletic competition with the princess's hungry suitors, wins many events and the princess's heart; a parental problem develops, but, lo and behold, the stranger turns out to be a prince himself. Surely he is going to marry her? But he moves on. The *Odyssey* stands at the dawn of literature, but in the way it plays upon convention, it is already an experimental work.

Huckleberry Finn, on the other hand, is an interestingly subversive book, written when the conventions of letters and of education were already settled. Huck, in his uninstructed semi-innocence, is like a product of Rousseau's state of nature. To such a mentality, books and ideas are tricky things, and they may well serve man's entrepreneurial skills rather than his finer instincts. This is evident at the very start of the book, with Tom Sawyer's rampant exegesis on pirate literature and on what constitutes conventional behavior for highwaymen. Later, the conventions of literature, and the pretentiousness of letters, are more savagely parodied in the persons of the bogus King and Duke, the two-man Shakespearean troupe that makes its felonious way downstream, pulling the simple but snobbish riverside towns with their performances as the great actors Garrick and Kean. But in Huck's relations with Jim, and in the problems that Jim presents to Huck's conscience, we see the sternest criticisms of education and the kind of moral sensibility that it instills. Huck ponders the religious lessons that he has learned, and reaches the conclusion that, as Jim is actually Miss Watson's property, it is Huck's moral duty to make sure Jim is returned to her. By helping Jim run away, Huck is collaborating in theft. But when he reflects on Jim's kindness to him—letting him sleep when it was his turn to stand watch—and on his sheer human companionship, which seems to Huck and to us *fully* human, he decides that he must continue to be bad (despite the prospects of "everlasting fire" as a punishment) and not return the slave to his owner. It is perhaps the stifling sense of moral probity, as much as the uncomfortable clothes that sometimes he is forced to wear, that constitutes "sivilization," the very idea of which keeps the noble young savage reckoning "I got to light out for the 'Territory.' "

Oedipus Rex, King Lear, and *Death of a Salesman.* One might take these as a trilogy, to establish the definition of tragedy across time. Once more, like Odysseus and Huck, all three of the protagonists in these plays are rootless; Oedipus seems to have found a resting place in a foreign land, but must leave it in darkness before the end, Lear rattles around his kingdom, without a home, and Willy Loman is a traveling salesman, dreaming of a settled place in the country.

The story of Oedipus is perhaps the most famous of a host of "supplanting myths." An infant son—whose birth is seen, often as the result of a dream or oracle, to threaten the reigning king—is exposed to the threat of death, but survives and in almost every case, topples a dynasty and establishes a new order. Cyrus, Moses, Romulus and Remus, and Jesus of Nazareth are some examples; Otto Rank, in his great essay, "The Myth of the Birth of the Hero," deals with fifteen versions of the story in world literature and refers to others.

What would be particularly challenging to Sophocles' Greek audience is the shifting of the tragic scene down a generation, so that the hand of fate, which seemed so evident in allowing Oedipus to triumph over his parents' cruelty in sacrificing him, is now seen to have trapped him in the same parental bind. It is his parents, after all, who finally bring him down. The circles of fate are very tight and very vicious.

In all these plays, there is a very evident stress on light and dark, on seeing and on blindness. Teiresias tells Oedipus:

> I say, since you have taunted even my blindness,/ That you have eyes, but do not see the evil you are in. . . . (411–412)

The theme of delusion, then, looms very large, and in every case the delusion is directed to those who are closest to the protagonist—to his family, whether he recognizes them or not. Is this the central kernel of tragedy, the essential *hamartia,* which Aristotle writes about in his *Poetics?* Is it true that man only becomes tragic when he becomes blind about those he loves, or ought to, but does not? In the case of Lear and Willy Loman, the generational delusion is not directed back toward the parents but forward to the children, Lear rejecting one daughter and being rejected by two, and Willy and Biff Loman destroying each other by the false expectations they hold for each other. In both these plays, the search for love is a kind of *ambition* on the part of the hero toward his children, a search for status and recognition, which is seen in the end to be misplaced. Lear's journey from the intemperate king, through madness, to the "very foolish, fond, old man," who rediscovers his daughter Cordelia ("Do not laugh at me; for, as I am a man, I think this lady to be my child Cordelia"), is an extraordinary progression from the childish to the childlike, from the capricious to the vulnerable; but when all the bombast of the king's madness and the storm finds its quiet resolution in the discovery of love, it is too late. But the resolution stays with us, and combines with the simple lines of the story to convey the impression that, for all the Sturm und Drang we construct upon it, love should be a simple thing.

From two kings, we come to the Salesman. Arthur Miller, in critical notes he wrote on the play, takes issue with Joseph Wood Krutch's attribution of the death of tragedy to the disappearance of aristocracy:

> In this age, few tragedies are written. It has often been held that the lack is due to a paucity of heroes among us, or else that modern man has had the blood drawn out of his organs of belief by the skepticism of science, and the heroic attack on life cannot feed on an attitude of reserve and circumspection. . . . I believe that the common man is as apt a subject for tragedy in its highest sense as kings were. (*Tragedy and the Common Man*—1949)

Here again the theme of ambition is very strong and perhaps more straightforward than in the other plays. Ambition is the vehicle that will help Loman escape from his life on the road to something grander and more settled. If he cannot do it himself, his son, the athlete, will achieve it. Interestingly, it is the modern playwright who is the most lenient with his hero's dreams and delusions; Willy's dreams are essential for Willy's life, sustaining him through the bleakness of his day. As Charley says for his epitaph, "Nobody dast blame this man. A salesman is got to dream, boy. It comes with the territory."

Romeo and Juliet, Persuasion, and *Portrait of a Lady.* These works contain definitions of three heroines, all at different stages of their lives, who, had they met, would have liked each other. Juliet's youthful passion carries her from child to woman overnight before our eyes. The play captures the extraordinary rapacity of sexual passion, its kind of meteoric self-consumption, leaving lovers out of breath and out of pace with normal time—"Gallop space, you fiery-footed steeds," Juliet cries to the sun, "towards Phoebus' lodging; such a waggoner/ as Phaethon would whip you to the West,/ and bring in cloudy night immediately. . . . Come gentle night, come loving, black-browed night, Give me my Romeo. . . ." The sexual charge that this play carries is indeed astonishing, but it should not obscure for us the skills with which Shakespeare develops his plot, especially in the steering of the whole theme of interfamily feud indoors toward the apparently inevitable conflict that young love finds with parents and authority. The previously supportive parents and the friendly nurse become Juliet's enemies, and almost gaolers, after the death of Tybalt; they do not know her secret (the nurse does, but does not seem to have betrayed her) and yet they act as though they did, and as though her refusal to marry Paris (when just a few days earlier her father pronounced her too young to marry him) is now a kind of perversion. Her father's fickleness serves to underline for us Juliet's constancy: we realize that with her lover absent, and with all her familial support withdrawn, she has become a woman, and a tragic one. (We note that the definition of the characters of Juliet and Lear would stand on their own as tangible proofs of the range of Shakespeare's imagination.)

From Juliet, we turn to the more measured passion of Anne Elliot in *Persuasion,* who had been advised against an early engagement when she was nineteen and followed the advice, but lived to regret it: She "had been forced into prudence in her youth," but "learned romance as she grew older." There is a lovely delicacy in Jane Austen's portrait of the quiet dignity of the woman who knows and accepts that her fate in life is probably going to be made for her in large measure by others. And yet as Wentworth and Anne approach each other warily for a second chance, we sense the depth of her yearning, both for physical love and for a shared sensibility. At the very climax of the work, in a conversation overheard

by Wentworth, Anne talks to his friend Harville of the sad dependence of
women:

> We certainly do not forget you so soon as you forget us. It is perhaps our fate
> rather than our merit. We cannot help ourselves. We live at home, quiet,
> confined, and our feelings prey upon us. You are forced on exertion. You
> have always a profession, pursuits, business of some sort or other, to take
> you back into the world. . . .

Later in the same conversation, Anne comments that the poverty of the
woman's world extends to an absence of literature which makes her case:

> Men have had every advantage of us in telling their own story. Education has
> been theirs in so much higher a degree; the pen has been in their hands. I will
> not allow books to prove anything.

And then the final modest claim:

> All the privilege I claim for my own sex (it is not a very enviable one, you
> need not covet it), is that of loving longest, when existence or when hope is
> gone.

This drawing room conversation is a consummate construction by
the novelist, channeling sensitivity, desire, intelligence, and near despair
into such a distilled form that the drama of it is almost painful. Anne Elliot
fortunately found a genius to tell her story; or is it the story of the novelist
herself?

Finally and briefly, is Isabel Archer, in James's *Portrait of a Lady,*
whom I would be inclined to crown as the all-world heroine; for generosity of spirit and for openness to experience and courage, there are few to
touch her. Her very virtues lead her to make her mistake, marrying the
still-born aesthete Gilbert, but they are large enough to let her live the
consequences without being crushed. But like Dorothea Brooke in *Mid-
dlemarch,* which had influenced James, she possesses an unquestioned
acceptance that her role in life should be as the support of a gifted,
preferably scholarly man—though in both cases, the men turn out to be
worthless. *Why* is Isabel attracted to the dead Gilbert, and the marvelously ironic and perceptive, but dying, Ralph? I think the answer is probably in James, rather than in Isabel. The sexuality, which the reader
knows she has, seems to have escaped her author, whether from Victo-
rian scruples, or from James's own indifference. No matter! The face she
turns to us is so brilliantly lit with courage, warmth, candor, intelligence,
and the highest decency, that we can supply the details for the rest.

It seems to me that this trio of women from previous centuries poses
an essential dilemma that reaches all of us still—their quality is so much
greater than the possibilities their world has room for: how did they
achieve the quality, and how could they fulfill it?

POLITICAL THEORY

There is no aspect of our lives that calls so urgently as the world of politics for a firm knowledge of where we have come from, and of how hard-won and slow the gains have been. The volatility of the political climate around us, where every issue at every level of a complex society is polarized and clouded with either barely articulate grievances or rhetorical slogans and code words, demands the sharpest analytic mind and also the strongest commitment to what we believe.

We begin with Plato's *Republic,* which raises, in the most seductive way, almost every question of ethics, politics, metaphysics, epistemology, and aesthetics (though I happen to believe that it gives many of them the wrong answer). The versatility of his mind is as inspiring as its authoritarian bent is depressing. But it was Coleridge, I think, who said, "Wherever I go in my mind, I meet Plato on the way back," so he makes a good starting point for one who would be well educated. The *Republic* as a whole takes its place, and a very important place, in a running debate referred to as the *Nomos/Physis* debate, which had gained in intensity from the middle of the fifth century B.C. The issue of this debate is the nature of goodness. Are normative rules mere matters of convention *(nomos)*, artificial devices conjured up to regulate, and put a brake on, man's behavior and his basic instincts in society? Or are moral values themselves inherently *natural* values, built into human nature *(physis),* so that their violation is not merely the abuse of an external code (which a man may only regret if he gets caught), but an internal abuse, which in some sense damages the man himself? A strong body of opinion had favored the *nomos* side of the argument, and it is represented in the *Republic* by the very belligerent sophist, Thrasymachus, who scores some palpable hits but does not get to develop his argument as thoroughly as he might.

Plato and his spokesman Socrates stand unequivocally on the side of *physis*: justice, which serves here as an archetype for all goodness, is a natural harmony of the soul, coordinating the activity of all facets of human behavior. But in Plato's mind, it is a harmony that amounts to a kind of *knowledge,* like all virtues, and this is the mainspring of his political theory. In Plato's work, the answer to the question, "Who ought to rule?" is, "The man who has the knowledge of justice, and therefore can regulate all the different classes of society"—in short, the Philosopher King. For Plato, if you don't know *in the truest sense,* then your opinion is trivial and to be discounted. He believes, then, that there is an intrinsic title to govern to be found in the qualities of the ruler. And this idea of intrinsic title (whether based on the ruler's virtue, his power, his divine right, his papal election, or his genetic heritage) reigned virtually unchallenged in practice throughout the West for 2,000 years—apart from small, temporary pockets of enlightenment, and the odd gesture of public relations.

In the second half of the sixteenth century, though, especially in France and in Holland, a concerted groundswell of theory starts to build, that challenges the established view. In England in the seventeenth century, after civil war and the execution of the king, that theory finally breaks through to practice. Hobbes, with his three books culminating in *Leviathan* (1651), is a crucial and fascinating figure in this change.

Hobbes's overall theory is certainly more repressive and absolutist than Plato's, except in one essential detail. The Sovereign in *Leviathan* is above the law and can do almost anything to his subjects, including kill them, and the subjects should acknowledge his rights to these extremes. The reason he must be allowed such rights is that the subjects have in fact given them to him: faced with the state of war, which is the natural state of man, with his insatiable passions and unrelenting competition for power, all men try to win peace for themselves, by transferring all their rights against each other to the Sovereign, whose sole function is to maintain order in society. But an important transition has been made. For all the potential for oppression that Hobbes writes into the Sovereign's mandate, there is one thing that has sold the pass to democracy: the Sovereign finally gets his title from the people. Government can henceforth only be justified by the governed.

It is from there only a short step to Locke *(Second Treatise on Government)* writing at the end of Hobbes's life and establishing the basic principles of democracy as we recognize it today. The mandate of government is not to assume the rights from the governed but to protect their rights; the rights themselves are not transferred, because they are inalienable. Persons in the state of nature are equal and free and not essentially at war with each other; but it is still more to the convenience of each to form a contract to enter into a regulated society. For Locke, it is absurd to imagine that one would enter upon an arrangement that left him less protected than when he started. Whereas Plato and Hobbes believed that government needs the protection of absolutism against the aberrations of individuals who threaten society's stability, Locke reverses the formula: the citizen needs constitutional guarantees against his government's abuses. To Locke we owe many of our contemporary notions of inalienable individual rights and political freedom and equality, as well as some of the more specific details of our political life, such as the separation of powers and regular elections. All of this should be engraved on our souls by the American Declaration of Independence and the Constitution— which constitute the first national adoption of what had been left for a century as simply a code of theory. What is particularly interesting is how such a basic idea as the inalienable right of equality, once ratified, serves as a constant social and political irritant, challenging and embarrassing all the institutional inconsistencies that survive in practice long after its adoption—slavery, racism, sexism, and so forth. How many more incongruities must we resolve if we are to live up to Locke and Jefferson?

Finally, a teacher must read Marx (*Capital*, vol. 1). Quite apart from global polarities, we are all raised under his shadow as a theorist. It will be impossible for any historian, from this century on, whatever his political stripe, to ignore the economic factor in the historical process, and Marx is largely responsible for that. The politics cannot be ignored either; two ideologies currently divide the world, and whatever our skepticism, and however we "vote with our feet" by the way of life we choose to follow, we must understand the principal premises of both.

Marx is a difficult writer to absorb; the corpus is huge, and the ideas evolve in a bewilderingly diverse polemic with different targets and accents at different phases. But everyone should try to come to grips with at least two of the central pillars of his theory, the labor theory of value, and the concept of class alienation.

The labor theory of value had been first hinted at by the liberal Locke and fully developed by the supposedly conservative Adam Smith and others. But it is Marx who follows its premise to a relentless conclusion: if it is true that what gives a commodity its value is the labor that a workman, whatever his status, invests to make it a finished product, then why is the economy of a nation not organized so that the profit on the sale of the commodity is returned to the workman who gave it its value?

The second question is even more fundamental: Is it true that there is an absolute rift in society between those who have property and those who do not, between the capitalist, who owns the means of production, and the proletariat, which has nothing to sell but its labor? Marx may have been influenced by his dialectical assumptions to see these distinctions as absolutely clear-cut—thesis and antithesis, whose ineluctable clash in revolution would finally produce the synthesis of the classless society.

Marx saw the industrial world of the nineteenth century as the final phase of class conflict: the dehumanizing conditions of the workers and the pressure of competition between capitalists seemed likely to produce an explosion which would blow it all away. Historically, it is interesting that Marx seems to have been right that only a clear-cut distinction between the haves and the have-nots produces revolution but wrong that the conditions are most likely to be found in an industrial society. There the sheer level of aspiration in the workers to improve their situation, along with strategic concessions in labor relations by the proprietors, have diffused the tensions and created the polite buffer zone of the middle class. But in feudal peasant societies, the distinction between haves and have-nots has been more exclusively defined, and there the revolutions occur.

SCIENCE FOR THE HUMANIST

The teacher of humanities is today sometimes regarded as the representative of a minority culture: it is assumed that the age we live in and particularly the culture we live in as Americans are by now technologically and scientifically oriented. It is not clear that the lives of the bulk of the population are much more closely attuned to the actual achievements and processes of science than they were a generation ago, but they are more consciously spent under its aura. If humanities teachers are to avoid a kind of ghetto-minded defensiveness about their fields, they should engage the world of science, investigate some of its signal achievements, and discover how the scientific mind operates and what questions it asks of *them*. And they should remember what William James wrote: "You can give humanistic value to almost anything by teaching it historically. Geology, economics, mechanics are humanities when taught with reference to the successive achievements of the geniuses to which these sciences owe their being." A number of classics make clear the indispensable essentials of science as a human endeavor: Galileo's writing (Stillman Drake edition); Darwin's *Origin of Species;* Freud's *Outline of Psychoanalysis, Three Essays on the Theory of Sexuality,* and *Civilization and Its Discontents;* Herbert Butterfield's *The Origins of Modern Science;* Alexandre Koyre's *From the Closed World to the Infinite Universe;* and Thomas Kuhn's *The Structures of Scientific Revolutions.*

Galileo completes the Copernican revolution and leaves the scene set for Newton, hence founding the modern scientific mind. To the ancient world, the apparent permanence and regular movements of the celestial bodies, their bright sameness, were evidence for the belief that they were "other-worldly," divine spheres of crystalline perfection which must be guided by their own music and not by earthly physical laws. Galileo, with his newly designed telescope fixed on the moon (see "The Starry Messenger"), was able to prove such pieties false; the surface of the moon is rocky and uneven; there are mountains which cast shadows, and deep valleys and rifts. The implications are that the heavenly bodies are, instead of impregnable perfections beyond our ken and reach, flawed compositions just like the earth, accretions of earthly matter and therefore susceptible to the same laws that govern it. The universe, thus lowered in status, is henceforth open to man's scrutiny and hypotheses. One of the most interesting and moving aspects of Galileo's writing (cf. especially his letter to the Grand Duchess Christina) is his own determination to reconcile his scientific findings with his faith; in his view, God gave man a mind to use in exploration of His creation. The depth and range of his faith makes the blinkered vision of his Inquisitors all the more appalling.

Darwin's *Origin of Species* again advances a theory, like Copernicus', which appears to fly in the face of both primary experience and orthodox religious belief: the species seem to be fixed but are not. What changes them is the process of natural selection. Darwin was impressed by the Malthusian formula that population expands geometrically, the food supply only arithmetically. Because of this, a species has to change to survive. The competition within a species for the same dwindling food supply (animals of the same species will have the same eating habits) is so intense that only those individuals will survive that have the benefits of some advantageous modification that leaves them better adapted to their environment and therefore gives them the edge in the competition. The useful modification is not "earned" but is the result of the random mutations that interbreeding produces. It is *nature*—the whole ecological complex in which the animal lives—that pronounces a particular adaptation useful, selects it for survival, and perhaps perpetuates it in the narrower genetic pool of a diminished population. Darwin thus endorses Herbert Spencer's tag, "the survival of the fittest"—an unfortunate slogan, seized on by Social Darwinists and others, as cause for self-congratulation and justification for all manner of social ruthlessness. Darwin himself would have disowned these constructions on his work. In his later book, *The Descent of Man,* he plays down the motif of "nature red in tooth and claw," and allows room for the law of mutual aid, for social supportiveness between species.

Freud's theory, like Galileo's and Darwin's, again argues the unexpected. Sexuality does not begin at puberty, when the sexual organs develop and become active, but in infancy. The sexual energy (libido) of the infant first fixes upon those areas of the body whose activities are associated with pleasurable satisfaction—the oral, anal, and genital zones. The baby is narcissistically self-absorbed at the outset, but as he grows he must come to realize that certain satisfactions lie outside his control: they are in fact provided by his mother. The mother therefore becomes the first love-object of the child and a little later the source of his first trauma. The competition with his father for exclusive possession of the mother is a struggle that the child, in the course of regular development, must lose. The need to supplant the father, the guilt at the resentment one feels at the father, whom in other ways one loves, and the fear of the powerful father's reprisals are what constitute the Oedipus complex. It is astonishing that such melodrama is seen as a normal part of growing up. (It is worth commenting, and I think a valid point of criticism, that it is hard to state Freud's theory except in terms of boy-child and mother; it is a very male-oriented hypothesis.)

But on a larger scale, and with more tragic implications, Freud sees the whole interaction between the insatiable appetites of the individual's libido and his conscious ego (reinforced by societal and parental norms— the superego) as leading to a set of compromises that are in principle frustrating: our love objects inevitably fail us, are unable to support the burden of the yearning we impose on them; our creative drives are always stultified by the need to conform; in the face of civilization, we must all ultimately be discontent.

Finally, the three other works listed under this section all deal with problems in the history of science and use them to elucidate the actual operations of the scientific mind. Butterfield's book is a lucid, historical exposition for the most part and makes clear the sharpening of the empirical method, the process of induction, the formation and testing of hypotheses with predictable results, the removal of "blocks" to insight. On this latter point, Kuhn's book stresses the importance of the correct "paradigm" or model as the key to the solution of certain problems, new models opening up the road to new experiments: when you start thinking of light as a wave, rather than an accumulation of particles, whole new lines of investigation emerge. Koyre's work plays ingeniously upon the element of riddling and paradox that is part of the excitement of science; he emphasizes the kind of unexpectedness that makes science seem a respectable cousin of magic, the insight that not only enlarges but often, as we have seen, reverses previous opinion. Newton, one discovers, spent a fair amount of time on alchemy and saw no discontinuity between that and his mathematics.

TEACHING AND TRADITION

Thomas Paine, the Englishman who loved America, wrote in *The Crisis* in March 1780:

> . . . There is something in the extent of countries, which among the generality of people, insensibly communicates extension of the mind. The soul of an islander in its native state seems bounded by the foggy confines of the water's edge, and all beyond affords to him matters only for profit or curiosity, not for friendship. His island is to him his world, and fixed to that, his every thing centers in it; while those, who are inhabitants of a continent, by casting their eye over a larger field, take in likewise a larger intellectual circuit, and thus approaching nearer to an acquaintance with the universe, their atmosphere of thought is extended, and their liberality fills a wider space.

At one level, of course, this is merely the polemical Paine contrasting English insularity with American, "continental" expansiveness. But, as Paine himself indicates, the passage admits of wider application: no matter where we live, we are offered a fundamental choice. On the one hand we can cloister ourselves in the closed circle of what is familiar, in the small pocket of time that is allotted to us, keeping our problems, fears, and dimly perceived aspirations to ourselves, without any content except the one we give them. Or else we can, as Paine suggests, "take in a larger intellectual circuit," and see how through the vast expanse of history men and women have tried to make sense of their worlds, in the same way we must try ourselves, and have passed their visions on to us in some great work of art, which still lives because it moves us still. The human predicament does not change much in its essentials—every generation must face the challenges of growth and love and death—and the range of feeling we bring to it does not change much either. The nursery rhymes we sing, the fairy tales we tell, the very games we play as children, have their roots somewhere mysteriously deep in the human spirit and produce, almost as it were spontaneously, a vivid flowering in every generation of children in virtually every land.

We should not be troubled by the fact that our lives are patterned with ancient ceremony. We will never, whatever our genius, contrive a whole new range of human feeling—we love, fear, hope, and grieve as human beings always have. To come to terms with a tradition, I take it, is to accept with gratitude, but never uncritically, what the experience of the past offers us and then to discover for ourselves where we can see further, redefine, advance to new conclusions, if not to the threshold of the promised land. We cannot remake the world, unless we know what it has been; by taking our place within the tradition in this way, we hand on to our own children the record of our striving and our hopes for them. Every parent tries to do this, but there are some who, because of their particular ability at doing it and the depth of their commitment to do it, are called on to teach all our children. We salute them and wish them well.

NOTES

1. "Core Curriculum" is a fairly condensed piece of academic jargon. I use it here in its tighter sense, as practiced by Columbia, Chicago, and St. John's Colleges: its assumptions are not merely that a series of explicit, interconnected requirements must be met (literature, social and political thought, etc.), but that each of these requirements should be spelled out in detail with a set syllabus of major works to be read. Where general areas for study are indicated but the student is left free to choose one or two from a number of courses in each area, this does not amount to a "core curriculum," but to "distribution requirements." The recent, busily promoted reforms at Harvard are of this kind, though they sail under the flag of "core curriculum."

The Intellectual Lives
of Teachers

Edwin J. Delattre

> Education has been the subject of innumerable treatises. They have all
> . . . received part of their character from the habits acquired by their
> authors from the mode which was fashionable in their own education.
> There is a fashion even of sentiment, and wherever there is a fashion
> there is bigotry. I wish we could get rid of fashions in thinking.
>
> —Benjamin H. Latrobe, "Thoughts on a
> National System of Education," 1798

The fashions of education are not only fickle; they are also unconsidered
and thoughtless. Yet however mindless they become, they seem always
to recur to these basic questions: What should teachers learn? How
should they learn it? What should teachers teach? How should they teach
it?

This essay is about these four questions, as they apply to in-service
education for secondary school humanities teachers. It tries to avoid
surrendering to the fashions that make American schooling resemble a
pendulum gone wild—concerned one year with "values" because of Vietnam and Watergate, another year with "careers" because the job market
is down, another with "technology" because nuclear energy production
and video games are in the news, yet another with "excellence" because a
national commission stresses that other countries are getting ahead of us
in one educational race or another. The essay tries also to show how true
excellence is possible in American secondary schools.

My argument is straightforward:

First, the purpose of formal education is to nurture and cultivate certain specific powers of mind and heart which have application in all human endeavors.

Second, no one can begin to do an adequate job of nurturing these powers in others, particularly in the young, who is not permanently cultivating them in himself or herself; that is, no one not engaged in ongoing self-improvement of the mind can resist the bigotry of fashion and the poor teaching that follows from it.

Third, in-service education must be designed in acknowledgment of these truths.

Fourth, schools must (yes, *must*) encourage, support, and pay for continued study and learning by their teachers, principals, and superintendents.

WHAT SHOULD TEACHERS LEARN?

In order to answer this question, it is necessary to think big—much bigger than is customary in education generally or in the education of educators particularly. For the question means "What specific powers of mind and heart are to be nurtured by formal education?"

The answer, broadly put, is the powers of mind exhibited in the practice of the divine arts, the liberal arts, the fine arts, and the useful arts. These arts have come into existence through concerted efforts of human intelligence since the beginnings of man; they are the disciplines of mind, and they contain the dimensions of intellect that touch and move the heart.

To use more familiar language, the divine arts are theology and related studies. The liberal arts (traditionally classified as the quadrivium of geometry, astronomy, arithmetic, and music, and the trivium of grammar, logic, and rhetoric) can be thought of today as including the natural and social sciences, mathematics, music, and the disciplines of the humanities such as philosophy, literature, languages, and history. The fine arts are the plastic arts and the remaining performing arts, and the useful arts are essentially manual, occupational, and technological skills.

Every educated person has a grounding in at least the fundamental methods of inquiry, discovery, expression, appreciation, and application in these four types of art. The American poet and author Mark Van Doren observed that an educated person is one who could refound his own civilization, and that requires breadth of mind. Notably, every time a teacher walks into a classroom, every time a teacher thereby takes responsibility for the way hours in the life of a student's developing mind are spent, the teacher is in the act of refounding civilization, the act of building the future. Thus, teachers, above all, must aspire to be educated people in the sense that Van Doren meant.

It is only through such breadth of mind that anyone can hope to see problems in their full complexity, imagine solutions to match that complexity, or understand the artistry and vision of other people. Depth of mind matters, too, of course, whether in history or physics or welding; but it is not enough, because by itself even the most profound specialization cannot grasp far-reaching consequences, it cannot apprehend interconnectedness, and it cannot avoid the bigotry of fashion to which minds without breadth are always susceptible. These first two points can be appreciated by considering advances in our knowledge of ancient civilizations realized by combining studies in anthropology, history, astronomy, and chemistry—advances never achieved by any of these disciplines in isolation.

The third point is most important. Breadth of mind is desired for itself by every self-respecting mind, on the grounds that no such mind will willingly deny itself the range of intellectual powers that typify humanity. Teachers must have such respect for themselves, and they must exhibit it in the presence of their students, or else they will teach terrible lessons by the example of their own intellectual negligence. They will teach that breadth of mind is unimportant, or that it is fine to study only what one finds interesting, as though being interesting and being important were the same. Worst of all, they may leave the impression that the arts beyond the teacher's ken are unworthy of attention.

This last is the lesson where bigotry reveals its ugliness. It is evident in schools where teachers whose expertise is limited to the useful arts publicly disdain learnedness as impractical and pointless, unrelated to student self-interest, while teachers limited to the humanities claim that only study of their disciplines makes people fully human—as though being human were an achievement. What rot and nonsense on both sides! No one with any experience of intellectual fulfillment can ever view coming to know as pointless, or its joy as impractical; and no one who has ever looked at a newborn child can doubt that it is fully human. To grasp both forms of artistry is to become immunized to the bigotry of fashion, to the simplistic idea that education should be reduced to some narrow goal of getting a job, or of becoming a "sensitive person." It is the fate of narrow minds to be the victims of fashion—or worse, the perpetrators of it.

Everybody owes it to himself to avoid this fate. It is the business of teachers to help others learn to avoid it. And so, teachers must learn to be practitioners, learners, students of all the arts of intellect. They will no doubt emphasize only some of these arts, but they must be intolerant of their own ignorance of the others. They must have a grasp of the intellect as a whole. This, they must learn.

How Should They Learn It?

The objections that can be anticipated to the first section of this essay are obvious. It will be argued that the essay expects too much, that it is utopian, that it demands more of teacher education than can possibly be offered, that there is not enough time, that the daily responsibilities of teachers, principals, and superintendents are incompatible with such study and practice of the arts of the intellect. It will be asked why such breadth and depth are necessary, since not all of either can be brought into the classroom anyway. These sorts of objections deserve attention— not because they are persuasive, but because they are bound to be made.

For teachers to have a grasp of the arts of intellect, what must they be able to do? First, they must be literate. That is, they must be able to read seminal books with contemplative power: to understand technical and nontechnical arguments and tell the reliable from the illogical or flawed; to be familiar with the methods of experimentation, explanation, and prediction in the sciences; to know how to approach a painting or sculpture or dramatic performance; and to be able to express themselves clearly, even eloquently, in conversation, dialogue, lecture, and print, So, too, for principals and superintendents.

The primary obstacles to the achievement of such literacy by teachers, principals, and superintendents seem to be the curricula of the teacher training institutions where many of them go to college; the relative youth in which many enter the professions; the failure of the schools where they teach to promote the intellectual maturation of faculty members; the tendency in schools and colleges to think of teachers primarily as "facilitators" for the learning of others rather than as practitioners of the disciplines of mind; and the reinforcement of these curricula, practices, and tendencies by the certification standards of the various states.

The recently published *Paideia Proposal* of Mortimer Adler stresses the need for teachers to achieve the sort of breadth of mind discussed above, and to advance it in their students. The text argues that "present teacher training programs turn out persons who are not sufficiently equipped with the knowledge, the intellectual skills, or the developed understanding needed to guide and help the young" to grasp the fundamental arts of knowing and learning.[1]

Of course, there are many wonderful and exemplary teachers in American schools; not all schoolteachers are the products of lackluster training institutions, and many who are have gone far beyond anything the teacher training programs required them to learn. But it remains to be asked whether institutions that set out to train teachers can or will do very much to improve the educational opportunities they offer.

It seems unlikely that they will. The curricula of most such colleges, and the standards for teacher certification set by the states, are hostage to the vested interests of specific faculty departments within the teachers' colleges. The departments are not themselves devoted to the *study and practice of* the arts of intellect; they are geared to the *study of teaching about* these subjects and to designing curricula for children and adolescents. They emphasize becoming a teacher and not becoming a practitioner who teaches. In short, they operate with a diminished and demeaning view of teachers which is disrespectful of the development of their own intellectual powers.

These facts about the ways aspiring teachers are treated show up in the preoccupation of many young teachers with the immediately useful— the materials, lessons, simulations, and so forth that can ostensibly be used in their teaching "right away." In part, their preoccupation exhibits merely the impatience that often goes with youth, and the anxiety that goes with a new job, but it also tells much about what they have learned to view as important from their own teachers, administrators, and school consultants. This is why fashions exercise such powerful influence over their thinking, and thus can be so dangerous to them and their students.

If this account of training and certification is basically right, then the question becomes "What can teachers individually do for themselves as practitioners, as advancing learners; and what can their schools do to encourage their maturation as learners and also as teachers?"

For teachers to make headway individually, they must have two things: time to learn and the imagination to envision a program of study, a curriculum, for themselves. Some teachers, principals, and superintendents can and do manage both; but relatively few have the leisure or the knowledge required.

Many school administrators are neither scholars nor teachers and play no direct part in the intellectual life of their schools. The day-to-day responsibilities of administrators tend to pull them ever farther away from study in scholarly and scientific disciplines. Only the very best administrators are able to resist this tendency and the related temptation to suppose that administrative responsibilities are so demanding, important, and relentless that improvement of one's mind must and can be foresaken without harm to oneself and to the school or schools one serves. This is hardly surprising in a country where it is commonplace to think of moving from teaching to administration as a *promotion*! Benjamin Franklin knew better, as he explained when he said that returning to private life from public service was a promotion, since it meant that others could now serve him as a citizen. Administration is only a means to the highest ideals of education—sound teaching and learning. No more, no less. And no one is fit to implement such means who is not centrally knowledgeable about teaching and learning in his own case as well as others, because no person devoid of an intellectual life of his own can offer leadership for the intellectual development of others.

Teachers themselves are often overwhelmed by the daily business of school. They have numerous classes, multiple preparations, lesson plans, papers to assign and grade, disruptive students to discipline and try to teach, paperwork to do, and innumerable daily distractions from teaching and learning. Add to this that meager salaries often impel them to work weekends and summers at other jobs, and it becomes all too easy to forget that teaching well is inseparable from learning and from exhibiting advancing knowledge in the presence of students.

Precisely because so many teachers, principals, and superintendents have learned more in college about educational psychology and pedagogy than they have about humanities or sciences or arts, they do not know how to build a program of study for themselves. Many have been subjected to too many textbooks and not enough original books; some have never read basic and profound works on learning, knowing and teaching—have never been exposed to Deuteronomy, works by Plato, Aristotle, Loyola, Milton, Agassiz, Hadas, or Highet, not to mention Augustine and the intellectual predecessors of Dewey. That is, some cannot teach themselves in any systematic program of study because they do not know enough to design one, and their own teachers are not always qualified to do so for them.

For these reasons, it is imperative that teachers, principals, and superintendents become members of an intellectual community where their own imaginations can be challenged by the experiences and thoughts of others and where they can in turn contribute to others from their own learning; the community should embody shared purpose and aspiration and high educational standards. It is here that "in-service education" comes into play. For many teachers, a school can offer the first opportunity for membership in such a community. This is a crucial opportunity because it is far more effective for people to learn in the company of others than to try to learn all by themselves without much of a plan for broadening and deepening the mind. Efficacious solitude becomes possible later.

The fact is that too few teachers, principals, and superintendents— even the especially diligent and dedicated—have ever been brought to the study of great lecturers, great dialecticians, great theoreticians, or great exemplars of learning and personal character. As a result, many have high hopes for their students but not enough regard for themselves as learners. They admirably seek to contribute to the realization of ideals that are larger than mere self,but they do not have enough experience in enlarging their own selves. This is surely one principal cause of teacher "burn-out," for total investment in the learning of others does not have a clear simplicity of result to it, like painting a house or mowing a lawn, and it is easy to come to doubt one's purpose and effectiveness. Intellectual community and due regard for oneself as a member of such a community can build bulkheads against this kind of personal erosion. Nothing can replace the inspiration of a community of learners.

An intellectual community is brought to life in practice by shared and cooperative study of works that can reasonably be expected to move the spirit and improve the mind. Participation in such a community takes patience and effort (the very things teachers try to inspire in their own students) and preparedness to fail to learn all things quickly. "Intellectual community" means a group of people who think together. It suggests friendship in the sense that Aristotle meant when he said that the best friendships among men seem to consist in shared contemplation rather than, as in the case of cattle, eating in the same place. But if people are to think together, they must know or learn how to speak, write, listen, and read well. If they are to think together to any purpose, they must know or learn how to think reasonably, with capacity to gather and assess relevant evidence, and they must learn to identify ideas, questions, and methods worth thinking about. These are the necessary intellectual conditions of sound in-service programs.

To these must be added the necessary temporal and economic conditions. In-service learning must be nourished by schools and their administrators in several ways: teachers, principals, and superintendents must be given time for shared study. This means fewer hours spent teaching and more hours spent learning in order to improve the mind *and* to become a better teacher. Released time must be a normal budget line item. Time and money must be invested in the school's ultimate resource—individual teachers and administrators; that is, the school must come to see that its vitality as an institution depends on the vitality of mind of its faculty. (A longer paid school year for teachers could serve the same purpose with no absolute reduction of teaching time—though the proportion of time spent teaching would decline.)

This view runs against many powerful trends in education, such as confusing the immediately useful with the ultimately practical; and profound resistance to it is the norm.

It is for this reason that "in-service" is a dirty word in many schools, suggesting dreary, boring days in the presence of putative experts who have never worked "in the trenches," have never done their own homework in the arts of intellect, and who come to schools armed with "packages," "teacher-proof curricula," "sure-fire textbooks," video and audio materials—canned goods designed to do everything for everybody instantly. Whole days of in-service, even all the in-service days in a career, may be spent in curriculum planning, teaching methods (or, if you like, the latest gimmicks), without any attention to the intellectual lives of the teachers. Such days invest nothing in the minds of the people who serve the school. Yet a school is, by definition, a place designed for the improvement of the students, teachers, and administrators who work in it. The challenge is to make the facts resemble the definition.

Schools determined to contribute to the growth of intellectual community have to start someplace. Given the limited experience of most schools with truly useful in-service, it is best to start modestly. They can take specific problems or perceived needs in the school as the place to begin or they can develop far-reaching programs of study for all who wish to participate. In the following four sections are described two real problems in particular schools along with possible in-service solutions; a third school problem and a description of how the school designed an in-service program to combat it; and one sketch of a far-reaching program of in-service education.

The Goldilocks Case

In the spring of 1983, an elementary school in Santa Fe, New Mexico, became visible in the national media when, on "Law Day," a fifth-grade class conducted a mock trial of Goldilocks for criminal trespass, criminal damage to property, larceny, and burglary. A federal judge presided, teachers took parts in the drama, students served as jurors. Goldilocks was convicted of the first two charges and acquitted of the last two.

After her conviction, the judge explained to the students that he could, but would not, sentence Goldilocks to eighteen months in jail; rather he sentenced her to give twenty hours of work at an animal shelter, to sell pine cones to pay for Baby Bear's chair, and to try to make friends with Baby Bear. He then instructed the children that service on a jury was the most important act of citizenship. Children interviewed by the press said they had learned how difficult it was to be a lawyer and "never do anything wrong."

Clearly, all this was well-intentioned, an attempt by means of a simulated courtroom trial to give the youngsters a sense of due process and governments of laws rather than of men. But the lessons that were inadvertently taught are pernicious and could have been avoided by the thoughtful imagination of a knowledgeable intellectual community of teachers. What was taught, implicitly or explicitly, as the facts were made out to the students during the trial?

First, that the proper response to an eleven-year-old child who is lost, cold, hungry, lonely, and afraid and seeks shelter in the only dwelling she can find, is prosecution. Second, that parents such as the Bears care more about their rights and their chairs than they do about the

Golden Rule, about how they would have wanted other families to treat Baby Bear if he had been lost and frightened and had sought shelter. Third, that honorable day-to-day conduct as a citizen, treating one's fellows with kindness, generosity, and civility, is not so important as service on a jury. Fourth, that litigation is a better solution to problems than candid, patient conversation among interested parents and guardians. And fifth, that media celebration of the trial and conviction of a child, even though only in simulation, is no invasion of privacy. The simulation taught a bleak vision of parenthood, a shallow vision of citizenship, a crude vision of problem solving, and an uncritical vision of the rightful powers of the press.

Children deserve better than this. How could an in-service program have led to what they deserve? A community of thoughtful teachers could have posed for itself questions like these: What are the purposes and traditions of fairy tales and parables? What would be the best materials to use for simulated trials? What kinds of crimes should be first on the docket? Should the three little pigs be tried for murdering the Big Bad Wolf? For cannibalism? Or are there better vehicles to teach and learn lessons about due process and the law? What are the relationships among law, justice, mercy, and discretionary authority in the judiciary? What crimes should be prosecuted and when? To what extent should the media be involved and to what extent, with juveniles particularly, are confidentiality and privacy paramount? What are the responsibilities of jurors, and how did trial by jury come to be? Why are so many juvenile trials held without juries?

Now, obviously, some of these questions bear directly on classroom teaching while others are addressed to the intellectual growth of the teachers for their own sakes and as it relates to their overall maturation as teachers.

The program of study could begin with teachers, principals, and librarians gathering a rich array of fairy tales, parables, and copybook headings for study and discussion. They might read Bruno Bettelheim's *The Uses of Enchantment,* John Silber's "The Gods of the Copybook Headings," assorted parables from the Bible and from oral and written folk traditions, *Mother Goose,* and McGuffey's *Readers* along with McGuffey's *Teachers' Guides,* especially those published in the late 1930s.

With this background, they might turn to Hugo's *Les Miserables,* Hawthorne's *The Scarlet Letter,* Melville's *Billy Budd,* Plato's *Apology* and *Crito,* Martin Luther King's "Letter from the Birmingham Jail," Gandhi's "Plea for the Severest Penalty on My Conviction for Sedition" and the judicial response, Freund's *On Law and Justice,* Bolt's *A Man for All Seasons,* the United States Constitution, essays by the Founders on education and a free press; and they might attend to the etymology of words like "law," "justice," "citizen," "privacy," and "mercy." Perhaps they would review the Supreme Court decision in Trop v. Dulles on citizenship as a status and an achievement, one of Earl Warren's most eloquent opinions. They could consult with a nearby law librarian or law firm to learn more about nonjury trials in juvenile cases, and this might lead them to a review, for example, Patrick Henry's opposition to trial by jury of peers.

Should the faculty of this school undertake anything resembling such a program, they would be on their way to becoming an intellectual community that could make the dedication and good intentions of teachers come to life with intelligence and excellent judgment. They and their students would be inestimably better for it.

The "Careers" Case

In the winter of 1981, a prestigious independent secondary school in Washington, D.C., held its annual "Career Day," meant as a chance for students to think about their futures, their aspirations, their desires, and their options. The students and faculty were eager to ponder life after high school, yet it was clear that no student had been prepared for these discussions, and no faculty member could articulate clearly the differences between a career and a succession of jobs, work and employment, vocation and job, leisure and free time, career success and extraneous emoluments, and a profession and a nonprofession. It was also evident that students had been encouraged to indulge in the false, and highly destructive, dichotomy between "the classroom" and the "real world."

Had the faculty done the right kind of homework and thought clearly about the words they were using and encouraging their students to use without any explicit understanding, they would not have been susceptible to the fashions of usage in such trivial and uninstructive settings as print and video advertisements. Yet those usages were about all they had.

An intellectual community could have done masterfully with the proper homework. It could have begun by learning the meanings of the words "career," "success," "work," "leisure," "school," "profession," "professional," "real," and "job;" then by reading Thomas Green's "Ironies and Paradoxes"[2] (and perhaps my own "Real Career Education Comes from the Liberal Arts").[3] They could have crystallized some of the distinctions. They might have gone on to ask whether Thoreau was right to insist that we reserve the word "real" to refer to things that matter, and, if so, whether we should think of classrooms as less than real. What would be gained by referring to "the classroom and the rest of the real world" and what would students learn from this formulation? It would be useful for them to proceed from there to Mill's 1867 Inaugural Address at

St. Andrews University, A. E. Housman's 1892 Introductory Lecture at University College of London, Dewey's "Self-Realization as the Moral Ideal," and John Hospers' *Ethics* on instrumentality, practicality, and utility.

Had they undertaken such a program of study and reflection, they could have discussed with care before ever entering Career Day such pertinent questions as: How is a career man or woman different from an employed man or woman? What does it mean to have a career? How is the success of a career to be determined? How is it different from job titles and salary? Is there any difference between the meaning of "leisure" and of "school?" Is there any point to a job that does not include leisure, properly understood? If so, what? What is a professional? Why are professionals permitted by law to keep confidential their communications with their clients, patients, students, and congregants?

If the intellectual community had approached Career Day thoughtfully, it would have begun to form the habit of sustained reflection on issues of importance in the school. The quality of discourse would have been transformed, and the intellects of faculty and students alike would come in time to be appropriately challenged.

The "Values" Case

In the 1970s, teachers and administrators in a public high school in Virginia decided that literature and history courses for juniors and seniors did not raise enough worthwhile questions about good and bad character in individuals, about the nature of trustworthy and unreliable institutions, or about the criteria and identifying marks of right and wrong actions.

These faculty members, guided by some of their more experienced colleagues, were well aware that their goals could not be achieved by the popular techniques of "values clarification" and the dilemma exercises of "cognitive moral development" theorists. That is, they knew that values clarification did not address such questions but instead treated everything as a matter of taste and thereby did nothing to enable students to understand either the questions or the intellectual means of addressing them. They knew as well that for dilemmas—hard choices between truly reasonable and powerful alternatives—to be intelligible, it is necessary to grasp concepts and methods basic to the humanities, especially in ethics.

They already employed good syllabi in their courses, assigned first-rate readings and exercises for their students, and reviewed homework assignments with care. The question was how to extend their own command of philosophy, literature, and history so that they could understand issues of importance to them and nourish the abilities of their students most thoroughly.

Instead of implementing some fashionable teaching strategy in their courses, they formed a voluntary group, including several exemplary teachers, assistant principals, and some less experienced but promising teachers. The school provided them released time over a period of two years, and they went to work. They studied alone, worked together at school and in their homes, and studied with several visiting teachers and scholars who could help them plan and build a program of reading, reflection, and conversation for themselves that could lead to classroom work with their students. Visitors were supported by a modest grant from the National Humanities Faculty, but often came without compensation, while the school absorbed the cost of the released time.

The group read and reread books and essays already assigned to their students, such as Ibsen's *Enemy of the People* and other plays, Madison's essays in *The Federalist,* and other documents in American history. They began to read a few Platonic dialogues to come to understand dialogue as the cooperative pursuit of the truth rather than as debatelike competition. They learned why Socrates says that individuals must have knowledge, candor, and goodwill to participate in dialogue, and came to a fuller understanding of the standards of consistency, relevance, probability, and implication used to determine the logical quality of argumentation. They learned how to make the best and most trustworthy uses of evidence.

Some studied formal and informal logic and then helped others to learn. All read and discussed seminal works in ethics and political theory. They read Kant's *Foundations of the Metaphysics of Morals* (not nearly so forbidding as it sounds) and Kurt Baier's *The Moral Point of View.* They learned what it means to think of persons as ends in themselves and not as mere means to be used by others in pursuit of their own self-interest. They studied numerous philosophic positions and learned the differences between assessing actions and appraising the motives of those who perform or commit them; between right, justified, wrong, and excusable actions; they learned to explain the cardinal virtues of wisdom, courage, temperance, and justice, and they read Aristotle on virtue as habit and mean between excesses. They learned how to ask and treat questions about good and evil, right and wrong, validity and invalidity, soundness and unsoundness. That is, they learned much more than they knew about applying reason to normative questions.

They applied what they were learning to the syllabi. They became an intellectual community influencing classrooms throughout the school. If they were suspicious in the beginning of the merely fashionable, they realized in time that the relativism of values clarification was stale and uncritical and that the theory of cognitive moral development was as old as Plato and much more carefully tested than textbooks and manuals reveal. They came to know as only practitioners of the arts of the mind can ever know.

Most of these teachers are today practitioners of the humanities and other disciplines, continuing to learn and to teach. What they did has been done in many places, all of them with local idiosyncrasies, disadvantages, and limitations. It can be done, it can happen anywhere, given the patience, the determination, the willingness to seek assistance from colleagues, and the readiness of administration to lead.

The faculty in this school took what was already very good, and they had the joy of making it even better.

A Far-Reaching Case

While there exists no sustained in-service program intended to compensate for weaknesses in an entire faculty and administration and to foster institutionally an intellectual community, it is worthwhile to envision possibilities.

Suppose the following, admittedly unlikely, circumstances and facts: A certain school system is committed to the idea that all of its faculty should be encouraged to grasp the arts of intellect. The board and administration recognize that salary incentives to do graduate work are not very effective because the graduate curricula in colleges of education generally reflect the same nonacademic biases as do the undergraduate curricula, and the salary increases normally take effect only if the graduate courses are strictly aligned with the teaching area of the teacher and so are narrow. The board and administration harbor a conviction that building an intellectual community might lead to the development of sounder methods of evaluating teaching. But budgetary limits prevent the system from offering released time to more than a fraction of the faculty at any given time, so that at best revolving opportunities could be provided for teachers, principals, and superintendents to participate in seminars and other in-service activities.

How might such a system begin to build an in-service program which would enable, over time, everyone who wished, to participate? A competent, determined administration might proceed along the following lines: first, ascertain how much money is already budgeted for faculty development, evaluations programs, incentive increases, and seniority, and assess the results of previous expenditures of these funds. Then identify some budgetary flexibility and investigate potential sources of external funding for faculty development. As a result, the administration can determine what might reasonably be committed to a genuine venture into in-service education. Once this is done, the administration might convene a small group of respected teachers to work with administrators on a plan for released time distribution and in-service schedule for the system. Additionally, this group of teachers could be authorized—and required— to prepare a curriculum for the program, including bibliographies and schedules of events to be given to all faculty and administration.

The committee could begin its work by reviewing the programs of study offered at the best liberal arts colleges in America and the best university programs in liberal studies. They could also query the universities and educational centers where the most reliable work is being done in pedagogy—whether in learning and teaching to write or to read, and so on. They should, at the same time, consult notable practitioners of the intellectual arts. They might, for example, review the work of the Bay Area Writing Project, the programs at St. John's College at the graduate and undergraduate levels, the curricula of the National Endowment for the Humanities Teacher Seminars, the Integrated Studies Programs at Kenyon College and Notre Dame University, the programs described regularly in the *Liberal Forum,* and such other programs as they could uncover with the aid of a good reference librarian. They would need as well to prepare a good bibliography on educational programs, including David Riesman and Gerald Grant, *The Perpetual Dream;* Robert Ulich, *Three Thousand Years of Educational Wisdom;* Frederick Rudolph, *Curriculum;* selected essays of Montaigne, Dewey, Montessori, Jefferson, and Mina Shaughnessy; Mortimer Adler, *The Paideia Proposal;* and Cremin, *The Genius of American Education.* They would surely want to consider as well the education of ancient and modern figures they admire.

Such work would provide the beginnings for a program of study that teachers and administrators could revolve into and out of, as they were awarded released time, and for a thorough program of readings that could be used by other teachers on their own time, seeking guidance in faculty meetings and regularly scheduled in-service days, and in faculty lounges where so much time is presently frittered away. Not everyone will participate, of course, and some will be skeptical. So be it. Intellectual communities have never depended on unanimity of support or universal participation. And many of the nonparticipants will burn out anyway, as they do now.

What, though, about the objections? All this work, with no guarantee of an immediate payoff? All this money for an experiment? All this admission that school personnel need to know more? Is there any realistic reply to these objections, and others like them?

Take a look at the discourse being generated in 1983 on a national level by the report of the National Commission on Excellence in Education. The report, *A Nation at Risk,* alleges mediocrity in American schooling. The weaknesses it stresses and the causes it identifies have been known to every competent educator and informed parent for at least fifteen years. Like other reports of its kind, it neglects the fact that public expectations for schools—that they replace education in the home, and so on—are preposterous. It rightly stresses the incoherence of most school curricula, including the soft electives that undermine academic study. But there is nothing new in it. Discourse arising from it shows some promise on the subjects of teacher testing, evaluation, and state and local initiatives. Beyond these, the discourse about merit pay is a rehearsal of the same issue as it arose twenty-five years ago, and the Master Teacher idea is new only to the public. Master Teachers won't make any difference unless their excellence can be woven into the fabric of a coherent in-service program where the cooperation and enthusiasm of others are granted. AFT's Albert Shanker argues (*New York Times,* June 19, 1983) that excellence can be achieved only by improving the applicant pool of teachers by raising the salary scale. This may increase the available talent, but it will do nothing to insure that the talent is better educated. Of course, if students in teacher training schools come to demand better programs of study, there may be some gain. But this does not address the problem of continuing rigorous learning while serving as a teacher or administrator. Here the discourse seems sterile and worn, the remedies patchy. In-service programs broadly conceived for the long run have potential that none of the other remedies seem to have shown.

The best response to the objections is to insist on telling the truth. Administrators must have the courage to face the public squarely and say that without parental instruction at home and without school investment in the intellectual maturation of teachers, improvement is likely to be slight, as it has been in the past. They must have the courage to insist that teachers and administrators uninterested in intellectual work for its sake as well as for teaching are unwelcome. The issue is centrally one of courage in defense of educational standards, standards of learning that the administrators must themselves live up to.

If much in education has been tried and found wanting, then rejecting substantive in-service programs without offering promising alternatives is mere flight, unconscionable flight for anyone willing to accept a portion of the responsibility for education of the young.

WHAT SHOULD TEACHERS TEACH AND HOW SHOULD THEY TEACH IT?

They should teach sound habits of mind and exemplify sound habits of character. They should teach them with intellectual humility, with expertise in the subject areas, with an awareness of suitable methods of instruction for children and youths, and with the insistence that every teacher and student is expected to do his best.

Relatively little of the life of a young person is spent in school, and so materials must be chosen that emphasize the fundamentals of the intellectual arts. No time is to be wasted on useless study halls, free periods, or pointless electives. A seventeen-year-old, after all, has been alive for 149,000 hours, awake for something between 80,000 and 100,000 of these. Perfect attendance in school for twelve years, 180 days per year at 6 hours per day, yields school time of 13,000 hours. This is less than 9 percent of the life, roughly 16 percent of the waking life. Add three hours homework per day, and still less than 25 percent of the waking life is spent on schooling. Spend any of this on shallow textbooks, wheel-spinning classes, or undemanding homework, and the percentage drops so low that failure is virtually assured. If students are to achieve the beginnings of mastery of languages, literature, geography, history, mathematics, natural sciences, and fine arts, and any sense of the useful arts at all, there is absolutely no time to waste—especially if extracurricular activities, physical education, and athletics are to be included in the life of the school. Waste time, and experience is reduced to the point of futility in learning to read, write, speak, listen, calculate, observe, measure, and think clearly and accurately. Every time a teacher asks what to teach and how to teach it, the answer should be designed to prevent such impairments.

One way to approach this is to think in terms of competence to form reasonable opinions. For example, it is commonplace in schools to have students ask and answer topical questions. Current fashion has students form opinions about applications of technology in modern society, say with respect to nuclear energy and human safety or industrial production and maintenance of the environment. Before putting such questions to students, teachers should ask: What does a person need to know about mathematics, science, economics, history, and the evolution of technology in order to think competently about such questions, and how much can be expected of students at this stage in their development? What should students know about reasoning and evidence in this instance so that their judgments will not be uninformed, arrogant, opinionated, and foolish? What do students need to know about means and ends and about tensions between good ends that may not be simultaneously realizable in full, in order to see something of the relevant considerations here? Then the teachers can decide what to teach so that their students will glimpse the competence of reasonable, informed, educated people.

Perhaps they will arrange for the means-end dichotomy to be taught in shop, or in home economics, or in a careful reading of Friar Laurence in *Romeo and Juliet,* or by all three. A look at the writings of James Bigelow, who invented the word "technology," might be useful with secondary students, with a survey of industrialization and computerization since his time. Mathematics and science suitable for the level of students would be a component, all to be brought into application when the topical question is asked. This kind of teaching activates minds. Rushing into topical questions only invites and encourages incompetent judgment.

Naturally, it is possible to be so unrelenting as a teacher that too much is demanded of students, or the wrong things expected at the wrong time. John Stuart Mill may have been the best-educated person of his time, but he was nearly destroyed by the education of his childhood and youth; Margaret Fuller may have been similarly harmed. Robert Browning's poem "Development" is, by contrast, a touching account of good and wise pacing of instruction for a youth and merits the attention of teachers.

Above all, in teaching, three things must be remembered and understood:

First, teaching requires a "tremble factor." In ancient Rome, architects and builders were required to stand under their arches when the supports were removed. If an arch failed, they were buried under their own incompetence. Classrooms are every bit as real as arches, and failures of conscientiousness, of effort, of work worthy of oneself, should be treated as such—real and unacceptable.

Second, the "tremble factor" must be joined with Tchekhov's understanding of cats and kittens. Bertrand Russell explains the point nicely:

> . . . We must . . . try to think out ways by which young people's desires and impulses can be utilized in education. This is far more possible than is often thought, for, after all, the desire to acquire knowledge is natural to most young people. The traditional pedagogue, possessing knowledge not worth imparting, and devoid of all skill in imparting it, imagined that young people have a native horror of instruction, but in this he was misled by failure to realize his own shortcomings. There is a charming tale of Tchekhov's about a man who tried to teach a kitten to catch mice. When it wouldn't run after them, he beat it, with the result that even as an adult cat, it cowered with terror in the presence of a mouse. "This is the man," Tchekhov adds, "who taught me Latin." Now cats teach their kittens to catch mice, but they wait till the instinct has awakened. Then the kittens agree with their mamas that the knowledge is worth acquiring. . . .[4]

Obviously, no student will desire to learn everything that he must. But this is no reason that he or she should be taught so as to wish not to learn anything that must be learned.

Third, and finally, all excellent teaching—all—is done by practitioners of the intellectual life who teach. For these practitioners alone truly love the subjects. The young are seldom deceived about this.

NOTES

1. Mortimer J. Adler, *The Paideia Proposal: An Educational Manifesto* (New York: Macmillan Publishing Co.; London: Collier Macmillan Publishers, 1982), p. 60.

2. In Dyckman Vermilye, *Relating Work and Education* (San Francisco: Jossey-Bass Publishers, 1977).

3. "Point of View," *Chronicle of Higher Education,* January 5, 1983.

4. Bertrand Russell, "Freedom versus Authority in Education," in *Sceptical Essays* (London: Unwin Paperbacks, 1977), p. 145.

Teacher Education and the Predicaments of Reform

Gary Sykes

A paradox lies at the heart of teacher education in America. For nearly half a century critics of all persuasions have scolded, even reviled, teacher education as a benighted and ill-starred enterprise, the very heel of our schooling system. Yet over this period teacher education has remained largely unchanged in important respects despite a variety of efforts at reform. True, the institution of teacher education has shifted from the normal school to the teachers college to the multipurpose university, and the general educational level of teachers has risen. In 1961, nearly 15 percent of the teacher work force still held less than a bachelor's degree, while less than a quarter had earned a master's degree. By 1981, nearly one-half of all teachers held a master's degree (or more) while the other half were at least college graduates.[1] This may be counted true progress (although it paralleled a general rise in U.S. educational attainment over these two decades), but the debate over teacher education has never slackened, nor has the sense of malaise, of something badly amiss, lifted appreciably.

WHAT TROUBLES TEACHER EDUCATION

Teacher education involves a smorgasbord of enduring, unresolved difficulties along which critics in each era pass, making selections to fit the mood and spirit of the times. The central conflict has always involved the proper balance and relationship among what nearly everyone regards as the four necessary (and sufficient) components of a program: a strong liberal arts education, solid grounding in at least one subject area (particularly for secondary teachers), an introduction to education as a subject of inquiry and to an emerging science of pedagogy, and the opportunity to practice and experience teaching in a real yet controlled setting. So much appears self-evident as hardly to require elaborate justification for either individual parts or their constituency into a coordinated program of study and experience. Yet no practical synthesis has resolved the dialectics of this professional quadrivium, while the politics of teacher education have remained a zero-sum game featuring imperialist forays from the contending faculties of arts and sciences and of education.

An ambiguity of competence[2] lies at the core of this territorial dispute. Teaching, like many undertakings, involves the employment of both special and ordinary knowledge, but stands apart in its reliance on the extraordinary use of ordinary knowledge. Teaching style appears to depend largely on personality and on tacit, idiosyncratic approaches to human relations. To many, teaching, like parenting, is a "natural," "spontaneous," "organic" human activity. Knowing subject matter and caring about children are the primary ingredients for success, around which some technical embellishments can marginally matter. Given this basic view, the notion of a "scientific basis of the art of teaching,"[3] or of "sources of a science of education"[4] seems dubious, a mystification of an essentially simple, universal activity.

By another view, however, teaching is an enormously complicated act whose full import has eluded the increasingly sophisticated methodological and conceptual tools of the social sciences. In the last decade, however, progress has been made and the rudiments of a paradigm have emerged, giving promise for the steady advance that characterizes the coming of age of a scientific field. The great hope—a scientifically validated knowledge base, an emergent science of pedagogy—seems less forlorn now, and the modest successes with applications suggest that stronger links between knowledge and practice are in the offing. But these steps are neither widely known nor credited, and the grounding of competence in science is a project still open to doubt and to counterclaims about the kinds of knowledge most useful to the aspiring teacher.

There is, too, in teacher education an unhappy legacy to live down.

Visitors to college campuses have too often come away with a low opinion of the actual quality of faculty, students, courses, and standards in
schools and departments of education. The paint has long since dried on
this portrait of mediocrity, of insipid if not anti-intellectual fare, of pseudo
scientific "methods courses" and a "professional" jargon which apes social science. (Koerner labeled it "educanto.") While the fraternity of
teacher educators and researchers doggedly issues analyses proclaiming
an imminent millennium if only the resources will be made available and
the purposes properly fixed, the fleet of disconcerting reports sailing from
the nation's campuses has belied such optimism. Conservatives, peren-
nialists, and devotees of the liberal arts have gleefully contributed to or
seized on this literature to support their position, but a close look at
reports on education usually uncovers an indictment of higher education
in general, with the faculties of arts and sciences coming in for their share
of blame and criticism. Yet teacher education's position at the bottom of
the academic pecking order is undisputed—a terrible handicap for those
whose project is to raise up this enterprise via the fruits of science.

Complicating the indignities of internecine strife is the tenuous relation of teacher education programs to the schools. One dilemma here is
common to professional education in all fields: to accept the conditions of
practice, warts and all, preparing novices to fit a sadly imperfect status
quo, or to take a critical stance toward current practice, imbuing the next
generation with the need for change, with the imperative to make, not
take, the role assigned. In teaching, though, there is evidence that suggests that socialization plays a far stronger role than formal training in
shaping a teaching style. Research on the subject parcels formative influences into four sets of factors:[5] the "apprenticeship of observation" that
teachers undergo during their fifteen thousand hours of experience as
students;[6] the bureaucratic aspects of schools and the ecology of the
classroom;[7] supervisors' and colleagues' impress on teachers;[8] and the
impact of students as unintended agents of socialization.[9] So, while the
stance to be taken toward the schools is a genuine vexation to teacher
educators, alternately provoking calls for closer collaboration or ringing
manifestos to raise consciousness and stimulate reform, teacher education appears such a "weak treatment" as to make moot the argument.

As a practical matter, however, schools of education must nurture
relations with the schools, which after all serve as the training ground for
beginners, provide a shadowy extension of the faculty in the form of
"cooperating teachers," and supply the chief clientele for postbaccalaureate course work and the consulting that supplements faculty in-
comes. This relationship remains uneasy at best, with little coincidence of
interests. Schoolmen complain about how out of touch university faculty

are, students typically find only their practice teaching helpful, and the professors who know how it should be done express dismay at the gap between their ideals and the realities of life in the classroom. Each point of view is valid; but the means for reconciliation or accommodation have not emerged. Hence, these laments persist generation after generation.

The shifting tasks and protean agenda of the schools make the relationship between the universities and the schools as unstable as it is uneasy. The remarkable growth of the school system has created serious strains, as educators have come to be expected to serve the full spectrum of the social structure. Likewise the transformation of the secondary school into a multipurpose social service agency has complicated the teacher's role and expanded the domain of responsibilities to this larger, more diverse clientele. Underlying these changes, however, has been a deeper conflict over the priority of excellence, equity, or efficiency in the schools' mission. As the emphasis among these central cultural values has shifted from one era to the next, so too have the terms of criticism of the schools.

Teacher education is vulnerable in its own right to fluid social imperatives. While the training institutions must now prepare teachers for "the real world" of inner-city schools, for multicultural education, for educating the handicapped, for distinguishing the subtle bases for sex and race inequities in their own and others' behavior, for the computer revolution, and so on, they must also act affirmatively in hiring and admissions while maintaining high standards and producing a teaching elite capable of training the advanced manpower for mastery in world technology markets. Neither schools nor universities can serve up such a volatile brew. After a while, both institutions may be permitted a modest dispensation for hunkering down and resisting change.

The status, wages, and other valuables associated with teaching constitute a final difficulty for teacher education. Teaching has always suffered an equivocal status compounded of respect and disdain, reverence and mockery, as amply depicted in the writings of Hofstadter, Elsbree, Waller, Lortie, and others. Moreover, some evidence suggests that teaching's occupational status actually declined between 1963 and 1980; according to one survey, teaching lost more ground than any other occupation ranked.[10] One telling indication of this trend comes from a Gallup Poll item. When asked "Would you like to have a child of yours take up teaching in the public schools as a career?" 75 percent of those surveyed responded yes in 1969, 67 percent in 1972, and only 48 percent in 1980.[11] To enhance the status and prospects of teacher education independently of the teaching occupation seems unlikely. Similarly, proposals to extend professional education for teachers run up against objections that few students would be willing to undergo a genuine training ordeal such as medicine requires or bear the costs of further schooling for the meager annual salaries and lifetime earnings teaching supplies.

That teaching is the closest thing to a mass profession may alone preclude a more elite status. Until the last decade, teaching regularly consumed 20 percent of the college labor market (35 percent of the market for college-educated women),[12] and training institutions were hard-pressed simply to supply the requisite numbers, regardless of quality. Indeed, easy access to teaching has historically served as both a potent recruitment incentive for individuals and a guarantee that supply would not lag too far behind demand in a tight labor market. The route to sovereignty in the true professions of law and medicine—restricted access under the protective mantle of a meritocratic ideology—was never available to an occupation whose single, overriding imperative was growth.

TWENTY YEARS' WORTH OF REFORM IN TEACHER EDUCATION

The oft called-for transformation of teacher education has failed through no lack of effort. Nearly everyone, it seems, has tried to reform teacher education; and our history is filled with task force and commission reports, with studies and recommendations, with association resolutions, government programs, foundation initiatives, legislation, and the rest. Teacher education has been the target for improvement both as an end in itself and as a means to effect other sorts of change in the schools and in the society at large. No assessment about what ails teacher education has yielded a consensus on what should be done, though, and the profession has proven vulnerable to a variety of enthusiasms, most of which have left little trace in their passing. A brief look at four reforms—The Master of Arts in Teaching, the Teacher Corps, Competency Based Teacher Education, and recent state regulatory efforts—will serve to illustrate the trends over the past two decades.

Recruiting an Elite: The Master of Arts in Teaching
Beginning in the early 1950s and extending well into the 1960s, the Ford Foundation sponsored a bold new approach to teacher education. Over a fifteen-year period Ford committed some seventy million dollars in awards to over seventy universities to underwrite the establishment of a new teacher training program, the Master of Arts in Teaching (MAT). More specifically, Ford supported three types of programs: under-graduate training in a handful of liberal arts colleges, a five-year or fifth-year program, and the MAT. Most awards went to MAT programs to train secondary school teachers. These were alternatives, not sequels, to regu-

lar teacher education programs. They aimed at graduates of liberal arts programs and typically involved a summer school orientation on campus, then either a full- or half-time internship in a local school, supplemented by seminars and additional course work and perhaps a summer of course work after the internship. These postbaccalaureate programs resulted in a master's degree and a teaching certificate; the five-year programs yielded only the certificate but were integrated with the undergraduate course of study.

The significance of these programs lay not so much in their innovative approach to the education of teachers (although the programs accommodated a variety of experiments) as in their impact on recruitment. Ford's strategy was to enlist the elites among American universities to train a new cadre of teachers. Ford hoped that academically rigorous, selective programs at the nation's best universities would set a new standard for teacher education and would lure the best and brightest among college graduates. At the institutional level the elite universities would influence their less prestigious brethren via higher education's "snakelike progression" (David Riesman's phrase), the status hierarchy impelling lesser institutions to follow the leaders. At the individual level, programs offered both an inducement and the removal of a disincentive: to study with the finest faculty and peers at the finest universities, and to avoid the dreariness of education courses. The grant strategy, then, called for bypassing the existing system in favor of an elite alternative, and implicitly viewed the status quo as part of the problem.

Additionally, these programs aimed to strengthen the ties of teacher training to the schools and to the liberal arts. The internship provided an extended yet controlled opportunity to work in classrooms under apprenticeship conditions—a genuine improvement over the usual, meager practice teaching experience. And, most proposals promised a renewed commitment to a liberal education through involvement of Arts and Sciences faculty in planning and implementing the program. Beneath the diversity in individual programs lurked the fundamental assumption James Bryant Conant made in his study of teacher education: that a strong liberal arts education, an extended, well-supervised practicum, and a modest dose of course work in education constitute the ideal.

Essentially a recruitment strategy, the MAT suffered some obvious limits as a paradigm of reform. First, the allure of the program consisted not in some technical breakthough that the elites could model for others, but in the cachet associated with the places themselves. The glamor of Harvard's simply being Harvard was not available in Pomona, Pierre, or Des Moines. Furthermore, the strategy relied on counteridentification with the status quo. Ford was consciously elitist in culling universities east of the Mississipi and north of the Mason-Dixon line that represented a liberal arts tradition very different from that of the mainline teacher training institutions. The aim, in part, was to enrich the pool of liberal arts graduates willing to teach by skirting the standard course of teacher education. The immediate appeal of such a strategy to education school deans and professors was not readily apparent.

The MAT failed to spread much beyond those few institutions that received Ford funds. Evidence on numbers completing MAT programs is fragmentary, but one study reported that in the three-year period 1961–1962 through 1963–1964, 4,114, students graduated, as compared with an annual production figure in those years of some 200,000 new teachers.[13] MAT programs, then, accounted for less than 1 percent of the nation's new teachers.

That only a handful of MAT programs are left testifies to their tenuous hold in the elite universities. Declining student enrollments and the teacher surplus of the 1970s hastened their demise. But even though the MAT programs were lively and exciting while they lasted, and anecdotal evidence suggests they were successful in attracting bright liberal arts graduates to teaching,[14] the handwriting was on the wall from the beginning. Teacher training had little enduring appeal for either liberal arts professors or faculty in graduate schools of education who wished to get on with training administrators and researchers. The mission of training teachers never gained much legitimacy, never secured core support, never engaged the faculty in the crucial roles of supervising interns, spending time in the schools, or conducting the companion seminars and courses. Teaching's low status ultimately confounded the attempt to enlist higher education's elite, who returned gratefully to traditional pursuits after this brief flirtation with teacher training.

Welcoming the Great Society: The Teacher Corps

Prior to the 1960s, the federal government was little involved with teacher education, but in the late 1950s it began what amounted to a sizable investment in the 1960s and 1970s. National defense provided the rationale.[15]

Initial government ventures aimed chiefly at improving teachers' subject matter competence via in-service activities. The programs operated through the existing institutional structure and eschewed fundamental reform. But as the conservative tenor of the 1950s gave way to the social activism of the 1960s, the federal government sponsored a range of more far-reaching programs, often in conjunction with the decade's major equity mandates. The government initiated or intensified training expenditures in vocational, compensatory, and higher education, in special education, and in bilingual education. Much of the funding went to teachers' in-service; but a number of programs were aimed at preservice training as well. In 1967, Congress passed the first piece of comprehensive legislation aimed at the development of educators, the Education Professions Development Act (EPDA). The act consolidated several existing programs (e.g., Teacher Corps) and spawned twenty-five programs of its own. In its nine-year life (1967 to 1976), these programs accounted for expenditures of $781 million on a wide range of innovative projects.[16]

Over these decades Washington controlled the agenda for reform and set a brisk pace. Directly or indirectly the federal government provided the funds and mandates, the strategies, the leadership, and the influence networks through which flowed a powerful current of reform and innovation. By 1981 forty-three federal programs expended nearly $6 billion on personnel development with nine formula grant programs accounting for 90 percent of this total.[17] (The Reagan administration, however, has eliminated or consolidated and reduced the budget of many of these programs.) No other development in this period so profoundly influenced teacher education as this centralization of reform. The Teacher Corps represents a small but significant piece of this history, and is worth examining both in its own right and for its lessons about federal programmatic reform.

Created in 1964, the Teacher Corps was touted initially as a domestic Peace Corps. In its early years the project supported a two-year internship for liberal arts graduates who wished to serve in low-income schools. The original purposes included strengthening the education of disadvantaged children, attracting and preparing persons to teach such children through coordinated work-study experiences, and encouraging colleges and universities, schools, and state departments of education to work together in improving teacher education. The program's rationale stressed that there are critical differences between the skills, attitudes, and experiences required to teach successfully in low-income schools and in middle-class schools. The corps sought to recruit idealistic young people and to provide them with mediated entry to teaching in schools where they were most needed. The typical program involved from thirty to forty liberal arts graduates (interns) and five experienced teachers who acted as team leaders. Following a summer preservice training program at a college or university, each team was assigned to a school serving a poverty area. Interns spent some 60 percent of their weekly time in schools, 20 percent in academic work at the university, and 20 percent in community activities. This two-year course resulted in certification and a master's degree.

Due to its entrepreneurial leadership, the Teacher Corps enjoyed a chameleonlike existence over its sixteen-year history. Program guidelines emphasized a series of vanguard themes, including, "performance based teacher education, training complexes, portal schools, research adaptation, education of the handicapped, multicultural education, youth advocacy, basic skills, organization theory, and models of teaching."[18] When the teacher shortage of the 1960s turned into a teacher surplus in the 1970s, the program secured congressional authority in its 1974 reauthorization to work with in-service teachers, and in 1978 extended the time span of local projects from two to five years. Initiated as a service program, the focus shifted after 1975 to a demonstration strategy for training and retraining experienced teachers and teacher aides.[19]

The Teacher Corps had undergone seven major evaluations over the years, and its effectiveness as a reform strategy is unusually well documented.[20] During its ten years as a service program, the Teacher Corps, like the MAT programs, proved an effective recruitment strategy. Evidence from several projects in the early program cycles suggests that the corps successfully attracted bright, change-oriented college graduates. With backgrounds in the liberal arts, the early interns displayed academic aptitudes above those of graduate students in education (but still below the median of all graduate students).[21] Initially, the Corps attracted white, upper middle-class youth, but determined efforts to recruit minorities increased their representation in later cycles. Imbued with the spirit of the times, the new recruits were more change-oriented, politically liberal, independent, and aggressive than their veteran counterparts. However, those drawn to teaching exlusively by the Teacher Corps program were also most likely to drop out. While a majority of interns went into teaching upon graduation, most did not anticipate a career in the classroom but intended to take on other roles in education.[22] So it appears the Corps attracted a new breed of teachers but could not hold them long in the classroom.

Teacher Corps was less successful in altering institutional patterns within the schools, colleges, or universities. The program's early rhetoric urged the intern teams to serve as change agents within the schools, but the sources of resentment and resistance proved too strong. Veteran teachers regarded interns merely as apprentices useful in assisting with normal duties. Filled with the program's reform rhetoric, the interns sought greater influence and often threatened the regular teachers with their radical ideas. The intern status could not easily accommodate the dual roles of change agent and apprentice. Interns possessed neither the technical knowledge nor the formal position to support their posture, so the schools shrugged them off. Some interns became radical and alienated in the process, while others were co-opted.

Colleges and universities, too, made few concessions to the program and resisted a more enduring involvement with the schools. Teacher Corps projects stimulated the addition of some new courses and raised consciousness about the special problems of teaching in low-income schools but failed to promote closer ties with higher education. The interns were more critical of the universities than any other aspect of the program. They found their courses irrelevant and judged that their professors knew little about teaching the disadvantaged and were less academically qualified than their undergraduate professors. The faculty acutely felt their inadequacies in educating the interns but themselves had no contact with the schools, no relevant, special knowledge to impart, and no solid commitment to the projects.

Teacher Corps projects also had difficulty overcoming the social isolation between schools and universities and could not supply the incentives for true collaboration. Vested interests within the higher education community resisted new missions, new priorities, or any reallocation of resources. When changes occurred, they tended to be superficial add-ons. Boundary-spanning personnel—the project director, team leaders, or unusually dedicated university faculty—sometimes created effective partnerships, but, "the hoped-for 'hybrid' professional, trained in the social sciences but concerned with the application of knowledge to educational practice, seldom appeared."[23] In short,

> The institutions operated under different incompatible incentive systems and had independent publics and resources. The schoolteachers were precariously trying to maintain daily teaching schedules with inadequate resources, often in the face of challenges from both students and the community. They were not primarily responsible for training and resisted being used as laboratories unless they had been provided with assistance or other benefits. University professors were oriented to an academic status system and were insulated from the operational pressures of school teaching and from the unruly or dull classrooms. Therefore, they could not provide the practical guidance and necessary leadership that interns needed. The interns were trapped between the university, which controlled their professional certification and the schools, which controlled their professional *experiences*.[24]

Ambitious in scope, complex in conception and execution, the Teacher Corps took on a number of long-standing problems plaguing both teaching and teacher education: the difficulty of recruiting talented college graduates to teach in low-income schools, the lack of attention to pedagogy suited to disadvantaged and minority students, the remoteness of colleges and universities purporting to train teachers from the schools, the strong resistance to change in the public schools themselves. Like other helping professions in the 1960s, teaching proved vulnerable to government intervention on behalf of society's neglected and oppressed. The profession could not resist these external pressures; but in a decentralized system and without a consensus, federal authority was not strong enough to affect institutional patterns and reward systems. Working within the existing system, subject to the constraints of special interest politics and of organizational inertia within the schools, the program had but modest long-term impact.

Quest for Certainty: Competency Based Teacher Education

In the late 1960s a number of themes in our political culture converged in a reform known as Competency Based Teacher Education (CBTE). The movement toward this reform drew support from the U.S. Office of Education, from several state departments of education, from the American Association of Colleges for Teacher Education (AACTE), from a handful of vanguard universities eager to innovate, and from a group of educational researchers. These groups stimulated intense interest in CBTE for a time, but the reform failed to attract widespread support and faded away in the face of retrenchment pressures in the 1970s. CBTE, however, represents a persistent strain in American education: a powerful yearning for method, for system, for certainty. Moreover, the fact of this reform illustrates education's difficulty with establishing a knowledge base. It is, then, worthy of attention beyond its impact.

Competency Based Teacher Education was an attempt to gain technical control over the preparation of teachers, to ground a professional curriculum in science, and to establish its measure for purposes of public accountability. The method, behaviorist in spirit, had the straightforward appeal of an engineering feat. Steps in the process called for, first, the decomposition of teaching into a set of discrete competencies, empirically validated through their connection to learning outcomes; then development of a training program within which students would learn the appropriate behaviors, via practice and coaching; close evaluation of students to determine their mastery of the competencies, with additional training prescribed for those who required it; and finally, certification based on mastery of the mandated competencies.

Proponents of this approach did not claim that teaching is simply a finite bundle of skills, nor did they deny that teaching is an artistic activity involving improvisation. Rather they argued that effective teachers exhibit skills that can be precisely identified and transmitted. The business of an initial training program is to provide such skills to novices as the foundation for development of a mature teaching style. This rationale at once supplied an implicit critique of current practice, a powerful appeal based on culturally authoritative symbols, and an orderly agenda for progress.

Status-quo training programs suffered, according to competency advocates, from two major shortcomings: a failure to base the professional curriculum on empirically validated knowledge, and a lack of precision and specificity in setting forth the skills of teaching to be mastered. Teacher education was at once too abstract, too impractical, and too trivial. Coursework failed to connect theory to practice, while methods courses deserved their ill repute as whimsical collections of gimmicks. A competency-based approach would remedy these defects through introduction of scientific rigor. Teaching would be systematically analyzed, and its core elements extracted, then validated through research. The result would be a training program organized around a set of competencies enjoying science's imprimatur.

CBTE as a rallying point had a number of obvious appeals, the primary one being that it promised to establish the intellectual legitimacy of teacher education through a grounding in science. In an era marked by increasing accountability demands on public service providers, CBTE offered the means and a commitment from educators for such an accounting. A fully developed program would utilize social science's most powerful and sophisticated technology—testing—to monitor progress, to diagnose difficulties, and to certify graduates. Professional educators would have the tools to gauge student progress, to prescribe extra and remedial work, and to identify those who lacked all aptitude and should therefore be counseled out of teaching. Rigor, precision, and control: these were the virtues around which to reconstitute a course of training.

CBTE possessed a further virtue as well. The design of teacher education around a set of competencies was a development largely internal to schools and departments of education, strengthening their claim to professional standing within the university. CBTE was a technical reform involving an orderly agenda of research and development. If the movement's leadership could establish the paradigm's power and gain a consensus within the educational community on its general outline, then widespread, concerted efforts could go forward and "normal science" (in Thomas Kuhn's sense)[25] could take shape. Furthermore, a technical breakthrough would strengthen the hand of educators seeking to secure greater resources for pedagogical education. CBTE's proponents recognized that at the time there was no set of empirically validated, generic teaching competencies, but hoped that a sustained, united commitment to the approach from the profession would gradually yield such knowledge.

Creating competency programs required a substantial initial investment of faculty time and cooperation, but in the late 1960s several universities undertook such efforts, stimulated by modest funds from foundations and the U.S. Office of Education (which expended some $12 million, mostly for conferences, dissemination, model building, and the like). Some schools, including Weber State College, the University of Houston, Toledo University, and Florida International, recast their entire programs; others, notably Brigham Young University, the University of Texas-El Paso, and Western Washington State University, established alternative programs. There was never a careful account of how many institutions participated, but a 1972 AACTE survey of 783 institutions turned up 125 that claimed to have such programs, with 366 others in the developmental stage.[26] (What "developmental stage" meant, though, was not clear.) Another AACTE publication provides details on seventeen programs located in thirteen institutions, with the range of effort from modest experiments to total conversion.[27] The slender record suggests that the reform stirred up enormous interest, spawned a large volume of talk and publication, but had near negligible impact in the universities themselves.

Competency education's difficulties are instructive both for the technical problems that proved insurmountable and for the opposition that the reform provoked. The yearning for a knowledge base could not compensate for its absence. In the face of multiple conceptions of teaching, multiple interpretations of classroom realities, and multiple educational aims, the hoped-for consensus on a unifying paradigm never emerged. Without the discipline of relatively unambiguous, fixed ends, the technical project of securing the means-ends relationship could not advance. And the attempt to validate teaching competencies through their association with student outcomes soon provoked challenges on empirical grounds:[28] the evidence was impeachable and the research community divided on its worth.

Furthermore, the notion of a teaching competency itself proved more troublesome than helpful. There was no agreement on whether a competency was big or small, referred to "knowing how" as well as "knowing that," or was subject-specific or generic. The effort to provide behavioral specificity yielded nearly a thousand competencies by one reckoning.[29] To avoid the traditionally loose, abstract, and behaviorally unanchored accounts of teaching, competency logic drove to a ludicrously atomized conception which in the same manner failed to provide guidance to teacher training. Just as overwhelming was the task of assessment. Reform rhetoric promised both accountability and individualization via a measurement and tracking system to chart each student's progress toward mastery of hundreds of competencies. But the measures were fallible to nonexistent, and the management burdens enormous. In short, the behaviorist approach, so appealing in its promise of rigor, system, and method, could not carry the intended freight.

As the CBTE vanguard grappled with these problems, opposition also took form. Humanists quickly became suspicious of competency education on a number of counts. Harry Broudy, for example, worried that the approach reduced teaching to the imparting of information and thus sacrificed its other modes and dimensions.[30] He argued that teaching involves more than skillful behavior, that teachers must develop understanding of their actions as educators and must be able to consider ends as

well as employ skills. If teachers were to be more than craftsmen following set routines, asserted Broudy, then their education must include
theory and must aim at creating a capacity for reflection and flexible
action. Yet he saw little appreciation for this in the competency approach.
In his view, CBTE actually threatened to deprofessionalize teaching by
turning out proficient technicians, not full professionals.

Yet another critic feared a bias against intellect, against what was
"merely academic." He first asked, "Does competence based education
reduce the teacher to a coach merely drilling people to pass exams? Does
the competence approach kill all true education or deeper thinking?"[31] Not
necessarily, he thought. A more moderate rhetorical question expresses
his view: "Does competence based education lead students and teachers
to be predominantly pragmatic? Not simple-minded or trivial or blindly
mechanical, mind you, but does it lead to a slight narrowing in the range
of human styles, away from creativity, intuition, play, humor, and purely
disinterested curiosity? Is the spirit of competence, in short, the spirit of
instrumentalism?"[32] Thus did humanists come to characterize competency
education as at worst illiberal, anti-intellectual, and technicist, and at best
merely an admonition to teacher educators to think harder about what
they were doing.

CBTE was a bootstrap operation by declassé teacher training institutions to gain credibility and prestige in an era of accountability, a technical reform internal to the school of education, whose rhetoric drew upon
powerful cultural themes. Its proponents hoped this sort of inexpensive,
nonthreatening innovation would support their argument for a truly professional school and for more "life space" in the university. However, the
requisite technical knowledge never appeared at the party thrown in its
honor, and program conversion along competency lines proved more expensive than anticipated. One calculation, likely an underestimate, placed
the cost at $5–6 million per institution, with a total system cost over
twenty years of $100 million.[33] During CBTE's brief period of fashionabil-
ity, most institutions found it cheaper to adopt little but the rhetoric.

Faced with philosophical and political opposition and fraught with
technical difficulties, this reform's liabilities outweighed its benefits in the
eyes of most teacher educators. Championed by lesser institutions, CBTE
failed to enlist opinion leaders in higher education's pantheon. It was, in
short, a very shallow ripple on a large pond, one that illustrated the
difficulties in establishing a knowledge base for teaching and the danger in
premature sponsorship of an ill-conceived technical reform.

Crisis of Confidence: State Regulation of Teaching

As foundations, universities, and the federal government have all attempted to recast teacher education in various images, so too have state

policymakers intermittently taken an interest. Their tools, however, have been regulations rather than programs, funds, or new knowledge, and the history of state regulation reflects teacher education's uneasy regard among the public. State certification and licensing laws have the dual potential to protect the public interest via standard setting and to enhance professional status by restricting entry and requiring special courses of study. The legitimacy of such laws rests on the public's perception of an equivalence between these functions, but the relationship is weak. Without scientific breakthroughs or potent technologies, teacher education must rely to a considerable degree on trust that its mission is valuable and useful. Perceptions that the schools, hence the teachers, are failing threaten this trust and impel state regulation as protection *from,* not protection *of,* professional autonomy.

Over the decades, the states have tirelessly tinkered with the certification law. Early on, many states and localities used literacy tests to screen candidates. In the 1830s, for example, Illinois state legislator Abraham Lincoln voted in favor of a teacher exam,[34] which became common by the century's turn. But as schooling levels rose and normal schools sprang up, states began to require years of schooling, then courses in education for certification. By 1940 the course requirements approach had largely superseded examinations, with additive reform—more years of schooling, more required courses in education—the progression thereafter.[35] Twenty years later, however, Conant reflected much public opinion in labeling such policy bankrupt. The low repute of education courses made their mandate through state policy an embarrassment. States, it appeared, were conspiring with the "education establishment" to require a fraudulent set of courses that had failed to demonstrate their worth.

This mounting criticism posed a crisis of legitimacy for teacher educators. Their clients (the students) expressed great dissatisfaction, Arts and Sciences faculties decried the wasteland of teacher education, and policymakers were becoming uneasy. However, two events forestalled action. First, the teacher shortages of the 1950s and 1960s turned to a surplus. Enrollments declined in teacher education, and few new teachers entered the schools. Concern consequently shifted from preservice education to renewal of an aging work force already in place. And, second, the 1960s' preoccupation with equity and civil rights intervened to shift the ground of criticism and the agenda for public policy. Relevance and rights, not rigor, became the watchwords, and the critiques of Conant, Koerner, and Silberman[36] for the moment lost their salience. The locus of reform shifted, as well, from the state to the federal level and over the next decade state policy took shape largely in response to the cascade of federal initiatives.

Enrollment declines and the social ferment of the 1960s and 1970s merely deferred the fundamental dissatisfaction with the quality of teacher education expressed earlier. By the mid-1970s, public worry over the test score drop, over reports of lax discipline in the schools, and over a general decline in standards was paramount. The academic adequacy of teachers became an issue as the press reported cases of teachers who wrote and spoke ungrammatically and who could not spell. The suspicion also took hold that some training institutions, faced with enrollment declines, had lowered entry standards to maintain their share of students. The demand for quality control led to the reintroduction of testing in state after state, so that at present thirty-six states have mandated some form of test for entry to a teacher education program and/or for certification.[37]

Some jurisdictions have extended their concern for teacher quality further still. Georgia sends observers into beginning teachers' classrooms to rate their performance on fourteen teaching competencies. South Carolina has required increased practice teaching, more observation and evaluation of teachers, and additional credits for recertification. Oklahoma's new Bill 1706 similarly mandates more clinical fieldwork and an entry-year internship during which a committee composed of a principal, a consulting teacher, and a teacher educator regularly monitors the first-year teacher and recommends either certification or further supervision at year's end.

The states have emerged as standard bearer for teacher education. While the older "approved-program approach" to certification—i.e., graduates of approved programs were certified simply because they *were* graduates of approved programs—implicitly reposed confidence in the training institutions, this new body of law regulates teaching in the name of public protection. Through tests, the states have extended their influence indirectly to the curriculum of teacher education, as training institutions must now ensure that their graduates can pass the tests. States are no longer willing to trust the profession to set standards. They have intervened firmly and in the name of accountability. To some extent, teacher education's interests have benefited from the new legislation which they have helped shape, but in many respects state regulatory action reflects the lack of public confidence in teaching and the loss of esteem for teachers. By emphasizing basic skills and general rather than professional knowledge, the tests themselves are demeaning and seem to imply that any reasonably bright college graduate can teach.

For years teacher organizations have pressed a professional governance model on state policymakers, and a half dozen states currently support professionl practice boards with teacher membership. But vesting regulation of the teaching occupation in its practitioners enjoys no widespread support, and the unions' use of professional rhetoric and strategy is not credible anywhere. Unions exist to protect the rights of their members; but the rationale for professional control, especially among public employees, rests not on an assertion of rights but on claims of technical expertise and of the public interest.

The states, though, can do little else through a regulatory approach than set minimums and thereby symbolize a concern for standards. Though the most academically deficient will be denied access to teaching, at the program level little is likely to change. These recent state responses fail to address one of the fundamental dilemmas facing teacher education: that without additional resources, it cannot demonstrate its worth; yet without such a demonstration, it cannot secure additional resources. This dilemma ultimately frames teacher education's relation to the state and makes vivid the crisis of confidence.

PROSPECTS FOR AN ENLIGHTENED FUTURE

These various efforts over the years to reform teacher education achieved some limited and temporary success, but could not effect a thoroughgoing transformation. The enterprise as a whole seems fixed by a range of institutional, demographic, and economic forces at an unacceptably low level of quality, incapable of setting and enforcing—or even of articulating and projecting—high standards. Invidious distinctions of status among the institutions of higher education, among departments and schools within the university, and between the universities and the schools frustrate the search for a common cause. Despite decades of earnest labor and some progress, no research paradigm has emerged to order the pursuit of knowledge and no cognitive base organizes, unifies, and legitimates the professional curriculum. Inevitably the mission is shortchanged. Teacher education is underfunded and lacks institutional "life space." It is a small, old outboard propelling a very large cabin cruiser through the water at an unsurprisingly slow rate.

Several recent developments have complicated these woes. Unionism has replaced professionalism as a strategy for advancement among teachers. An overlay on existing status tensions, unionism has further estranged teachers from teacher educators in terms of their organizational interests and public posture, rendering even more suspect the rhetoric of professionalism. And, as enrollments in teacher education dropped 50 percent between 1972 and 1980, thereby threatening the survival of many programs, coping with decline superseded programmatic reform. Retrenchment proved inhospitable to the quest for excellence. Simultaneously the states intensified their regulation of teacher education, exposing its vulnerability to external control. This policy development revealed teacher education's inherent weakness in relation to the state:

the public confidence required for control over teaching to be vested in teacher education institutions has been based more on inattention than approval.

Most friendly critics appreciate that reforms of teacher education stand little chance unless linked to changes in the schools, in the teaching occupation, and in the policy framework shaping the whole enterprise. They emphasize that teacher salaries must be higher, that working conditions must better support teachers,[38] that teaching must attract and hold more academically able recruits, and that state policy—particularly allocation formulas to the universities—must supply more resources.[39]

If the past is prologue in teacher education, then widespread, comprehensive reform is unlikely. The prospect of converting teacher education to a postbaccalaureate program (whether integrated with the undergraduate curriculum or not) appears slim. To require an extended program of training for all new teachers without a corresponding increase in the rewards of teaching is not feasible: market pressure will continue to dominate standards. Likewise, no major reallocation or infusion of resources to teacher education is likely. The training venture has not gained sufficient warrant for this, in part because its rationale is derivative: teacher education exists to improve teaching. With ever-present arguments that both teaching and teacher education are underfunded, and without an impressive demonstration of the latter's potency, policymakers will most often direct funds to teaching itself. Finally, social science knowledge is unlikely to rationalize a technical transformation of the professional curriculum. No paradigm orders inquiry in education, no "sciences of the artificial" nor eclectic arts conjoin basic knowledge and design;[40] rather, the technical base grows fitfully and in small increments.

Short of ambitious reforms, though, teacher education has several modest prospects. Both the MAT strategy and the Teacher Corps demonstrated that special programs can enhance status, supply an esprit otherwise lacking, and recruit able college graduates despite teaching's low pay. For a limited number of prospective teachers a selective postbaccalaureate program highly regarded by the university and by the community will be attractive. The MAT approach never received much trial in the mainline institutions, yet might well serve as an alternative on more campuses.

Efforts to extend training into the first year of teaching point to another promising trend. State-mandated induction or intern programs such as Oklahoma's join the university and the schools in providing more support, supervision, and evaluation for first-year teachers, a step intermediate to and less costly than a full extended program. Intern programs have several virtues: they are job-related, do not defer income for young teachers, can involve experienced teachers in passing along their lore, and provide a performance base for certification. The Teacher Corps experience underscored the importance of boundary spanners between universities and schools, and the new state mandates may help provide a framework within which such positions will develop. They appear crucial to effective collaboration.

Finally, the gradual accumulation of usable pedagogical knowledge provides a more spacious avenue for technical improvements in the professional curriculum. For some time advocates have faulted the training programs for failing to stay abreast and failing to use the best available knowledge, arguing that the translation and use of knowledge, not its quality or quantity, are the fundamental problems. Progress in the coming decades, then, will take the form of better knowledge use in the training program, and stronger connections between research and training.

The Neglected Dimension

Interpreted in broad outline, teacher education appears trapped in a force-field admitting only small movements in any direction. Yet other histories and intepretations are available. This broad interpretation of teacher education's status omits consideration of the individual institutions where stories of success and failure, triumph and tragedy, progress and stasis have played out over the decades. A bit of determinism often accompanies history as global sweep, denying the choices and maneuvering room actually open to individuals. But let us step down from the slow movements of history and the grand stategies of reformers to the prospects for renewal and excellence in particular institutions and glimpse other possibilities.

Worry o•er what is lacking in teacher education often centers on such things as funds, status, standards, life space, and knowledge, with corresponding attention to these resources in reform proposals. Yet this emphasis on the instrumental neglects an important dimension in the lives of individuals and institutions. What is most fundamentally missing in teacher education is both a conception and conviction of its value. The enterprise of preparing teachers in our society is not esteemed, and the consequences of this lack of esteem are devastating. Without sufficient caring we have no appreciative framework for teacher education, no shared conception of quality, no capacity to recognize or vocabulary to describe excellence, nor occasions to celebrate it. The process of educating teachers is essentially invisible, a sure sign of its undervaluation in our culture.

The outward manifestations of this problem should now be clear, but there is a toll on the inner life as well. Every professional practice requires a discourse continuously enriched through reference to transcendent ideals. Central to human services is a sense of mission powerful enough to inspire and sustain, to give meaning and significance to the work. Without occasions for pride and a sense of connection to important values, the vicissitudes of human service work can be great. As any teacher will acknowledge, working with others has both a light and dark side, an inevitable feature in the pursuit of ideals that at once compel but admit no easy realization. Teaching can provide joy and fulfillment, but can be frustrating and enervating, too. Visions of excellence nourish the light side, enabling buoyancy and resilience. Their absence leads to low morale, failure of nerve, loss of expectations.

Missing from the rhetoric of reform in teacher education is much attention to this expressive side, to the inner life of the enterprise. Consider, by contrast, the emphasis in some recent writing on management that hails the creation of corporate cultures as a hallmark of excellence.[41] In these accounts of successful businesses and business leaders, it is not technological breakthroughs or rational management schemes that matter, but attention to the human side of enterprise. The corporate exemplars stand for and communicate a set of values through rites and rituals, organizational sagas, and proud traditions filled with heroes and champions. The new language used to describe corporate life is remarkably primitive, smacking more of Margaret Mead on Samoa than of Harold Geneen at ITT. It is an anthropological language redolent of mythology and symbolism, a language appropriate to the centrality of values.

"Companies succeed," claims one observer, "because their employees can identify, embrace, and act on the values of the organization."[42] So, too, do programs of teacher education, yet preoccupations there are unrelievedly literal, instrumental, and parochial. The rhetoric is too often plaintive, too seldom inspirational. Needed is not another six-point program of reform complete with arguments pro and con and steps toward implementation, but eloquently rendered visions of excellence. To repeat: what the leadership has most sadly neglected in teacher education is not resource calculations or the mechanics of reform but reasons and ways to care.

This concern for value, for meaning, is no mere froth on the bracing brew of hard-headed practice. Rather it is something more serious, more fundamental to the life of an institution. Although I have argued that the larger predicament of teacher education is in a sense tragic—the show must go on but with no promise of greatness on a grand scale—there is room for affirmation and progress at any institution that prepares teachers. But the starting point for those who are interested—the university president, the dean, the professors—must be with the value of the enterprise itself, even in the face of public indifference, narrow institutional confines, and resource poverty. Teacher education needs its heroes, its sagas, its proud traditions that embody and convey what is valuable in the undertaking. This, I judge, is the place to start.

NOTES

1. National Education Association, *Status of the American Public School Teacher, 1980–81* (Washington, DC: National Education Association, 1982), p. 21.

2. For this phrase and the related ideas, I am indebted to David Cohen. See his unpublished manuscript, "Commitment and Uncertainty," May 1982 (available from D. Cohen, Harvard Graduate School of Education, Harvard University, Cambridge, MA 02139).

3. N. L. Gage, *The Scientific Basis of the Art of Teaching* (New York: Teachers College Press, 1978).

4. John Dewey, *The Sources of a Science of Education* (New York: Liveright, 1929).

5. For a good brief summary of evidence on teacher socialization, see K. M. Zeichner and B. R. Tabachnick, "Are the Effects of University Teacher Education 'Washed Out' by School Experiences?" *Journal of Teacher Education* 32, no. 3 (May–June 1981), 7–11; and K. M. Zeicher, "Myths and Realities: Field-Based Experiences in Preservice Teacher Education," *Journal of Teacher Education* 31, no. 6 (November–December 1980), 45–55.

6. See chapter 3 in Dan Lortie, *Schoolteacher* (Chicago: University of Chicago Press, 1975).

7. Research by Wayne Hoy and colleagues emphasizes how the bureaucratic aspects of school shape teachers' pupil control ideology. See W. Hoy, "The Influence of Experience on the Beginning Teacher," *School Review* 76 (1968), 312–23; W. Hoy, "Pupil Control Ideology and Organizational Socialization: A Further Examination of the Influence of Experience on the Beginning Teacher," *School Review* 77 (1969), 257–265; and W. Hoy and R. Rees, "The Bureaucratic Socialization of Student Teachers," *Journal of Teacher Education* 28, no. 1 (January–February 1977), 23–26. A variety of studies explore the structural characteristics of classrooms that affect teachers. See, for example, P. Jackson, *Life in Classrooms* (New York: Holt, Rinehart, and Winston, 1968); R. Dreeben, "The School as Workplace," in R. Travers, ed., *The Second Handbook of Research on Teaching* (Chicago: Rand McNally, 1973); R. Sharp and A. Green, *Education and Social Control* (London: Routledge & Kegan Paul, 1975); and W. Doyle, "Learning the Classroom Environment: An Ecological Analysis," *Journal of Teacher Education* 28, no. 6 (November 1977), 51–55.

8. See D. Edgar and R. Warren, "Power and Autonomy in Teacher Socialization," *Sociology of Education* 42 (1969), 386–399; for a study of superteachers see G. McPherson, *Small Town Teacher* (Cambridge: Harvard University Press, 1972). See also R. Parelius, "Faculty Cultures and Instructional Practices," unpublished manuscript, Rutgers University, September 1980.

9. See, for example, W. D. Copeland, "Student Teachers and Cooperating Teachers: An Ecological Relationship," *Theory into Practice* 18 (June 1979), 194–

199; and S. S. Klein, "Student Influence on Teacher Behavior," *American Educational Research Journal* 8 (1971), 403–421.

10. G. R. Reinhart, "The Persistence of Occupational Prestige," paper presented at the Southern Sociological Society, Louisville, KY, 1981.

11. "The 12th Annual Gallup Poll of the Public's Attitudes Toward Public Schools," *Phi Delta Kappan* 62 no. 1 (September 1980), 38.

12. National Center for Education Statistics, *Projections of Education Statistics to 1988–89* (Washington, DC: NCES, 1980), pp. 63–64.

13. James Stone, *Breakthrough in Teacher Education* (San Francisco, CA: Jossey-Bass, 1968), pp. 156–157.

14. For example, Stone, ibid., p. 158, reports that in 1961–1962 and 1962–1963, 2,187 teachers successfully completed experimental programs, of whom 78% were teaching in the subsequent year. During the same period 16,117 completed the conventional program in these same institutions, of whom only 49% were teaching in the following year. He further reports that a six-year follow-up of University of California-Berkeley MAT graduates, 1956 to 1962, reveals a sizable number still teaching, with a similar report from Harvard in the first decade following World War II (under President Conant, Harvard had established its MAT program before the Ford Foundation became involved).

15. Wayne Welch, "Twenty Years of Science Curriculum Development: A Look Back," in *Review of Research in Education,* ed. D. Berlinger, vol. 7 (Washington, D.C.: American Educational Research Association, 1979), pp. 282–306.

16. Roy Edelfelt and Margo Johnson, "A History of the Professional Development of Teachers," in *The 1981 Report on Educational Personnel Development* ed. E. Feistritzer (Washington, DC: Feistritzer Publications, 1980), pp. 44–56. See also Don Davies, "Reflections on EPDA," *Theory into Practice,* 13 (June 1974), 210–217.

17. Feistritzer, pp. 134–135.

18. Edelfelt and Johnson, p. 54.

19. Gary Sykes, "An Overview of the Teacher Corps Program, 1965–1982" (Washington, DC: U.S. Department of Education, unpublished report, undated), pp. 22, 25.

20. For a succinct review of six of these seven studies, see G. Thomas Fox, "Limitations of a Standard Perspective on Program Evaluation: The Example of Ten Years of Teacher Corps Evaluations" in James Steffenson, et al., *Teacher Corps Evaluation* (Omaha: University of Nebraska, 1978), pp. 11–86.

21. Ronald Corwin, *Reform and Organizational Survival: The Teacher Corps as an Instrument of Educational Change* (New York: John Wiley, 1973), pp. 81ff.

22. See Corwin, p. 93, and Fox, p. 54.

23. Corwin, p. 378.

24. Ibid., pp. 370–371.

25. The distinction between "normal" and paradigm-shattering science is made in Thomas Kuhn, *The Structure of Scientific Revolutions* (Chicago: University of Chicago Press, 1970).

26. W. Robert Houston, "Competency Based Education," in *Exploring Competency Based Education,* ed. W. B. Houston (Berkeley, CA: McCutchan Publishing Corporation, 1974), p. 4.

27. Iris Elfenbein, "Performance-Based Teacher Education Programs: A

Comparative Description," PBTE Series, no. 8 (Washington, DC: AACTE), October 1972.

28. See, for example, R. W. Heath and M. A. Neilson, "The Research Basis for Performance-Based Education," *Review of Educational Research* 44 no. 4 (Fall 1974), 463–484.

29. See Normal Dodl, et al., *The Florida Catalog of Teacher Competencies* (Tallahassee, FL: Florida State Department of Education, 1973).

30. Harry Broudy, "A Critique of Performance-Based Teacher Education," PBTE Series, no. 4 (Washington, DC: AACTE, May 1972).

31. Peter Elbow, "Trying to Teach While Thinking About the End," in *On Competence: A Critical Analysis of Competence-Based Reforms in Higher Education,* ed. Gerald Grant et al. (San Francisco, CA: Jossey-Bass, 1979), p. 125.

32. Ibid.

33. Bruce Joyce, *Estimating Costs of Competency Orientation* (New York: Teachers College, Columbia University, 1973).

34. This historical fact is cited in Joseph Cronin, "State Regulation of Teacher Preparation," in *Handbook of Teaching and Policy,* ed. L. Shulman and G. Sykes (New York: Longman, 1983), p. 178.

35. See Willard Elsbree, *The American Teacher* (New York: American Book Co., 1939), chapter 24.

36. These three authors overlapped substantially in their critique of the status quo in teacher education. See James B. Conant, *The Education of American Teachers* (New York: McGraw-Hill, 1963); James D. Koerner, *The Miseducation of American Teachers* (Boston: Houghton Mifflin Company, 1963); and Charles E. Silberman, *Crisis in the Classroom* (New York: Random House, 1971).

37. J. T. Sandefur has been tracking the development of teacher competency tests. He reports that the turn to teacher tests began in 1977, and that of the 36 states involved, 21 test or plan to test applicants for admission to teacher education programs, while 28 states test or plan to test prior to certification. Ten states now also require some on-the-job assessment, usually a one-year internship or induction program for beginning teachers. See J. T. Sandefur, "Teacher Competency Assessment Plans 'Little Short of Phenomenal'" (Washington, DC: AACTE Briefs, November 1982).

38. See Donna H. Kerr, "Teaching Competence and Teacher Education in the United States," in Shulman and Sykes, pp. 143–144, and Hendrik d. Gideonse, "The Necessary Revolution in Teacher Education," *Phi Delta Kappan* 64 no. 1 (September 1982), 15–18.

39. B. O. Smith, "Pedagogical Education: How About Reform?" *Phi Delta Kappan* 62, no. 2 (October 1980), 87–90.

40. See Herbert Simon, *The Sciences of the Artificial.* (Cambridge, MA: The MIT Press, 1969); and Joseph J. Schwab, "The Practical: A Language for Curriculum," *School Review* 58 (November 1969), 1–20, and "The Practical: Arts and Eclectic," *School Review* 59 (November 1970), 493–542.

41. See, for example, T. E. Deal and A. A. Kennedy, *Corporate Cultures* (Reading, MA: Addison-Wesley Publishing Co., 1982); and T. J. Peters and R. H. H. Waterman, Jr., *In Search of Excellence: Lessons from America's Best-Run Corporations* (New York: Harper and Row, 1982).

42. Deal and Kennedy, p. 21.

PROFESSIONALISM AND QUALITY TEACHING

Teachers and
Professionalism

Jon Moline

People often speak of teaching as a profession and of teachers as professionals. Those of us who teach are flattered by this. We think it good to be called professionals, perhaps because we think that in calling people professionals one is saying that they are good at what they do or that what they do is good. Not only do we think it is good to be or to be called professionals; we also think it is good to become more like professionals. The process of becoming more like professionals is called "professionalization," and some think it is a means to achieve excellence among teachers and in their teaching.

It is not altogether clear why people say or think such things. It is not clear whether they are true or false. It is not even clear how one could tell whether they are true or false, for it is not clear what they mean. In this essay we shall ask. We shall start at the beginning, as it were, and ask basic questions about the variety of things it may mean for a person to be a professional or for an occupation to be a profession. We shall then examine the answers to these questions in the hope of shedding light upon the sources of excellence in teachers and in teaching.

I will conclude that *most* teachers are not professionals in any interesting sense; that the *best* of teachers do approach professional status, and that if certain obstacles can be overcome, teaching can be improved by making it more like a profession. But careful analysis will be required before it will be clear what these conclusions mean or why they are warranted.

PROFESSIONALISM

There is a bewildering variety of people who are labeled professionals and an equally bewildering variety of lines of work called professions. There is a long list of people and occupations eager for professional status. Many cities have police unions that call themselves Professional Policemen's Associations, and there are similar organizations of fire fighters. It was believed as early as the turn of the century that eventually all workers' labor unions would be included among the recognized professions.[1] An insurance company affiliate, calling itself "Mutual Association for Professional Services," has as its slogan, "Professionals serving professionals." By 1964 there were so many people who wanted to be known as professionals that a slightly incredulous sociologist published a paper entitled, "The Professionalization of Everyone?"[2]

If the proliferation of claims to "professional status" causes confusion, one may become even more bewildered upon noticing that in calling an occupation a profession we are not always saying that what the "professionals" in that occupation do is good. The usual journalistic euphemism for one occupation is the "world's oldest profession," and one hears of professional pickpockets and even professional assassins. It might therefore appear that whether it is a good thing to be a *professional x* depends simply on whether it is good to be an *x*. If so, one might wonder why teachers think it is flattering to be regarded as professionals. And one might doubt that we can throw any light on excellence by pondering what professionals and professions are.

We have stumbled across a confusing ambiguity. Surely teachers do not aspire to be professionals merely in the sense in which pest control specialists are. Nor do teachers wish to be regarded as professionals merely in the sense in which Billie Jean King and Terry Bradshaw are. We do not always mean the same thing when we speak of a person as a professional. How can we tell what we do and do not mean?

Meaning shows in contrast. "Professional" in the confusing sense

encountered thus far contrasts with "amateur." To call people professionals in this sense is not to say that they are good at what they do. It is
simply to say that they are paid for doing it. Members of volunteer fire
departments may be fully as good at fighting fires as paid (and in that
sense "professional") fire fighters. Amateurs have sometimes brought
fresh or even revolutionary insights to a discipline. Charles Ives was not a
professional musician for most of his composing life, and Charles Sanders
Peirce was unable to obtain a position that would allow him to be a
professional philosopher. Socrates refused all pay from those who regarded themselves as his students. Albert Einstein did his most famous
work as a lowly patent office clerk, not a professionally employed theoretical physicist. In sports also, professionals are not necessarily better than
amateurs. Pro-Am tournaments in tennis and golf are not always complete
mismatches, and one could mention several pairings of NFL football
teams with college teams that might embarrass the professionals.

Thus the "nonamateur" sense of "professional" is plainly not the one
in which teachers might be flattered to be known as professionals. It is
known that teachers are paid for teaching. So it is obvious that teachers
are professionals in that sense. Yet there remains a sense in which it is not
so obvious that teachers are or can be professionals. This is the more
honorific sense, the one associated with a certain excellence. What is this
sense? What does it mean to call people professionals not by way of
remarking that they are paid for what they do but by way of praising and
honoring them in a special way?

Again, meaning will show in contrast; but again, it will be important
not to seize upon the wrong contrast. With whom then do we contrast
professionals in the honorific sense? There is a two-fold contrast. We
contrast such professionals, first, with people who have an occupation,
trade, or job; and second, with the sorts of pseudo professionals whom we
call quacks or charlatans. We shall consider these two contrasts in turn.

We speak of what the barber or computer programmer "*does* for a
living." We speak of what the professional *is*—a physician, attorney,
priest, pastor, or rabbi. These are our paradigm professionals. When
teachers are flattered to be called professionals, they are probably thinking of these.

A physician may well be an employee of an organization, even a
bureaucracy, but even then we do not think of the physician simply as
having a job. We think of what he or she *is*. This sense of "is" is almost the
timeless, durative one, and contrasts with its counterpart in "He is a
grocery clerk," which is immediately interpreted in terms of what the
subject does, probably on a temporary basis. Contrasting what a physican
is with what a grocery clerk does for a living is not just a piece of snob-

bery. It marks an important distinction, the distinction that lies at the root of our ideal of a professional. This is the distinction between a job and a calling.

A person engaged in a business—managing a McDonald's Restaurant, for example—has a job, and may well have trained for it carefully at McDonald's Hamburger U. in Chicago. That job may be very time consuming. The person holding it may approach it with the intensity of a workaholic. Even so, this person's relation to his or her job is in some important respects unlike the paradigm professional's. A paradigm professional has an entire way of life, not simply a time-consuming job. This way of life engulfs not only the hours of one's day and the "time on task" but the years of one's life. Becoming a professional changes what one is and is expected to remain. What one *is*, one is twenty-four hours a day, year in and year out, including vacations and "off hours." Once one is a "professional" in this sense, it is virtually impossible to jettison the designation.

Becoming a professional also changes one's aspirations. In the paradigm professions of law and medicine it is not considered advancement to accept a "promotion" to an administrative position, however lofty. It is considered the abandonment of one's career, and perhaps even the betrayal of one's ideals. Thus competent physicians rarely become hospital administrators or research grant facilitators no matter how well these positions may pay. It is notoriously difficult to interest physicians in running for political office. They wish to get on with the practice of medicine. Our respect for paradigm professionals is founded on the professionals' more or less single-minded dedication (some would say "calling") to a life governed by a service ideal.[3]

Mentioning a service ideal is still not precise enough to distinguish paradigm professionals from others, however. This may again be appreciated best by contrast. Consider a series of ads run by a plumber of my acquaintance, H. J. Pertzborn. Mr. Pertzborn advertises on the radio that he is "the last of the family plumbers." He does not, I think, mean that he is the last plumber whose son has gone to work for him, and whose wife minds the store. He surely knows that this is not true. I believe that he intends us to think of him as being like our family physician.

What sort of likeness might there be between a plumber and a physician? Your family physician cares for your family's health. Your family plumber cares for your family's household pipes and fixtures. A few family physicians still make house calls. Plumbers certainly do that, sewage systems not being very portable. Plumbers commonly advertise their willingness, like family physicians, to provide skilled service at any time, day or night, as needed. Plumbers as well as physicians, then, may also live by a service ideal. Are plumbers therefore professionals in the honorific sense in which physicians are? They are not. Why?

One might think that the difference lies in the type of a skill or knowledge involved in the service. This is a promising thought, but it needs careful statement. The difference does not lie in the extent of the knowledge, or simply in its being arcane, though a professional's knowledge is both extensive and arcane. There is a great deal of knowledge which is more arcane than that of the physician or attorney—e.g., that of the high-energy physicist, the topologist, the cosmologist, the radio astronomer, and the Montague semanticist. For all their arcane knowledge, each of these specialists contrasts with the amateur, not with someone who simply has an occupation.

One might then think that arcane *knowledge* coupled with a *service* ideal will capture the difference between physicians and people who are professionals in the sense in which the plumber is. Again, these are necessary but not sufficient to distinguish the paradigm professional from everyone else. The computer-repair technician provides arcane service based upon arcane knowledge, but he or she is a professional in the nonamateur sense, not the honorific sense in which the physician is.

Where then do we find the distinctive character of the professional in the honorific sense? Perhaps it is found in the particular type of service relationship he or she has with clients. This is not simply a service relationship; it is fiduciary. This means, of course, that it involves trust. *Black's Law Dictionary* describes a fiduciary relationship and the people in it: "On the one side there is an overmastering influence, or, on the other, weakness, dependence, or trust, justifiably reposed. . . ."[4] The service station people who provide routine auto service for me have neither the knowledge nor the commitment to justify a fiduciary relationship; they know this, and they know that I know it also. Moreover, they do not want to be responsible for my car in the way that a fiduciary relationship with me would demand. Fiduciary relationships are grounds for malpractice suits if abused, not simply complaints to the Better Business Bureau.

We demand of paradigm professionals that they take their trust seriously, believing themselves bound to act in equity, good conscience, and good faith, "with due regard to the interests of the one reposing the confidence."[5] We back up this demand with extraordinary sanctions: loss of medical licenses, disbarment, and defrocking.

Professionals cannot take this trust seriously without acquiring and using extensive arcane knowledge. But as we have seen, this knowledge is not sufficient for professional status. We expect professionals not simply to know how to diagnose and treat our ailments but to want to do this above almost all else. We expect them to be worthy of our trust. We demand that they turn themselves into people with a special character.

Thus we demand of professionals a certain self-restraint, a willingness to pass up what might seem to be opportunities to serve their own advantage at the expense of the weaker party. We have learned not to expect this of people in the service station business, or even in many of the trades. The professional has what Plato termed a *techne,* usually translated as "art," but translatable also as "profession." What distinguishes the possessor of a *techne* is not the ability to get large fees, for many nonprofessional people have this; what distinguishes the professional is the trained ability and willingness to serve the interests of the weaker party, the client.[6]

This appeal to a service orientation involving arcane knowledge, service based upon it, and a fiduciary relationship with clients is not yet sufficiently precise, however, to distinguish the physician from the computer service technician. More needs to be said about the extraordinary *subject matter* with which we trust paradigm professionals such as physicians. About what do I trust my computer-repair person? I trust him to fix my machine. Computers require very arcane knowledge to service, and they are increasingly important to us. Yet a defective disk-drive or even the loss of the information on a disk would pale in personal significance beside a defective kidney, a deteriorating marriage or business partnership, or a troubled soul—matters on which we consult paradigm professionals. We trust paradigm professionals with personal matters, problems in areas near and dear to us. These matters we would prefer to deal with ourselves if we could. We permit physicians and surgeons to touch our bodies and the bodies of members of our families; we allow attorneys to have access to our wills, our financial records, and much else of an intimate nature. Some of us consult members of the clergy on our most embarrassing shortcomings. Whatever the descriptive, sociological truth may be about the service orientation of actual physicians, attorneys, and members of the clergy, what we demand of them is adherence to an ideal of service *in areas of intimate concern to us.* To the degree that we trust paradigm professionals we do so because we believe that they have both arcane knowledge about matters of overwhelming importance and the dedication to use it for our benefit. Both are required to render them worthy of our trust.

We trust some paradigm professionals for another reason as well. Their licenses merely *allow* them to provide certain services. Contracts or implicit contracts with patients legally obligate them to do so. But there is more than one way of discharging a legal obligation. Some may be discharged in a perfunctory, self-protective way rather than in a spirit of concern for the client's overall welfare, a spirit which can never be precisely described in a contract. Professionalism is not at bottom a matter of licences and contract obligations. Thus many professionals have bound themselves to their service role not simply by contract but by an oath that, if it is taken seriously by the professional, can secure far more than any contract could. The spirit of the Hippocratic Oath has long pervaded the training and practice of physicians and provides perhaps the deepest insights into the spirit of professionalism. Consider some of the words of this oath:

> I will use treatment to help the sick according to my ability and judgment, and never with a view to injury or wrongdoing. . . . Into whatsoever houses I enter, I will enter to help the sick, and I will abstain from abusing the bodies of man or woman, slave or free.[7]

These standing intentions and commitments of the physician—the intentions and commitments one must take as one's own in order to *be* a physician—are not simply to the patient or to the patient's family. Elsewhere in the Hippocratic Oath, the physician undertakes a commitment to the art of medicine—to improving it and teaching it to worthy successors. The attorney, also, is not simply an employee of the client. He or she is an officer of the court, with commitments more extensive than (and sometimes in conflict with) clients' demands for services. The pastor, priest, or rabbi as well is committed not only to the members of a particular congregation or to people seeking services but to God and to a tradition that he or she has sworn to teach to others. A commitment to something larger than the patient and larger even than the art of medicine—a commitment to something divine—also is explicit in the Hippocratic oath.[8]

Professionals emerge from their training professing to know what is best for us in their areas of expertise. They profess to know better than we do. And we trust them to the degree that we believe both that they do indeed know better than we do what is in our interest and that they are more committed to helping us achieve this than they are to almost anything else, even their own financial interest. Thus we are prepared to go along with them many times even when they prescribe unpleasant courses of action or treatment we would otherwise ardently wish to avoid.

This trust is seldom blind. We are not inattentive to professionals' past record of success or failure in treating the sorts of problems on which we consult them. If they professed to know how to treat such problems but had no record of success, we would view them not as professionals and not even as amateurs. We would regard them as quacks or charlatans.

We have learned by costly experience that one fairly reliable sign of quackery is an overwhelming desire to gratify the client or patient at all costs. Paradigm professionals, though, have a clear and insistent grasp of the distinction between what *pleases* the client and what is *good for* the client. This has been true in medicine since ancient times. Plato's Socrates generalized upon this when he denied that rhetoric, as it was conventionally conceived and practiced, was a profession *(techne)* because it "aims at the pleasant, and ignores the best."[9] T. H. Marshall of the London School of Economics noted that

> The client . . . is often ignorant. Authority passes to the professional, who must give him what he needs, rather than what he wants. The client, unlike the customer, is not always right.[10]

One source of the dignity of the paradigm professional is his or her unwillingness to go to great lengths to attract or please "the consumer." We trust paradigm professionals to distinguish what is truly good for us from what we perhaps childishly and unrealistically prefer. George Bernard Shaw reinforced this distinction by remarking that "There are two tragedies in life: One is not getting your heart's desire. The other is getting it." Paradigm professionals might, as one commentator suggested, make their slogan not *Caveat emptor* (Let the buyer beware) but *Credat emptor* (Let the buyer trust).[11]

To the extent that professionals take seriously the training, knowledge, objectivity, and service ideal that make them fit objects of trust by those in positions of relative weakness and relative ignorance of their own good, they will understandably take a dim view of people who attempt to address the problems they do without these prerequisites. They will typically be ready to point out the ignorance, the faking of the service ideal, and ulterior motives of quacks and charlatans.

Both resistance to quacks and the transmission of professional knowledge and professional service ideals are much easier with some form of organization. Hence it has been typical for each profession or aspiring profession to organize itself in ways which set its members off from others both psychologically and otherwise. They form a community within the community. One of the main functions of this professional community is to enforce knowledgeably the high expectations of the larger community toward the profession. This function cannot be performed unless professionals assess the behavior of other members of their professional community. William J. Goode has argued that no community exists unless members evaluate the behavior of other members.[12]

Community, intensive training, a strong service ideal in areas of intimate and almost universal human concern, and fairly successful efforts to enforce the dictates of the service ideal are key factors in the prestige or status that paradigm professions have come to enjoy. Special forms of address such as "Doctor," "Father," "Pastor," "Rabbi," "Your Honor," and "Counselor" remind such professionals that the rest of us want them set apart from nonprofessionals. We want our attorneys to be more trustworthy than our newspaper carriers. We deliberately set professionals apart because we expect far more of them than of ordinary people. As Goode points out, "The advantages enjoyed by professionals thus rest on evaluations made by the larger society, for the professional community could not grant these advantages to itself."[13] Thus professionals acquire their professional status not simply from the previous professionals who trained them but from the larger community that endorses and sustains that status.

Such relations between paradigm professionals and members of the larger society plainly would be difficult if not impossible to maintain if professionals disagreed extensively with the larger society on matters of good and evil. The authority and respect we grant them are plainly conditional and not blind. We expect them to know better than we do what is good for ourselves and for others whom we place in their care; but we are not totally awed by their authority or unable to spot symptoms of the sorts of gross ignorance or malfeasance that lead to the loss of medical licenses or to disbarment. We are especially alert to signs of lack of common sense. Precisely because professionals' alleged knowledge is arcane and the commitment to the good of the weaker party difficult to assess, we try to be alert to signs that this knowledge and commitment are not what they are professed to be. We are interested in such disquieting symptoms wherever they occur.

TEACHER PROFESSIONALISM

Already one will have noted quite an array of obstacles that stand in the way of teachers' being or becoming professionals today. These obstacles may be divided into two sorts—internal and external. The internal obstacles show up in the thinking and discourse of teachers. The external ones may be seen in the thinking, discourse, and institutional expectations of school administrators, school board members, certifying authorities, legislators, and other leaders who are in a position to encourage or discourage professionalism. These two sorts are equally important, and strongly reinforce each other.

Chief among the internal obstacles to professionalism in teachers is a widespread failure to understand the distinction between needs and wants, between what is good for students and what students happen to like. This failure is never complete, and seldom entirely conscious; but it is real, and devastating to professional status. Physicians, attorneys, and members of the clergy profess to know better than we do what is good for us, and we think they are right. If we did not, we could not trust them. Teachers—especially public school teachers—are not widely trusted as professionals because many parents and others have come to believe that teachers do not know better than they what is good for their children. Some students think so, too. How did this happen?

Teachers have themselves, some of those who taught them, some of those who are in authority over their schools, and some teacher-organization leaders to blame for this. Whether they have been taught to do so or have simply picked it up from popular culture, some teachers have come to regard the notion of what is good for students as "a matter of opinion," "subjective," or "for the students to choose." Telling students what is good or bad for them strikes such teachers as "authoritarian," and they will stoutly maintain that we must not "impose our values upon students." To express before students one's disapproval of virtually anything strikes such teachers as "indoctrination," and they accordingly strive to maintain complete neutrality on all questions they label as "matters of value preference." Some may even deny that there is any such thing as "knowing what is best," claiming that what is best is always a "matter of opinion," not a "fact."

A physician with a similar attitude would have few patients. In time, teachers with such attitudes may be in danger of having few students, as parents realize that such teachers do not hold professional views about the good of students. No profession can diverge very far from the larger community in its views about good and evil and still be viewed as a profession; for it is precisely to help us with difficulties about various kinds of good and evil that we consult professionals. We consult them because they profess to *know* better than we do about certain kinds of good and evil, about how to find or to avoid these. One who claimed to be a professional but professed not to see any intrinsic difference between good and evil, leaving the choice or the labeling of each up the client, would quickly be seen as a quack, a person more akin to the prostitute than to the ideal of the physician. A group that claims to be a professional organization but that undermines the distinction between good and evil or systematically confuses the two will come to be seen as antiprofessional.[14]

We demand *results* of professionals, and though they are the acknowledged authorities on how to achieve those results, they will not long remain so if they confuse being an authority—which is a good thing—with the evil of authoritarianism. Nor will they remain so if they do not respect the desire of those who pay them to see those results achieved. Their professional status as trusted authorities is forfeited if they express uncertainty about whether there is any "objective" difference in "value" between curing cancer and ignoring it, or between winning a lawsuit and losing it. If, perish the thought, your daughter develops anorexia nervosa, and your physician passes this off lightly as "simply a matter of her personal choice about her weight," insisting you must "respect" this choice, you will probably think the physician mad.

But what, you may say, is so clear-cut in teaching as the curing of a disease or the winning of a lawsuit? Perhaps one suspects that the reason physicians and attorneys have the status they do as professionals is that the *ends* they are to achieve are both clearer-cut and less controversial than those of education. Now it is surely true that the ends actually pursued in many American *schools* in the past few decades are neither clear-cut nor uncontroversial. But it is not true that the ends of *education* are particularly volatile or vague. Unsound judgment is a great evil, both for its possessor and for his or her society, much as a contagious disease is. Traditional education aimed at combatting this evil and professed to know how to go about it. Much contemporary schooling rejects this aim and makes no such profession. The crucial fact here is not that contemporary educators pursue this aim differently or criticize earlier conceptions of it, but that they reject it altogether. Inculcating sound judgment is eschewed.

Traditional education also viewed ignorance of facts as a great evil, and set out to cure this by imparting knowledge and skills to students, whether the students found these congenial at the moment or not. Knowledge was viewed as good and ignorance as bad; and since something's being good was distinguished from its being pleasant (especially from its being pleasant to the immature), educators were able to maintain an attitude parallel to that of paradigm professionals. They made no sharp fact-value distinction, recognizing that a fact is essentially a claim that can be argued for rationally, tested by exploring its concrete implications, and defended before judicious people in the face of criticism. By that standard, many claims that would be regarded by some recent teachers as expressing "matters of personal values" are straightforwardly factual. It is a fact that rape is an outrageous wrong. The category of "personal values" is empty. Teachers who assign to it the very matters of acquiring solid knowledge, developing sound character, and forming good work habits forfeit professional status and respect.

The second obstacle is a result of the first: without the distinction between the good and the merely pleasing, teachers will not have any basis for forming a *professional* community. In the paradigm professions, such communities are formed in order to protect clients from quacks and to protect competent practitioners from being confused with quacks. But teachers who fall at the first obstacle say, in effect, that there cannot be educational quackery, any more than there can be quackery in cafeteria management. In their conception of education, schools are to provide a smorgasbord at which students may consume or not consume what they like. The good teacher provides an attractive, well-prepared variety. Incompetence is possible, on this conception. But quackery is not. Such teachers can scarcely form a community to protect themselves from being confused with quacks. Protection of professional standards among such teachers cannot exist because they have not such standards. Standards are necessary for assessment of behavior to take place. If it is a necessary condition of a community that members assess the behavior of other members, then teachers who have no standards of quality in their subject matter and in the teaching of it cannot form a community. In some schools there are, of course, external administrative and institutional barriers to the formation of professional communities by teachers, but these are redundant where the internal barriers are so formidable.

A third chief obstacle to professional status for teachers is that some—far from possessing well-tested arcane knowledge—have very little knowledge of subject matter, and that they know a great deal of bad educational theory. This isn't entirely—perhaps not even primarily—their fault. In the schools of education they attended, they were encouraged to take courses on what passed for educational theory and required to take courses on teaching methods but may not have taken any courses at all in the content that the schools that employed them assign them to teach. There are no methods for teaching what one does not know. Consider the confession of one former teacher:

> As a schoolboy, I always presumed that my teachers were experts in the subjects that they taught. My physics teacher must, of course, be a physicist, and my history teacher a historian. I knew that my music teacher was a musician, for I had actually heard him play, and, during a dismal year in military school, I could see with my own eyes that the Professor of Military Science and Tactics was a bird colonel. . . . Even when I became a schoolteacher myself, quite by accident, I imagined that I had been chosen for the work because of my knowledge of the subject I was to teach. It turned out not to be exactly so, for I was soon asked to teach something else, of which my knowledge was scanty. No matter, I was told. I could bone up over the summer. Eventually, I was asked to teach something about which I knew nothing, nothing at all. Still no matter. I seemed to be a fairly effective teacher and at least smart enough to stay a lesson or two ahead of the students. That's just what I did. No one saw anything wrong with that, and the students never caught me. It was nevertheless depressing. . . .[15]

What is wrong with what this teacher—Richard Mitchell—was asked to do? Why was it depressing to do it? The answer is not exactly that he did not know the material he was teaching: he "learned" it as he was teaching it, or slightly in advance of teaching it. That is, he presumably crammed and learned what was in *the text* well enough to present it and pose some questions about it. But learning what is in a text well enough to "stay a

lesson or two ahead of the students" and learning a subject are far removed. Even further removed are teaching what is in the text and teaching the subject matter or discipline.

One does not know a subject matter or discipline unless one is in a
position to catch mistakes in the textbook, or devise intelligent, disciplined, and informed alternatives or at least supplements to what it says.
The level of mastery this requires varies with the grade level taught; but in
middle school and high school classes it can easily surpass the level
achieved even by an undergraduate major in the subject being taught—
and relatively few states require even a major for certification in many
subjects.

Not knowing the subject matter well enough to teach it is not the
worst of the teaching situation described by Mitchell, however. Much
learning is a solitary affair, not simply the result of teachers pouring their
knowledge into empty heads. But how does such a solitary learner come
to *want* to master a subject matter? One picks up such a want from
someone who already has it, from a teacher who loves that subject matter. And here it is simply false that love is blind. One cannot infect
students with love of a subject matter or discipline unless one knows it
fairly well. To encourage the love of a subject requires encouraging questions about it, serious questions posed in the realistic hope of finding good
answers, perhaps from the teacher, or from resources the teacher can
recommend knowledgeably. Such a hope will not be realistic unless it is
gratified fairly regularly. It would be a rare teacher in Mr. Mitchell's
unfortunate situation who could regard student questions with anything
but dread. Such a teacher is simply not in a position to feed and guide an
inquiring mind, for the inquiry will quickly outstrip his meager resources.

If teachers or coaches in such dismal situations regard becoming
assistant principals or curriculum facilitators as professional advancement, not as a betrayal of their professional commitment, we should not
be amazed. They did not acquire either professional-level mastery of
subject matter or a professional commitment to a life of teaching in their
years of teacher training. This willingness or even eagerness of many
teachers to escape the classroom poses another obstacle to their professionalization. No one could blame an ill-prepared teacher for wishing to
escape the teaching of what he or she neither loves nor knows thoroughly.
Such a wish is a sign of fundamental honesty. But a commitment to the
lifelong practice of one's profession is a standard feature of the paradigm
professions.

Until teaching is made nondepressing for conscientious people, it will
not be a profession in the sense in which medicine, law, and divinity are.
And that will not happen until those teachers who do know and love the
subject matter they teach are suitably rewarded in tangible and intangible

ways—in salary, greatly reduced class size, relative freedom to teach what they think best, and public recognition. Once there is a critical mass of such teachers who recognize one another, they can organize themselves into a paradigm professional organization for the encouragement and protection of the high standards they have set. But each of these steps will require the overcoming of obvious external barriers to teacher professionalism.

Professional teachers will cherish and merit not simply professional pay but autonomy such as physicians have in deciding on their patients' mode of treatment and attorneys have in arguing cases. The *Wall Street Journal* for February 23, 1983, quoted the principal of a rapidly improving ghetto junior high school in Baltimore as having said that he prefers to give his teachers great autonomy because there is no one method of teaching that works for all teachers. His task, he notes, is "to assure teachers of a disruption-free environment in the classroom." Such a strong principal is widely agreed to be a key element in a quality school, and only the strong can both grant autonomy to others and demand that it be used responsibly. Teachers will not merit such autonomy, though, unless they keep the ends of education as clearly in view as physcians do the ends of medicine.

Responsible parents care deeply about their children's well-being and know that inability to speak and write the standard language of our nation, ignorance of history, mathematical illiteracy, and unsound judgment are evils. If the subject matter on which we trust professionals must be of intimate and nearly universal importance, then the well-being of our children certainly qualifies; the evils of ignorance and unsound judgment deeply affect that well-being. We would treat these evils ourselves if we thought we could, but for various reasons many of us judge that we cannot, and so we have paid those who profess to know better than we do about ameliorating these evils to treat them for us. Those teachers who profess this truly are the professionals, and they merit rewards commensurate with their professionalism.

Singling out good teachers for reward is a formidable and potentially divisive task, but not so divisive as the demise of the public schools that may result if we do not undertake this risk. If the ends of education are "the pursuit of knowledge and the exercise of the mind in the cause of judgment," then it is not beyond the ingenuity of those expert in testing and measurement, aided by intelligent parents and school board members, to determine which teachers have been outstanding. One finds out by looking for solid improvements in teachers' own *knowledge* of the subject matter that is the core of sound education—history, mathematics, the competent use of the English language and foreign languages, for example—and by looking and testing for their success in teaching that subject matter to their students.

How well a teacher has done in pursuing this knowledge with students *in the cause of judgment* may not be fully known for a long time, but there will be important early symptoms, such as the incidence of gross errors of judgment shown in student infringement of the rules of the school and the laws under which we all must live. The cause of judgment is the cause of wisdom, the opposite of folly, and as Thoreau remarked, "It is a characteristic of wisdom not to do desperate things." Judgment, like love of a subject matter, is picked up at first from one who loves it enough to cultivate it.

Obviously any attempt to judge a teacher's success by such standards is open to abuse, especially to abuse by administrators. But why let administrators be the sole evaluators? There are teachers who are capable of spotting the best of their own number. Let the evidence of teaching excellence be gathered in the form of standardized achievement test scores, subsequent records by students who have been in the nominee's class over the past few years, and testimonials by students, past students, and parents. Give the evidence to a committee of teachers chosen for their fair-mindedness and good judgment, and let them make the judgment. This is the way Distinguished Teaching Awards (carrying a $1,000 prize) are decided upon in my university and many others, and I see no reason to think that a similar procedure could not work well in secondary or elementary school settings.

LEARNING AND PROFESSIONALISM

Plainly any serious attempts to encourage professionalism as described in this essay are likely to have the entire arsenal of educationistic and ideological curse words fired at them. "Elitist" is only the first. How are we to respond to charges or elitism?

I hope that my physician, my attorney, my pilot, and so forth, are all of elite quality, and that my children's teachers are also. If elitism consists in aspiring to encourage the pursuit of knowledge and the exercise of the mind in the cause of judgment, then there could be no finer compliment paid to an educational proposal than to call it elitist. The alternative might be labeled mediocritist. Is this what the critics want? As for curses, I have one for those who persist in combatting the pursuit of knowledge and the exercise of the mind in the cause of judgment as "elitist:" may your physician be someone taught as you favor teaching.

One telling standard for any educational proposal to meet is the effect it is likely to have on the love of learning. As Sir John Lubbock remarked, "If we succeed in giving the love of learning, the learning itself is sure to follow." Those who have acquired a love of learning will often be able to teach themselves, or they will seek out others who can teach them. And again, students have their love of learning kindled by coming into contact with the love of learning in a teacher who shows it in teaching what he or she loves. Students may have their love of learning doused by repeated contact with teachers who do not love what they teach.

It is a truism that one who loves something tries to get more and more of it. Teachers who have loved learning in their subject areas will very likely have acquired more of it, and those who have acquired more of it will probably have done so because they love it. Such teachers approach the stature of paradigm professionals, and these professionals set the educational standard to which we should look in the education of the next decade.[16]

NOTES

1. S. and B. Webb, *Industrial Democracy* (London: Longmans, Green and Co., 1902), pp. 825–826, quoted in Harold L. Wilensky, "The Professionalization of Everyone?" in *American Journal of Sociology* 70 (September 1964), 137.

2. Wilensky, ibid.

3. Here see Nathan Glazer, "The Schools of the Minor Professions" *Minerva* 12 (1974), 356. Even additional academic degrees typically have little or no effect upon a physician's self-esteem or reputation among other physicians, even when these physicians serve on medical school faculties. The same is true among law faculties. The first professional degree is trumped by nothing at all in their estimation, for it is the degree necessary and sufficient for the practice in which they fulfill their lifelong service ideal.

4. *Black's Law Dictionary,* 4th ed. (St. Paul: West Publishing Co., 1951), p. 1375.

5. Ibid., pp. 753–754.

6. Plato, *Republic,* I, 345E–347A.

7. Hippocrates, The Oath, in *Hippocrates,* trans. by W. H. S. Jones, vol. 1 (London: W. Heinemann, 1923), p. 299.

8. Here I am indebted to Dr. Leon Kass of the University of Chicago Medical School.

9. Plato, *Gorgias,* 501A.

10. T. H. Marshall, "The Recent History of Professionalism in Relation to Social Structure and Social Policy," *Canadian Journal of Economics and Political Science* 5 (August 1939), 330.

11. Everett C. Hughes, "Professions," *Daedalus* 92 (1963), 657.

12. William J. Goode, "Community Within A Community: The Professions," *American Sociological Review* 22 (1957), 198.

13. Ibid., p. 196.

14. The AFT and NEA have dissimilar records on this. See Chester E. Finn, Jr., "Teacher Politics," *Commentary* 75 (February 1983), 22–41.

15. Richard Mitchell, *The Graves of Academe* (Boston and Toronto: Little, Brown and Co., 1981), p. 19.

16. Portions of this paper appear in another form in "Professions and Professionals," in *The Humanities and the Profession of Medicine,* ed. Alan R. Dyer (Research Triangle Park: National Humanities Center, 1982).

The State's Responsibility for Teacher Quality

John T. Casteen

Governments regulate schooling because they see education as an essential public service. Since poor schools and poor teachers threaten the public welfare while good ones enhance it, there must be effective "quality control mechanisms." Historically, it has fallen to the state to provide them. In recent decades, teachers' organizations have frequently called for a transfer of quality control from the state to the members of the occupation. "Professionalism" is the banner under which this call is issued.

Education is too important to the public welfare for the public, acting through the state, to relinquish responsibility for its quality. The question is, how best can the state insure that the schools and the teachers in them are as good as they can be?

STATE REGULATION AND PROFESSIONALISM: BACKGROUND

The history of state regulation of teaching predicts, in a number of ways, today's issues and anticipates some of the problems in addressing them.

The early formulators of American school law did not tarry over large questions of philosophical purpose. To prescribe a curriculum, to define physical standards for schools, and to set competence standards for teachers were viewed in essentially practical terms. Especially in the West, where earned collegiate credentials remained scarce until the land grant and normal colleges matured, practical demonstration of competence to teach made sense to just about everyone and led to creation of certification systems. Indeed, the major disagreements had to do with just how the localities would join forces in addressing competence, not with whether to gauge it.

Regulation of teaching moved generally from the Pacific to the Atlantic. Standards set in the West tended over time to assert themselves in the East, when (sometimes fifty years later, and for vastly different motives) officials there came to terms with the state's role in education and began setting standards for teacher qualifications and creating normal schools to prepare would-be classroom teachers.

This was not a coherent historical development, however, nor was it a process concerned overmuch with the "profession" of teaching. Rather, as the states assumed responsibility for schooling, they addressed pressing public needs—needs perceived as best met at the state level for reasons of practicality, not of constitutional mandate or of philosophy. The public needed ways to determine the competence of employees who lacked formal credentials, but who, for good or ill, would significantly influence the community's welfare. Even today, most states base their approach to regulation in essential distrust of the labor market.

(Here, a distinction is in order. Some commentators have suggested in recent years that our approach to teacher regulation derives from the essential sexism of a system in which men control both the machinery of regulation and the schools, while women work in the classrooms. History belies this analysis, I think—though there is sexism aplenty in education, as elsewhere. States like Oregon dealt with no existing labor market demography when they wrote their certification laws. They simply needed "competent" teachers before they had established colleges and universities to train these teachers. Apparently, most candidates for certification under the early examination laws were men, not women. So the impetus seems not to have been essential distrust of women as teachers, but distrust of incompetents, pretenders, or imposters.)

The growth of professional schools of education in the state universities between the world wars brought a second dimension to state regulation: state regulation as an object and, in time, a result of political strife between different elements of the education community striving to control the schools. The normal schools, schools of education within universities, and "professional humanists" were the main disputants.

State regulation becomes primarily a matter of demanding certain formal credentials—courses to be taken, degrees to be earned, and the nature of the department, school, or institution from which credit could be earned—rather than of "competence" proven by passing certain kinds of tests. Certification via educational credentials is a relatively late development in the history of teacher certification in America, and it arose largely out of the institutional efforts of schools of education. It is interesting to note that the present movement toward teacher certification via testing parallels both the original concerns that led to certification—lack of faith in the educational backgrounds of those who would teach—and the earliest methods of certification.

Without drawing overly fine distinctions, one can probably say that the state university education programs that developed with support from John D. Rockefeller and others differed from those of the normal schools and teachers colleges in at least two ways. One was their emphasis on other school activities in addition to teaching—school administration and finance, for example. The other, and for our story more important, was the potential for alliances with and wars against the liberal arts and other professional faculties in the state universities. Because of where they were, these new education faculties faced opportunities and hazards not known to the earlier teachers colleges—competition for students and funds, for instance, and comparisons of scholarly achievement were hazards created when education faculties came into the universities.

Much of the modern debate over control of the school derives indirectly from these century-old developments in higher education. Even as education faculties moved into the universities, lines between the elements of the education community were being more clearly drawn. Each component had its own interests in what was taught in the schools and who would teach it. Disagreements and shifting power relationships among these parts of the community have shaped state regulation.

While debates on what state regulations should, in fact, consist of—how many hours of what kinds of courses, taken where, supplemented by what sort of "practice"—raged on, the alternative conception of quality control known as "professionalism" arose. "Professionalism" as a movement to give regulatory power to teachers and remove it from the state—the peculiar sense of the word often used by educators, but rarely by sociologists or by the better established professions—was not created by the leaders of the teachers' union, though today it has largely been taken over by them. Rather, it probably derives from two unrelated sources: the self-consciousness of those in higher education who worked in the 1920s and 1930s to define a national agenda for teacher education; and the desire for autonomy by teachers whose schools adopted over the course of a long half century the suggestions about teacher education put forth in 1892 by the NEA Committee on Secondary School studies—the famous "Committee of Ten."

The development of schools of education, which began in earnest only at the turn of the century, led to a class of university professors whose sole subject was the teaching of teaching. These schools had to create their own constituency, secure their own institutional place within higher education, and construct for themselves an area of expertise to which they could lay unique claim. These needs of the education faculties were well served by the idea that school teaching ought to be a "profession," since it was easy to argue that a profession needed specialized professional training and depended on a body of arcane knowledge. At the same time that schools of education were developing, the ideas of the Committee of Ten were being carried out in a number of secondary schools. In addition to explicit calls for more highly trained teachers, the Committee called for a curriculum of clearly delineated, logically "sequenced" courses. Teachers who eventually taught such courses tended to feel themselves better qualified, by virtue of their specialization, to determine what happened in the school than the politicians and other officials who had previously controlled academic decisions. This, too, fostered a sense of—at least a yearning for—professionalism.

Under these two influences, educational standards for entry into teaching grew stricter. Teachers without baccalaureate degrees virtually disappeared. Graduate education became customary preparation for teaching after the entry level. In-service training, formal internships, and sundry other quality-control mechanisms appeared and in time came to be routine elements of the teacher training program. The teachers who raised the professionalism issue saw—or thought they saw—an end of the era of uncertainty about the qualifications of applicants for teaching positions, the very uncertainty that originally led Oregon and other states to regulate teaching by way of entry examinations.

Oddly, though, few attempted to explore the governance issue in its largest context. Advocates of professionalism debated how to license persons upon their entry into teaching—but rarely discussed how to govern the classroom, how to improve the curriculum, or how to guarantee that available books and other materials could support effective teaching. Worse, educators debated mostly with each other. They did not attract the attention of political leaders with the power to change the system. Advocates of professionalism, then, were mostly absorbed with the issues that state regulation already addressed, but they asked neither whether conditions still called for state regulation of entry nor what larger issues a real professionalism movement would address. The advocates of professionalism who were located in schools of education, in particular, did not address the fundamental issue of professionalism in the larger sense of peer governance of the profession. Rather, the teachers college professionals were concerned primarily with strengthening their own control over the occupation of teaching. Schools of education did not assign high priority to equipping prospective teachers for self-governance, and they certainly did not offer to relinquish the franchise over entry into the profession that they were, in fact, seeking to strengthen. The net effect was that educators created no real agenda or political base for professionalism.

Perhaps that is why professionalism of the sort educators have advocated has never yet supplanted—or even become a credible alternative to—state regulation. In the first place, teachers themselves have hardly supported it. Obvious disparities—in salaries, status, and conditions of work—between teaching and the other occupations commonly called professions are still facts of life in most states. In most states, easing of such disparity is impeded by the fact that schools compete for resources with other government commitments. This competition must discomfort educators, since our communities' populations are aging and older voters generally favor expenditures for human services and health care over expenditures for education. In this environment, most teachers seem to have set aside the issue of professionalism in order to concentrate on more pressing matters, such as lost purchasing power or the prospect of widespread layoffs. Quality control concerns teachers less than survival.

The political world, meanwhile, is inclined to view proponents of teacher professionalism as merely another special interest group with its own agenda for self-aggrandizement, a set of partial truths to explain away embarassing inconsistencies, and transparent (but not high-minded) motives for wanting to control the schools. Given the choice, thoughtful legislators and governors avoid aligning themselves with such blatant special interests. With provocative exceptions, the unionists who are today's professionalism advocates rarely speak credibly about teacher quality or about how best to enhance school effectiveness or classroom practice. Two decades of special pleading make for a lot of baggage in state politics.

STATE REGULATION AND PROFESSIONALISM: NORMATIVE ISSUES

We are now in an era when most people want improvements in teaching and learning, and the question we must face is whether these improvements are likely to be brought about by new state regulation or by some form of teacher self-governance. We must be clear that the state's responsibility for improving education is not at issue. But does the state best discharge this responsibility by regulating the occupation of teaching directly, or might not some form of partnership between the state and the occupation—some form of limited professionalism, if not the complete autonomy that teachers' unions want—serve best to control the quality of teaching?

We begin by asking whether external regulation, imposed on the occupation by the state, has worked. A case can probably be made that it has. If one compared the credentials of those who served before the onset of regulation with those who serve now, it would seem clear that the regulated teachers are stronger. They have baccalaureate degrees, which implies more years of study. Their transcripts display both general education and specific training to teach their subjects. They continue to study subjects thought to be appropriate to their teaching fields. This set of *post hoc, ergo propter hoc* observations is not conclusive, of course; but in a different context we could show, I think, that past improvement has correlated credibly with state regulation.

We would have to say, though, that while state regulation has done much to keep wholly unprepared teachers out, it has not done much to attract the very able in; it has in fact often discouraged the brightest and best prepared; and it frequently withholds from teachers a legitimate measure of self-determination, insofar as most states exclude teachers from the licensure boards that set teaching standards. Moreover, in recent years, in response to public demands for greater accountability in schooling, state regulation has brought greater centralization of authority and creation of new layers of vertical authority. Apologists for these trends in regulation speak of concern for new populations, enhanced managerial effectiveness, and clearer lines of accountability. The facts, though, are that such developments do not make the occupation of teaching more attractive, and that it is not at all clear that the managerial authorities in whom greater control has been vested have the training or knowledge of academic subjects necessary to enhance teaching.

States have much experience in "partnerships" with occupational or professional groups. We might suggest that the state's responsibility for education would also be well served by the development of such a partnership, in which the teachers controlled the central educational activities of the school—including curriculum design, selection of materials, hiring and promotion of teachers, in-service and continuing education, and teacher discipline—within general rules set by or in counsel with the state. These general rules might need to be more prescriptive than are analogous rules for other state-regulated professions: professionalism needs to be modified, even as an ideal, when the concept is applied to teaching, because teachers stand in such a different relation to the state than do the paradigm professionals. Law does not mandate that citizens go to doctors or lawyers, much less that they go to them eight hours a day, one hundred eighty days a year for eight to twelve years, even less that they be assigned to a particular doctor's care. School children are assigned to specific teachers for vast periods of time, and can hardly—unless they can afford private schools—opt out of these assignments.

The state must, I think, continue to regulate entry into teaching by setting both academic and ethical standards. The public interest justifies mechanisms to assure both competence (a concept mentioned in all licensure laws with which I am familiar) and good character (a concern in some other professions, such as law and medicine, but not in all). Teachers may enforce these standards, but few legislators will or ought to deliver up the standards themselves to be formulated by teachers.

The state's interests in the conditions under which people who have met the entry requirements continue to teach is complex. Standards for promotion and tenure are involved, and the state itself usually sets basic levels of remuneration. The state's responsibility for quality teaching is greater than its responsibility, perhaps, for quality legal counsel, for reasons I have made clear. Lawyers are rarely disciplined for incompetence; we assume that people will simply learn not to use the incompetent lawyer. The same holds for physicians. Teachers must be regulated for competence, though. The "client" has little or no choice. There is no "marketplace."

States have been inclined to vest control of the continuation in teaching in "managerial" personnel who are accountable directly to one or another public board. Nonetheless, once states have set general standards of competence and comportment, making clear just what is expected of teachers, the public interest is probably best served by granting to teachers' peer governance bodies—which, of course, would have to be created as part of a move toward greater teacher self-governance—responsibility for designing the mechanisms and executing the procedures of promotion and tenure reviews and competency proceedings. The state would reserve to itself only the power to insure that these procedures are fair and efficient and that teachers subject to them are treated in accordance with the large principles of due process and equal protection. Generally speaking, the greater the span of control assigned to teachers, the greater the prospect that the public interest in improved teaching will be well served through collegial activity.

To pursue the idea a bit further, consider two models of teacher self-governance. The first would organize teachers by school or groups of schools. (I would prefer here to speak simply of faculties, much as we do in higher education, but the varieties of school organization in the elementary and secondary grades can make "faculty" a meaningless term.) A local school division might be a self-contained unit; the jurisdictional arrangements, though, matter less than the paramount principle that aggregations ought to be small enough to sustain *genuine communities of interest*.

This unit of aggregation matters because it defines an academic community. The self-governing faculty of a school or district would remain accountable to the board that controls the budgets and through the board to the voters whose taxes fund the budgets. Each faculty would monitor its own results, and report on a prescribed schedule to its board and to the general public. Each faculty would be responsible for improving (or removing) its weaker members and identifying (and rewarding) its stronger members. Each would govern tenure, but with the specific obligation also to identify and discharge members found less than competent.

This scheme would not necessarily separate teachers by disciplines. Rather, *it would seek to build collegiality by making the faculty, however defined, the primary arbiter of its own membership.* Faculties might choose to subdivide themselves by disciplines, grade levels, or perhaps by other schemes, but the unit of aggregation would be the faculty.

The principle that collegiality entails power to control membership in the *collegium* is fundamental to self-governance. Insofar as administrators are necessary for the governance of the schools, these should be seen as leaders or agents of the faculty, not rulers set over it by outsiders. They should participate in whatever forum the faculty uses to set policies, and they should carry out policies and decisions reached by the faculty. The model by which the faculty should be governed, in short, is collegial, not managerial.

The unit of aggregation, then, would be the faculty of a school or district. The mechanisms by which this aggregation governs itself can be left largely to the determination of the faculty. Whether the members choose to elect a faculty parliament or senate, to select officers who are vested with the authority of the group, or to set principles by which certain teachers automatically become members of governing committees (e.g., all senior teachers serving on bodies that attend to hiring, promotion, and competency proceedings) is less an issue of state concern than that the faculty, by some means, insures that the general principles of competence and sound character are enforced rigorously and fairly.

This scheme would not necessarily require changing the rules governing portability of credentials, but it could. Those rules are not uniform now. Whatever vices or virtues they have might well carry forward under this proposal. On the other hand, states that do not adopt this proposal might decline to accept credentials from states that do on grounds that no basis exists for accepting faculty assessments as valid. Individual states or even localities that implement it might require secondary substantiation of credentials from other jurisdictions in the form of acceptable scores on examinations or probationary service in the receiving school system. But portability is not a central issue. Teachers will never achieve significant advances in self-regulation if each state waits for all other states to act before deciding how to proceed. Reasonable prospects of portability or reciprocity already exist within many regions of the country. A state that wants to test the proposition that teachers can improve schooling by governing themselves ought to proceed on its own.

A second model of academic self-governance might organize

teachers by disciplines (English, mathematics) or levels (primary school, middle school, upper school). The state could enter into contracts with the professional organizations that already exist to serve the disciplines. This scheme poses the obvious danger that the English or history (or math or physical education) organizations might evolve into pressure groups interested primarily in self-aggrandizement. But it also promises to give teachers greater control over the curriculum. Disciplines that now lack well-developed groups would have motives to develop them. Secondary school teachers, who now have relatively little discourse with colleagues in the colleges and universities, might well come to participate in academic debates about their disciplines. This scheme might even make possible the establishment of separate teacher examinations for each of the disciplines since the professional organizations that would make and administer the exams are controlled by members of the disciplines. Since in-service training or continuing education would be designed by leaders in the discipline, we might expect courses with more academic than pedagogical purposes. This scheme could also foster "pride of ownership" in courses. Teachers engaged in governing admission to and promotion within their discipline would thereby contribute their expertise directly to improving the discipline itself.

The two schemes are not mutually exclusive. Any system of collegial governance at the school level must assume that senior teachers in each discipline would be the chief judges (and mentors) of new teachers in the respective disciplines.

Each of these schemes, like the classical governance model of liberal arts colleges, builds authority from the bottom up. In the colleges, specialists within disciplines judge their own peers; departments exercise veto power over their own membership; deans and provosts balance the competing interests of many departments in distributing finite numbers of tenure slots, raises, or other resources. Public school teaching differs, of course, in requiring licensure as well as degrees. This difference necessitates arrangements for portability of credentials and the like. But it does not in the end invalidate for application to the schools the model by which university faculties govern themselves, which can work if teachers assume responsibility for their part and administrators and board members accept the terms of the implied contract.

Either of these schemes can enhance the prospect for radical reform of the internal management of our public schools. Building new machinery to support better teaching and greater autonomy for teachers makes little sense if we do not also eliminate or substantially modify the verticality of the structures in which teachers work. Teachers who control their own curricula and police their own membership may well discover that they do not need hierarchies of principals, vice-principals, assistant superintendents, and the like in order to run good schools. They may, indeed, discover that functional collegiality makes for a better school.

State regulation of teaching will continue under either scheme, but the character of that regulation will inevitably change if states share substantial authority with the teachers themselves. State regulation of the practice of law or social work is often vested in "professional practice" councils or standards commissions, public bodies composed primarily (sometimes exclusively) of practitioners and charged with defining and requiring good practice. In the case of nursing, the state commissions often include physicians, hospital administrators, and representatives of the general public. Some commissions are responsible only for licensure examinations. Others actively regulate practice. The standards set forth by these bodies take on the force of law in many states. In some states, legislatures codify and enact regulations originally formulated by occupational regulatory groups. Teachers organizations could be empowered and regulated according to similar arrangements. Because the analogies between teaching and other licensed occupations are imperfect, regulatory mechanisms will diverge from the precedents, too. But there should be little difficulty in discerning where divergence is needed and then designing suitable procedures.

PROFESSIONALISM AND UNIONS

Saying that greater teacher self-regulation can effectively serve the state's need to foster high quality education is pointless, unless we assess the political conditions that would be needed to gain adoption of proposals for greater teacher self-regulation. As I have said, one of the prime obstacles to self-regulation is a lack of credibility suffered by teachers' associations in the eyes of politicians. Insofar as the concept of professionalism appears to be only a foil for rampant teacher self-interest, politicians of a thoughtful sort will remain unimpressed. When groups advocating professionalism appear to violate the fundamental notions of what the public construes to be professionalism, the concept itself looks like such a subterfuge. Too often, teacher unions have resisted the basic tenets of professionalism, at least insofar as professionalism includes a serious system of quality control.

Yet the unions are powerful forces, especially in the Northeast and the Middle West. It would be foolish either to condemn them out of hand or to overlook their influence. In the states that permit collective bargaining, reform is all but impossible without the unions. In states that have seen frequent work stoppages—Pennsylvania, for example—neither school boards nor teachers can afford to back a movement that lacks union support. If either of the aforementioned schemes of self-regulation in tandem with general state regulations is to be effected, unions must be taken into account. Either could incorporate union participation, if the unions were willing to accept the specific sort of limited aggregation assumed in each scheme. This concession may not come easily. Organized labor typically exercises power built on *mass* aggregation of membership, not aggregation by specific professional duty.

Nonetheless, the unions may find it in their own interests to take part in reforms such as these, perhaps even to lead them. In education, union power derives from success in bargaining (in collective bargaining states) or in lobbying legislators and bureaucrats and organizing voters (in those and other states). Neither scheme that I have proposed would diminish either power base. Both may even enhance teacher power by enabling faculties to deal on more equal terms with administrators (who sometimes ignore faculty groups *because* they see them only as aggregations of employees rather than as professional communities). Union representatives could continue under either scheme to function much as they now do. And teacher-leaders could assume functions that now go begging— comparing instructional styles, conducting faculty seminars on current scholarship, or even learning the disciplines of others. There is no inherent reason that professional self-regulation by teachers cannot coexist with unions.

With or without new structures, professional self-governance will require of the teacher unions one major concession—but it is one that they will likely have to make soon in any case. The unions will have to accept forms of merit pay or master teacher designations, and perhaps other performance-based compensation schemes: i.e., they will have to accept the development and application of *meaningful criteria of professional performance* by teachers and the concomitant differentiation of compensation. The unions will accommodate these changes regardless of their posture on faculty governance, simply because these changes will be made with or without union backing. The combined weight of a half dozen or so national task forces and commission reports and the efforts of many governors and legislators have made "merit pay" a movement that now runs on its own momentum.

Tactically, the unions would do well to support merit pay/master teacher initiatives in return for greater self-governance for faculties—as well as for solid commitments from political leaders to support salary scale increases in excess of the consumer price index. That is, the exchange must include both power for teachers and more nearly adequate compensation in return for acceptance of master teacher programs.

Why does merit pay matter? Faculties that take on the obligations of self-governance without acquiring also the capacity to reward excellence

risk becoming mere enforcers for administrators or boards, mere func-
tionaries doing the tasks of nonprofessional regulators. If the profession is
to control its own quality, *professional* distinctions—based on criteria of
excellence that members of the profession are uniquely qualified to formulate and apply—must be matched by distinctions of professional reward. Visible markers of excellence must exist. Moreover, if salaries are
to improve overall in an era of limited public resources, master teachers
must establish the targets toward which other teachers' salaries move.
The public and its elected officials will raise teacher salaries for excellence. Without such optimal marks, teachers' salaries will inevitably continue to lag. With them, we may expect all salaries in time to be raised as
the level of pay required to secure and hold excellent teachers rises, since
too great a disparity between normal and superior salaries will be attractive to no one.

THE TIMING OF REFORM

One can make many objections to any suggestion to deliver more power
over professional qualifications and school curricula to teachers. One can
say, for example, that the public distrusts teachers so profoundly that it
will not tolerate professional self-governance, or that the practical barriers to real reform make the effort fruitless, or indeed that the very
faculties that might gain the most by such reforms are so completely in
thrall to competing special interest groups that they cannot participate.
Each objection has some validity.

Still, the timing is right for major reforms, and not even schooling's
harshest critics propose eliminating teachers altogether. (Indeed, efforts
to make use of new technologies in teaching depend more on the teachers
than on the technologies.) Political leaders have often looked in vain for
forward-looking leaders of the profession to be their partners in the reform effort. Individual teachers have contributed in many ways. Some
organizations have also. But real leadership of the kind that can capture
imaginations and deliver solid results has been absent from the teaching
forces of most states. Collegial self-governance within faculties could do
much, I think, to foster development of the leadership that we now miss.

Perhaps it is with regard to this missing ingredient that the humanities
can hope to make their largest contribution to school reform—and also
stake their claim on the future of schooling in the nation. The sorts of
training that characterize preparation in the humanities disciplines are
conducive to certain of the skills that leaders of teachers will need. Such
leaders must be linguistically adept, well-versed in the motivations and
concerns that shape the actions of others (e.g., administrators and fellow

workers), shrewd in articulating conceptually the ways that concerns can be met, and practiced in conceiving of multiple alternatives and evaluating their several attractions. While training in the humanities surely does not force people, even teachers, to become good at these things, it can provide the resources for those who are inclined, by will or temperament or conviction of duty, to lead. Teachers of the humanities in schools and colleges have too often been inward-looking or defensive, trying to protect their own domains without trying to exercise leadership over, and assume stewardship for, the entire academic community. This is a serious mistake. If the humanities have any utility, it must lie in knowledge and skills in the areas of human relations, understanding, and concern that are manifest in, *inter alia,* the efforts of people to shape the lives of their communities—including their working communities. One would think that "professional humanists" will understand this and willingly put to work in the schools the resources of their own training and fields of devotion.

Whether or not the leadership of the schools comes from the teachers of the humanities, the remainder of this decade is ripe for the sorts of reform I have outlined. To the extent that humanists fill the need for leadership, our disciplines and their uses to a free society will flourish.

Epilogue: A School Administrator's View

Peter R. Greer

In the late 1960s, I taught in a humanities program for the "noncollege" student. Later, in a small Massachusetts school system, I served as humanities coordinator for grades seven through twelve. I became a school visitor for the National Humanities Faculty, then its associate director. From 1969 to 1974, I read hundreds of schools' descriptions of their needs and hopes for their humanities programs, and I visited dozens of these schools, from McAllen, Texas, to Anchorage, Alaska, and from Creek Reservation School, North Dakota, to Great Neck North, New York. Now I oversee the school system of a growing city.

The late 1960s and early 1970s are often recalled as the golden years for the humanities in the schools. At least, everyone talked about the humanities, or talked about something going under the name of the humanities.

"Humanities" was usually the name of a specific elective course, taught by at least two teachers. Most schools attempted to put together a course involving literature, history, art, and music. Any course with four teachers representing those four areas was considered bold and visionary. Such a course was thought first-rate if there was a double class period, scheduled back to back, with common planning periods for the teachers. These teachers were tyically college-oriented, because the texts and other materials were at about an eleventh-grade or better reading level, and it was assumed that only the "better" students were fit for these "finer" studies. The courses themselves were organized in several ways: chronological, thematic, or by cultural epoch. In the latter approach, a decade—say, the Roaring Twenties—might be closely studied through its literature, history, and other depictions or creations, depending on the expertise and enthusiasms of the contributing teachers. Regardless of the approach, they would "team teach" the course. Typically, this meant turn-teaching, with each member of the teaching team presenting a fairly independent minicourse.

The community was usually supportive. Parents wanted their children to go to college, and such courses were regarded as good preparation. The humanities teachers were normally the liveliest in the school, and their course themes were interesting and relevant: prejudice, war, suicide, freedom, civil disobedience, violence, destiny. Moreover, the students brought home good messages.

Teachers would improve their teaching of the humanities via regional and national conferences that provided virtually the only available assistance in planning, developing, and teaching general humanities courses. Neighboring colleges were not much help, as the scholars there either demanded expensive honoraria, had scant knowledge of precollege classrooms, or evinced little confidence in working with classroom teachers. Publishing companies spewed out textbooks that utilized "a humanities approach," with come-on titles such as *The Nature of Prejudice: A Humanities Approach,* but were of no real help in curriculum development.

The humanities conferences themselves were often spectacular. They were offered with the same frequency as those we now see on computers. It was common to offer a humanities conference, or session on the humanities, in conjunction with a larger meeting or convention— e.g., the Association for Supervision and Curriculum Development, American Association of School Administrators, National Council of Teachers of English, and the various humanities councils. I attended humanities conferences where weather balloons were used as movie screens for the showing of art slides from multiple slide projectors and where I could learn about teaching art in the humanities by the use of fan cards. The conference titles were themselves catchy: "Grooving with Zeus," "Fun, Freedom, and Frolic in the Humanities," "Spider's Webs and the Humanities." I could also go to a humanities conference and watch a professor slap bananas to his forehead to the tune of "Sewanee River." I could learn how the joining of dance with the study of logarithms was indeed the humanities. Most conferences demonstrated "models," but this was ineffective, for most teachers refused to take up someone else's model. To have done so would have meant that teachers had similar knowledge, similar schedules, similar support, and similar methods and materials.

Any conference that stressed academic content was on shaky ground. In Reno, Nevada, I was asked to be very brief because very few would stay for my talk on "The Importance of Content to the Humanities." In Atlanta, a session on *The Federalist Papers* drew three participants. Next door, there were over one hundred participants at a session on values clarification. "Process" rather than content, subjective feelings rather than classic knowledge: these were the objects of interest.

Two schools of thought about secondary school humanities could be found among college professors of the humanities. First, there was the group that concentrated on humans and their relationships. Before you could study the humanities, you had to understand group processes and go through sensitivity training or T-groups. This cadre typically studied "relevant" themes such as violence or racism, or tried to predict the future. Students had to voice feelings and get their thoughts out in the marketplace of ideas, whether or not the ideas had any facts to back them. Values had to be clarified, and the teacher was not to dominate the classroom. A splinter group pushed local history and folklore as humanities. Tape recorders, personal diaries, and the search for older citizens became the tools and methods of the classroom. Teachers had to be "humanistic," i.e., nice to students.

A second group of professors pressed for courses systematically presenting our Western heritage. They maintained that students should study Plato, Pericles, and Shakespeare. Pupils had to learn how to write well and how to read a text carefully and accurately. This group believed that classroom teachers had to know more about their subjects so they could lead their students in the study of important matters. College professors, it was believed, had to work closely with classroom teachers in improving the teaching of the humanities through content. This contingent of professors was seen as traditional and thus as not relevant.

Neither group of professors had much of an understanding of how actual high school humanities classes functioned or of the conditions under which teachers, students, and administrators worked. Everyone attempted to be a Johnny Appleseed of the humanities, and there were few sustained collaborations between colleges and school professionals.

During the golden years, there was little evaluation of the impact of humanities courses. It was, after all, difficult to define the humanities, and it was bad education to apply a scientific method to the humanities, since so many courses focused on affective goals rather than on content or cognition.

There were, to be sure, some humanities courses of substance and rigor. But the foregoing account represents what I understood to be the norm.

From about the mid-1970s to about 1982, the humanities offered a dramatic decline in the schools. The cycle of interest seemed to have run its course. There were still proponents of the humanities in classrooms, and there remained leaders who were enthusiastic about the teaching of the humanities, but conditions had generally changed. Schools were pinched for money. Hence, schedules were not as flexible, classes were larger, textbook budgets were tighter, and electives were reduced. Often the community was also more critical of the public schools and more traditional in its educational values. What money was obtained from the property tax was to be used for "basic" courses, special education, bilingual education, computer education, and vocational education. In some enlightened schools, there was also "gifted education." But almost everywhere, the focus was on "skills" and methods or "process." Everyone was talking about mastery learning, minimal competency testing, and time-on-task. The school's image had to be improved. The humanities were seen as nonutilitarian fluff. They made for poor public relations.

The humanities grew dormant in many schools but did not die. Now sentiment seems to be changing, once again; the cycle has gone through another turn, and humanists are coming out of hibernation. Interest in the humanities is reviving, but it is different from before. It is an interest, now, in more substantive courses containing solid information and structured patterns of thinking.

What is the state of the humanities in the schools now, and what are the problems and prospects facing advocates of the humanities? The two conferences from which this book emerged brought together many of the staunchest advocates of secondary school humanities programs in the country. I attended both, and I think the study of these conferences says much about where the humanities stand today.

The emphasis in Atlanta and Denver was indeed on the centrality of subject matter and the teacher's ability to stand before his class without "peddling from an empty wagon." Some speakers even dared to suggest a core curriculum for the humanities, including exemplary texts. Individual subjects, namely history, literature, and foreign languages, were closely scrutinized; rather than focusing on interdisciplinary aspects of the humanities, the integrity of the individual disciplines was stressed. "Humanities," it was emphasized, is a collective term comprising the disciplines, not the name of a separate or contrived entity: Long-term collaborations between universities and high schools were also stressed rather than brief "cameo appearances" in the schools by visiting scholars.

Several issues of concern to participants, issues that will influence the humanities agenda for years to come, were manifest at the conferences. A working definition of the humanities was not addressed. There were few female and minority presenters, and hardly any minority group members had applied to attend. This raised questions of how many minorities see the humanities as important elements of education. There was the lingering question of whether the humanities are only for especially able students. Questions were also raised as to the place of the non-Western world in the humanities education of America's students. There was still an uneasy relationship between the high school teachers, teacher educators, and humanities scholars. Of particular note was the contention by many practitioners that advice from professors may be vitiated by lack of evident understanding of how high schools operate. Worse, teachers felt that the schools were again under attack by some professors who visit a few schools, look for evidence of bad teaching, and report their findings with an "I told you so" attitude.

The Vanderbilt conferences raised other timely issues as well. High standards and rigorous requirements were urged. The development of master teacher programs and their significance for the humanities were discussed, and the establishment of networks of humanities teachers was proposed. Complicated questions about the humanities and bilingual education were debated. The need for teaching all our students the interrelatedness of ideas was reinforced. A common—indeed, ubiquitous—query was how teachers of the humanities can show that the humanities are valuable to the society and are important to students' lives. The importance of the humanities, in light of the reports of the National Commission on Excellence in Education and other education task forces, was closely examined. Questions of relevance versus rigor, standardization of curriculum versus flexibility, and indoctrination versus relativism in teaching values were studied. Many participants were outraged by stories of principals who placed needless obstacles in front of teachers of the humanities: there was broad agreement that more principals needed to take part in more conferences on the humanities.

Overall, these two conferences represented positive efforts by responsible educators engaged in the humanities to work out directions for reform. But they were not isolated events, comets flashing across an otherwise dark sky. Besides conferences of this sort, other recent developments give evidence of a quickening in the humanities. For one thing, there are highly regarded people talking and writing about the importance of the humanities. Many of these people have the attention of high school teachers, college professors, and foundations. These people generally know of each other's work, sustain each other, influence their own colleagues, enjoy excellent reputations among the nation's teachers and, together, are beginning to make a difference. If it weren't for the constant utterances, publications, publicity, and persistence of these educators, the humanities would be in much deeper trouble in the 1980s.

But these are still individuals. Not one major national organization— e.g., the American Association of School Administrators, the National Association of Secondary School Principals, the National Council of Teachers of English, the National Council of Social Studies, or college-based organizations—is today speaking forcefully and sensibly on behalf of the humanities. Few foundations are funding school-based humanities projects—or if they are, it is the best-kept secret in American education. Most colleges and universities still have not made any determined attempts to work closely with schools that want to improve their teaching of the humanities. For their part, the schools have not made determined attempts to identify willing professors or to bring about closer relationships with neighboring universities. One force tending to bind these two groups is that the National Endowment for the Humanities looks more favorably on applications that show evidence of attempts at higher education/school collaboration. NEH is a small federal agency, but it is uncommonly well led at present, and by action and example it can prod, cajole, guide, and legitimize important reform efforts.

Meanwhile, most schools are still suffering from severe image problems as a result of popular pressures that have led to competency tests, greater emphasis on "the basics," vocational education, and the like. Resources barely cover courses mandated by law and public pressure. If any money is left over, it goes for computers and building maintenance. In-service training and staff development monies for humanities teachers are exceedingly hard to come by. Since many administrators and teachers still view the humanities as something interdisciplinary and team-taught, courses in the humanities appear expensive and complicated. Many superintendents hire new teachers on the basis of ability to bring about good discipline in the classroom. "Give me a teacher who has teaching skills, good discipline, and the ability to supervise extracurricular activities— those are more important than subject matter" is a common attitude found among administrators.

Overworked teachers whose principals and superintendents are unsympathetic to (or even ignorant of) the humanities cannot devote attention to learning more about their subjects until summer, if then. After-school time and in-service days are not conducive to learning or attractive to teachers. Favorite one-day in-service topics for teachers are "School Climate," "Tension and Burn Out," "Teaching Reading," "Mastery Learning," "Child Abuse," "Time on Task," "Affective Learning," "Alternative Education," and something about computers or discipline. You can't ask teachers to study serious new texts in one-day stints. Staff development in the humanities is most effective when designed and conducted by teachers and administrators working together over an extended period of time, including sustained study of texts that are relevant to the issues at hand. But such in-service programs are rare.

The present context for the teaching of the humanities then, includes both promising developments, represented in part by the people at the Educational Excellence Network conferences, and debilitating reality in much of the education community. This situation calls for considerable nerve on the part of educators and the public if the humanities are to become healthy and vigorous in our nation's schools; but it makes the display of such nerve reasonable, or at least not foolhardy.

Much of the responsibility properly rests with schools administrators, who must have the nerve—and acquire whatever knowledge is needed to exercise it competently—to insist on high-quality humanities programs. Recent research persuasively demonstrates the key role that administrators' instructional leadership plays in the quality of a school. This leadership is crucial to effective humanities programs. What, exactly, do school administrators and policymakers—including superintendents, board members, principals, district directors and coordinators, and sundry lieutenants and assistants—need to do? The possibilities are vast, limited only by the scope of one's imagination and the extent of one's energies. I will mention just a few.

To begin, we must insist that "the humanities" are part of the educational birthright of all students and then spend time on the difficult task of devising ways to teach all students eventually the same core curriculum. Naturally this will require us to enlist qualified and willing teachers who are well-versed in their disciplines. The unsatisfactory alternative—if we have those who prize method over content—is the hiring of teachers who may look like pedagogical sharpshooters but who regularly end up firing blanks in the classroom.

Further, we should demand that our professional organizations devote serious time and attention to the humanities. Key officials in such groups as the National School Boards Association, American Association of School Administrators, National Association of Secondary School Principals, and Association for Supervision and Curriculum Development, must be pressed into the efforts to strengthen humanities programs. These well-placed advocates can bring the considerable prestige and resources of their organizations to the effort of providing school administrators with guidance. Actual reform depends finally upon "grassroots" administrators, of course; but the national organizations can do much either to facilitate or impede the efforts of local "movers and shakers." Hence, if these organizations are not moved by their own leadership, they must hear from their membership that more attention needs to be given to issues in the humanities.

School board members, for example, can fairly insist that some sessions of National School Board Association conferences be devoted to explanations of issues in the teaching and content of the humanities disciplines. Association publications should also provide space for thoughtful expositions of these issues. School board members would then be able to discuss intelligently the teaching of the humanities in their respective school systems. Since school boards set school policy, it is crucial that their members be capable of talking knowledgeably with superintendents and their staffs about the standards for selecting new teachers, the scope and sequences of the humanities disciplines individually and collectively, and the staff development plans that have impact on the humanities. Naturally, it is important that the school board members develop their own criteria and information with the help of a "disinterested party" such as their own national association, not from the very people who are responsible for the programs under scrutiny.

Superintendents and their designees also should look for and take advantage of opportunities to show support for the humanities in specific, concrete ways. Each administrator can team-teach a course once a week, for instance. This may mean dusting off some old college notes, perhaps spending some Saturdays at the public library, maybe even some formal study at a nearby college, but what a strong and clear signal this would be to the teaching staff!

Administrators can develop a fund for "internal sabbaticals" for humanities teachers (and, of course, others as well), which would pay for substitute teachers, perhaps some study materials, and incidental expenses (such as travel to the nearest research library) for teachers who are given release time simply to learn more about their fields. Superintendents could insure that humanities teachers make use of this fund by giving them professional credit only for study in the humanities disciplines, not for "Audio-Visual Methods" or "Guidance and Counseling." I note that in my own school district, teachers have asked that new incentives and rewards take the form of time and resources to study and discuss exemplary texts rather than what today is widely known as "merit pay."

If only we would look, we can find countless small ways to demonstrate our support for better humanities teaching. We can watch for—and circulate—notices of important conferences and new publications. We can encourage our principals and staff members, as well as our teachers, to attend conferences on the humanities and to share what they learn there.

We can also ask hard questions: Do our history courses include intellectual, cultural, and social history? Do they pay attention to the historical development and cultural significance of art and music? If not, what is needed to bring these into the social studies? Do we have people on our faculty who are cultivating serious intellectual relationships with the local college, museum, or library? How can we make use of such contacts to enrich our schools? What sorts of extracurricular guidance do our teachers give students who are especially interested in the humanities? Do our English classes read good literature, or are they mired in textbooks, contrived "readers" and magazines? When we ask questions, we must naturally be prepared to do something with the answers. It may take both nerve and money to do so. But superintendents (and other administrators) who want to support the humanities do not have to look far to see how to start.

Presently, there is far too little instructional leadership offered by administrators at all levels. School boards who hire, and administrators who work, on the basis of "management by objectives," single-minded budget-consciousness, and other purely managerial concerns offer little assistance to the humanities. Administrators should carry on active intellectual lives of their own, intellectual lives that give them appreciation for and competence to lead in the humanities. But we do not do this. I am coming to fear that we administrators are losing the habit of thought.

Education is an enterprise of the intellect and the spirit. But we have forgotten our mission and are acting like monks in a monastery who are fighting over who is responsible for filling the holy water font. We seldom take the time to discuss instructional matters, in the humanities or elsewhere, that are at the heart of any serious educational system. We hire administrators primarily on the basis of management style and ability to discipline and schedule—rather than on the basis of leadership, intelligence, and vision. We hire teachers on the basis of questions related to methods and discipline, rather than on how competent one is in his field. We wait for teachers to propose and then to develop humanities courses, rather than ourselves becoming leaders, actively encouraging and supporting such courses and their teachers.

We pay only lip service to the principle of content-rich staff development by looking the other way when frivolous sessions are held. We make believe we offer the humanities to all students since all are obliged to attend English and social studies classes. We lie down during contract-negotiating sessions and do not even attempt to identify ways to reward teachers who engage in serious study of their disciplines and thus enrich their teaching. Though we seldom take the initiative, neither do we relinquish our authority and ask teachers to suggest ways by which we could strengthen the humanities throughout the system and across the curriculum. Why don't we do this? Why don't we carve out time each month to re-establish the habit of thought in instructional matters? Why don't we dedicate staff meetings and faculty meetings to the content of education rather than its trappings and its mechanics?

Instead, we order paperbacks with the word "humanities" in their titles, we attend a few conferences, we scan the occasional article in a professional journal, we apply (more likely, allow others to apply) for a few grants—and then we wonder why students leave our schools with well-developed career plans but baffled by or heedless of timely and timeless issues, good books, and the quality of their inner lives. We act as if we were engaging in regular practice at the humanities rifle range; but most of the time *we are firing blanks instead of bullets, and we know it.*

Parents, politicians, and business leaders are ready for reform of our schools. Indeed, they are growing ever more insistent. The colleges to which we send many graduates are demanding improvement as well. A historic opportunity is at hand to strengthen public education across the United States. New interest in solid humanities teaching can be found in much of the education community. If, in this context, we fail to improve our high school humanities programs, a good deal of the responsibility will belong to school administrators. We need some help, to be sure, from those who write the laws, appropriate the funds, and influence public opinion—who establish the contexts within which we work. No doubt we would benefit from more help than we will get. But to blame external forces for the shortcomings of our schools, or to wait for others to rectify those shortcomings, is both irresponsible and unwarranted, as well as a wasted opportunity of truly enormous proportions. As administrators, we wield far more influence over the content and quality of our school programs than most people realize—more, indeed, than most of us are comfortable acknowledging. Hence there is no need to lose this opportunity and no satisfactory excuse for failure. What we can do to effect needed reforms in our schools is clear. The only serious question is whether we have the nerve to do it.

Conclusions and Recommendations: High Expectations and Disciplined Effort

Chester E. Finn, Jr.
and Diane Ravitch

> Plenty of people will try to give the masses, as they call them, an intellectual food prepared and adapted in the way they think proper for the actual condition of the masses. . . . Plenty of people will try to indoctrinate the masses with the set of ideas and judgments constituting the creed of their own profession or party. . . . Culture works differently. . . . It seeks to do away with classes; to make the best that has been thought and known in the world current everywhere; to make all men live in an atmosphere of sweetness and light, where they may use ideas, as it uses them itself, freely—nourished, and not bound by them.
>
> —Matthew Arnold, *Culture and Anarchy*

Between the ages of about fifteen and eighteen, most Americans partake of "high school" or "secondary" education. As the terms themselves imply, this means that what one learns in grades nine through twelve (or ten through twelve) is qualitatively different from what one has learned earlier. It presupposes that the student has already acquired a "primary" or "elementary" education and is therefore ready to undertake more advanced study, leading to more sophisticated intellectual skills, deeper

237

understanding, and a larger body of more complex knowledge. For many people, this leads on to the yet more advanced study encountered in college, perhaps even graduate school. But for others, whatever is learned in high school constitutes the end of formal education. Hence, as William Bennett observes in the Introduction, high school is the last opportunity we have to influence the education of *all* Americans.

This book is fundamentally an effort to influence the parts of secondary education known collectively as "the humanities." As is by now clear, we—together with most of the contributing authors, conference participants, and the leadership of the National Endowment itself—are profoundly dissatisfied with the quality of teaching and learning in the humanities to be found in most of American secondary education. While saluting the superb programs, stalwart teachers and remarkable schools that we have here and there encountered, we must nevertheless echo and underscore, with respect to the humanities, the dire words that the National Commission on Excellence in Education used to characterize the educational system as a whole: "We have, in effect, been committing an act of unthinking, unilateral educational disarmament. Our society and its educational institutions seem to have lost sight of the basic purposes of schooling, and of the high expectations and disciplined effort needed to attain them."[1]

The problems that beset high school humanities are in ways more serious than even the Commission's apocalyptic language would suggest. They have not yet seized the nation's attention as has the "crisis" in mathematics and science. They are not widely understood to be intimately related to the economic vitality, technological prowess, or strategic defense of the United States. They do not tap the veins of utilitarianism that constitute the circulatory system of much education policymaking. And, as problems, they are partly self-induced, the unintended consequence of our laudable determination to ensure that all youngsters acquire "the basics" before finishing school.

Thus before even suggesting correctives to some of the specific failings of high school humanities teaching today, it is necessary to examine three general conditions that tend to dissipate interest in them, to divert attention from them, and to mask the gravity of the situation.

First, for many students and schools, "primary" education now lasts well into the "high school" years. The distinction between elementary and secondary education has simply blurred. We do not contend that there can be or should be an abrupt intellectual transition from the one to the other. On the contrary, cognitive skills should develop throughout the educational process, even as the understanding of the humanities does. They are essentially interdependent. But when this interdependence is not well understood, *and* when policymakers dwell on mastery of "basic skills" as the only demanding intellectual standard that youngsters must meet, *and* when many such youngsters reach ninth or tenth grade without the level of mastery they should have attained in sixth or seventh grade, then there is little hope of squeezing enough time out of the high school day—or enough intellectual energy out of the student—to teach and learn the humanities at the level of sophistication appropriate to a secondary education. Even if there were, the student would lack a solid foundation of knowledge and skills on which to build. Simply stated, "high school humanities" (or biology, or mathematics, or art) is a meaningless concept if young people entering the high schools do not bring with them a *bona fide* elementary education.

Second, the humanities at every level fall victim to the vocational fallacy so widespread in American education: the assumption that if knowledge or skills have no self-evident usefulness in the workplace, acquiring them is unimportant. Basic skills have obvious uses, if only to fill out a job application, to read the directions for one's lathe, or to add up the bill before handing it to one's customers. Explicitly "vocational" courses have even clearer uses, for they openly seek to impart the lore and the techniques of particular trades and crafts. Science and math classes may be less obviously tied to earning a living, but many education policymakers, students, and parents are (in our view legitimately) convinced that such courses assist the nation to strengthen its scientific and technological endeavors while equipping individuals with credentials to participate in them. Less justifiably, a number of elective courses in seemingly marginal fields—family life, personal economics, even driver education—stake their claims to the attention of students and to the resources of schools on the assertion that those who take them will be better prepared for life in the "real world." But how is one to justify literature, history, or foreign language study? We shall argue presently that the humanities, too, are profoundly "useful" to the society and to the individual, but we acknowledge now that the utilitarian calculus we employ is more subtle, less self-evident.

Third, partly because their "usefulness" is not widely acknowledged, the humanities also suffer from an aura of elitism, dilettantism, even preciousness that can lead those persons who care for them to be wary of saying so in public and those persons with other priorities to dismiss the humanities as cultural playthings of the upper classes. This condition takes on special salience in the eyes of some minority group members and women, who are apt to decry the humanities as intellectual weapons brandished by upper-middle-class white males to intimidate other members of a pluralistic society.

Setting aside for the moment the important task of characterizing the "culture" that we believe can and should be transmitted—and that is itself transformed through the transmission—we turn to the allegation of elitism. For this is indeed perverse and in its perversity can be self-realizing. In every society we can name, apart from the truly barbarian, elites have always understood that to be master of one's own affairs and the affairs of others requires a rigorous education in the humanities. While knowledge of literature, history, and poetry and the command of languages may not substitute for brute force or tribal loyalty, it is not coincidental that determined members of the "ruling class" have consistently seized every opportunity for their children to acquire such knowledge. It is that knowledge and its associated intellectual skills that have enabled them and their descendants to rule, though not, we concede, with predictable humanity or justice. Ideas, words, information, the capacity to mold beliefs and values, the power of communication, the ability to understand the hopes and fears of others well enough to make use of them, the knowledge that enables one either to repeat history or to avoid such repetition as it suits one's interests—no shrewd ruler would allow his own children to trade these treasures for basic literacy or even for an understanding of biochemistry.

And through most of human history, whatever the form of a society's government or the nature of its social structure, only the progeny of elites *could* acquire more than basic skills and elementary knowledge. Until the dawn of the twentieth century in the industrial nations—and still today, in much of the rest of the world—secondary education was itself a possession of the upper classes. Whether one views this exclusivity strictly in economic terms—the children of the peasants could not afford to do other than scrabble for a living in the fields, streets, and sweatshops—or as the result of deliberate political decisions, the fact is that opportunities to acquire a serious education in literature, history, and languages have largely been confined to the children of the very classes of society that most valued them as guarantors of their own secure positions.

What the United States—and a few other prosperous liberal democracies—set out to do through its educational arrangements was to make these prized intellectual possessions available to everyone. We were so bold as to suppose that our foremost educational mission was to provide for every young person access to a complete and high-quality program of schooling. In Robert Maynard Hutchins's durable epigram, "The best education for the best is the best education for all."[2] Or, as Horace Mann put it earlier, "Education is the gateway to equality."[3]

As a society, we have understood that every citizen must have the education that is necessary for him to be free, to choose wisely for himself how to live responsibly and well. Though we have occasionally slipped into the false (if, for the educator, beguiling) supposition that years of schooling alone would bring virtue and benevolence, for the better part of two centuries we have at least recognized that ignorance brings nothing of value to anyone, rich or poor, black or white. Hutchins, Mann, Dewey, and Jefferson would all have dismissed as arrant nonsense the suggestion that the subjects we know as "the humanities" were suited only to the education of elites. In their day more than we perhaps now realize, the humanities were the essence of all education above the level of basic literacy; and common wisdom recognized that it was by acquiring such an education that the citizens of a democracy could best govern themselves, that the children of the poor might become members of the upper classes, and that the members of a free society could thereby become truly equal.

The spread of universal secondary education made realization of that dream possible, and those who today would deny the humanities as part of the educational birthright of every American are denying the very dream of a free and just society for all. For it is perfectly clear that contemporary American elites—whether they be defined in economic, cultural, social, or intellectual terms—are not about to deny their own children a secondary (and, generally, postsecondary) education that includes the best that the humanities can offer, even if they must seek out private schools, summer schools, tutors, or exclusive suburbs in order to provide it. Though one might fault certain aspects of the education that elites obtain for their children, there can be little doubt either that they are going to continue obtaining it or that it is going to continue to include serious study of the humanities. The important question for education policymakers—and for those spokesmen, lobbyists, and interest groups that seek to influence them—is whether the regular public schools attended by the vast majority of American youngsters are going to allow the humanities to be scorned and dismissed on the absurd ground that they are elitist, thereby ensuring that they again become the property only of those already most aware of their value and their power.

Well taught and well learned, the humanities are the strongest democratizing force that formal education can muster. "A free society," the Rockefeller Commission observed, "depends on citizens who are broadly educated. The humanities form a bridge between functional literacy and the higher intellectual and civic purposes of learning."[4] They liberate the mind, they inform the citizen, they hone the intellect, they supply criteria by which assertions and claims can be judged, and they train the analytic skills that give such judgments power. It is no surprise that totalitarian societies that recognize—and fear—the power of the liberated intellect pay such meticulous attention to the curriculum and pedagogy of humanities teaching in their schools. Young people who understand trigonometry, physical chemistry, civil engineering, or computer programming pose no imminent challenge to the regime; but those who have read the works of Aristotle, Epictetus, Erasmus, Voltaire,

Locke, Hobbes, Marx, Rousseau, Orwell, Zola, Gibbon, Dostoevsky, Kafka, Faulkner, Solzhenitsyn, Whitehead, and others of their ilk, under the guidance of teachers able to elucidate their messages about the proper ordering of a society and the relationship between man and the state, and who have thereby glimpsed the power of ideas and the ability of the trained intellect to sway the course of history—such people inevitably threaten any apparatus that would control them.

It is through their ability to liberate the individual, to democratize the society, and to toughen the intellect that the humanities also refute the allegation that they are not "useful." To be sure, the relationship between knowledge of the humanities and immediate employability is often indirect. Though we have yet to meet a lawyer, journalist, or public relations expert whose daily work does not draw upon the knowledge and intellectual skills we ascribe to the humanities, the lasting worth of the humanities is generally to be found at least one or two removes from the workplace itself. (By and large, that is true for math and science as well. Relatively few employment opportunities in modern "high tech" industries draw directly on one's knowledge of calculus, physics, or biology.) Does one understand the motivations and values that drive the enterprise in which one works? Does one grasp the cultural and attitudinal makeup of one's fellow workers, and possess the requisite blend of tolerance, appreciation, and ethical standards to work successfully alongside them? Can one communicate effectively with superiors, peers, and subordinates, as well as with the diverse "publics" that intersect one's work? Does one go home at night to recreational, cultural, intellectual, and civic pursuits that yield refreshment, renewal, and fulfillment, or are one's private horizons so limited as to produce bitterness, frustration, and ennui that inevitably blight one's daily work and long-term career? Does one see the linkages between one's own vocation and the complex modern economy of which it is a part?

Such considerations may not matter greatly to the worker who has learned to "shut off his mind" during his eight-hour shift in the office or assembly line, who regards his work as just a job rather than part of a career, and who feigns indifference to the larger affairs of his employer, his occupation, or his nation's economy. But even the most bored, cynical, and discouraged of workers is apt to have a strong desire for his own children (nieces, nephews, whatever) to embark upon careers with wider horizons, perhaps with greater status, surely with higher income. The familiar American determination to make a better life for one's children— the cumulative realization of which, in millions of individual cases, defines an open society in which "upward mobility" is authentic—remains vibrant, as does the understanding among people who themselves may not be highly lettered that an education of quality remains a necessary, if not always a sufficient, element of such betterment.

The humanities, then, can mount strong defenses against the charges of elitism and impracticality. But the public and private benefits they confer are not to be measured only in utilitarian or egalitarian terms. Their value must be tallied on other balance sheets as well.

We do not claim that study of the humanities in and of itself builds character, virtue, or good citizenship. That is too heavy a burden to lay on formal education.[5] The responsibility for nurturing those qualities in young people is shared by many institutions, including the family, the church, and the community, and is powerfully influenced by the ways the society itself works and the examples that it sets. The school is but a supplementary resource, yet it is a distinctively important one, for among the major nurturing institutions with which all young people have sustained contact, it is the most susceptible to design and control through the mechanisms of public policy. The content that the school sets out to teach, the ways it organizes itself for that purpose, and the people it selects to teach in it are all choices that need to be made with utmost care by a society that wants to maximize the prospects that its members will use knowledge for good rather than evil. The decisions we make about formal education comprise the surest mechanisms within the grasp of public policy and public institutions to encourage youngsters to grow in wisdom and virtue.

To study the humanities is to learn about the uses of ideas and language and about the ways in which these move human beings. It gives us the opportunity to reflect on what is moral and what is ethical. No one can study history or literature without a sense of what is good and bad, of what is right and wrong, and, in the very act of studying, that sense is deepened, tested, and refined. Knowledge of the humanities cannot guarantee that one will become wise, ethical, or moral, but it engages one in serious consideration of what it *means* to be wise, ethical, and moral. At least since the time of Aristotle, the paramount questions that everyone strives to answer are versions of the central issues posed in studying the humanities: What is a good person? What is the good society? Is it possible to be a good person in a bad society? How does one lead a moral life? What does it mean to be virtuous?

Study of the humanities conflicts not at all with the acquisition of cognitive skills. These, after all, are the keys that permit one to unlock the treasure chests of knowledge. Nor can we find any contradiction between the benefits we ascribe to the humanities and those that flow from the study of science. Education is not a "zero-sum game." Studying the sciences teaches one to exercise reason, to base conclusions on evidence, and consciously to weigh various alternatives. The student of the sciences learns—because this is embedded in the culture of science—that truth and honesty are bedrock values and that conflicting interpretations must be heard and weighed on the scale of those values. He learns, as the student of the humanities may not, that some statements are absolutely true, others entirely false, and that the choices he must make will oblige him to understand and apply criteria that distinguish the one kind from the other.

But if the sciences teach one what it is to understand and follow certain rules by which the universe is governed and by which some knowledge is ordered, the humanities teach one about freedom and wisdom. That these are linked by knowledge was understood by Alfred North Whitehead, who wrote that "the only avenue towards wisdom is by freedom in the presence of knowledge. But the only avenue towards knowledge is by discipline in the acquirement of ordered fact. Freedom and discipline are the two essentials of education. . . ."[6]

Consider, also, John Dewey on freedom:

Impulses and desires that are not ordered by intelligence are under the control of accidental circumstances. It may be a loss rather than a gain to escape from the control of another person only to find one's conduct dictated by immediate whim and caprice; that is, at the mercy of impulses into whose formation intelligent judgment has not entered. A person whose conduct is controlled in this way has at most only the illusion of freedom. Actually, he is directed by forces over which he has no command.[7]

And again Hutchins:

What is needed for free minds is discipline, discipline which forms the habits which enable the mind to operate well. . . . To determine the good and the order of goods is the prime object of all moral and political education. We cannot hope that one who has never confronted these issues can be either a good citizen or a good man. . . . An educational system which does not make these questions the center of its attention is not an educational system at all. It is a large-scale housing venture. It may be effective in keeping young people out of worse places until they can go to work. It cannot contribute to the growth of free minds.[8]

These are lofty statements, and it is their loft—so easily mistaken for airiness and then for emptiness—that often gives treatises about the role of education in general and the humanities in particular a vague and ephemeral quality and makes them difficult for policymakers to grapple with. So knowledge, you say, is its own end, and the humanities are important branches of knowledge. But—asks the superintendent or school board member—what does that have to do with the ninth-grade English curriculum, with the choice of textbooks for the world history course, with the difficult decision we must make about whether to commit scarce resources to more of those "in-service education" programs for teachers, or with the interminable argument over which students (if any) should be obliged to study foreign languages and for how long? I can agree with your general comments, says the university professor, but what bearing have they on my own research into the metaphors of Yeats, the theology of Catullus or the socioeconomic tensions that foreshadowed the Franco-Prussian War? I don't agree with much that you say, adds the director of teacher training at the college of education, for you pay too little attention to the "affective" domain and to adolescent socialization, but even if I did I would find it hard to see much relevance to my own institution's problems with conforming our own curriculum to the new statewide teacher certification requirements, or with recruiting students smart enough to get a passing score on the National Teachers Examination.

Among the many lessons we learned at the two national conferences held in conjunction with this project is that even those educators and policymakers who share our respect for the humanities, who agree that the humanities are not now as well taught in the nation's high schools as they should be, and who understand why it is important that they be better taught—even such sympathetic souls have a greater hunger for specific advice than for high-flown exhortation. So we turn now to a dozen of what we judge to be the most important conclusions and recommendations arising from this project and from our own reflections. Many of these echo—sometimes in different forms—the ideas and suggestions found elsewhere in this volume. Some are not to be directly encountered in the other chapters, but are assumed or implied by the authors. A few diverge from the views of our colleagues, for while we have felt obliged as editors to ensure a degree of comprehensiveness and topical synchronization in the book as a whole, we were not so bold or foolish as to expect that everyone would agree about everything.

1. The central problems of high school humanities teaching today arise from uncertain convictions, confused ideas, and irresolute standards, not from insufficient knowledge, weak techniques, or inadequate resources. That is not to say that every current teacher knows his subject thoroughly, that every lesson is a triumph of intellectual showmanship, or that every school is well supplied with books and materials, for none of those statements is correct. But even if we could wave a wand to make them true—something we would greatly relish—the most vexing doubts and anxieties that beset the humanities would remain. They derive, we think, from the general "sense of lost authority," to borrow Joseph Adelson's phrase, that settled over American education during the past quar-

ter century. "The weakened authority of teachers and principals," Adelson writes, "led to a weakening of academic demands. . . . A demoralization often took hold which diminished the will to set and abide by high expectations. During the late 1960's a sense of impotence overcame many of those managing and teaching in the schools, producing in turn an inanition of the purpose necessary for sustained academic effort."[9]

While manifestly not confined to the humanities, this "inanition of purpose" was particularly severe in English, history, and foreign language study. Not only did they have few self-evident "uses" and lack powerful external constituencies, but they also dealt—as it is in their nature to deal—with many of the most volatile, divisive, and intractable issues of our time. Should values be taught, and if so, whose? Are we the possessors of a single shared culture to be transmitted from one generation to the next, or are we a veritable United Nations of disparate traditions, argots, heroes, and mores, each demanding that "its own humanities" be transmitted? Have we a single conception of morality and code of ethical conduct that every young person should absorb, or is each to invent his own? Are we a nation with a single language of discourse, or should every group and individual be encouraged to make use of whatever tongue suits them?

Such questions do not admit of simple answers, and it is perhaps not surprising that if the nation as a whole could not answer them the ensuing confusion and conflict would permeate those quarters of the educational system charged with translating those nonexistent answers into curricula, standards and lesson plans. The result, predictably, was indeed a sense of "lost authority" among those who set and carry out educational policy. But if blame is to be meted out, it would be wrong to apportion too much of it to high school educators themselves, for this unhappy responsibility must be shared by myriad self-absorbed interest groups, by heedless employers, by covetous professional organizations, inattentive media, careless parents, and short-sighted public officials, by university faculties whose own weakening authority was trumped by enrollment exigencies, and by commentators and ideologues who did their best to keep any consensus from forming.

These problems have not yet been solved, nor has any sure consensus formed and, notwithstanding the crescent national interest in educational quality, it is clear to us that the uncertainties entangling high school humanities teaching have deep roots and stubborn tendrils. Indeed, it is clearer now than when we commenced our inquiry that many of the assumptions we made, and that we supposed virtually everyone else shared, about the nature, content, and worth of humanities study in the high schools are themselves still matters of intense controversy.[10] We cannot wish such controversy away, nor claim consensus where none exists. But we can at least state the problem clearly, and thus perhaps dissuade the reader from supposing that more knowledge, sounder technique, or greater resources alone will solve it.

2. The proposition that everyone should acquire the knowledge, insights, and intellectual skills that the humanities can impart is a profoundly liberal idea, necessary for a free society and a democratic polity, not an elitist doctrine or retrograde impulse. But it is liberal only so long as it is understood that the humanities embody knowledge, ideas, ways of thinking, and forms of communication that do not vary with the extrinsic traits of those learning them. It is the shared "human-ness" of all persons that gives meaning to "the humanities," which concern what people have in common with each other—and do not have in common with sea lions, magpies, or tarantulas. Conceding that the specific content of secondary school humanities courses in the United States—the books that are read, the language that is written, the history that is learned—will not be exactly the same as the substance of analogous courses in Kenya, Uruguay, or Taiwan—that the content, in other words, is affected by the cultural inheritance of the society in which the courses are given—the reasons for teaching such courses do not vary at all. Moreover, while there will be some variety in the texts and techniques of individual teachers, schools, and school systems across the United States, the durable lessons of all such courses—what Harry Broudy terms the "associative" and "interpretive" uses of the humanities—will not vary in any important respects and *ought not* vary.

For such lessons both *acknowledge* that, as human beings resident in the same country, we have much in common with each other, and *extend* those commonalities. Shakespeare speaks to Richard Rodriguez, the child of recent immigrants from Mexico, as loudly and clearly as to the descendant of seventeenth-century Puritans, and in so doing he brings them closer together. The nomadic life of the ancient Hebrews as recounted in the book of Exodus has few obvious similarities to the lives of the Polish factory worker near Chicago or of the black accountant in Atlanta, yet the Old Testament holds lessons—and reverence—for both, and thereby brings them closer together. The ideas and controversies that moved the Founding Fathers to compose the Constitution as they did took place long before the ancestors of most Americans even reached these shores, yet the reasoning set forth in *The Federalist Papers* has immeasurable implications for all 220 million of us.

Some people disagree. They insist instead that what one learns, and should learn, from the humanities will differ according to one's race, ethnicity, gender, political preference, or social class. But while noting this disagreement, we reject it as perversely—because unintentionally—

antidemocratic and essentially confining rather than liberating. If the desirable attributes of character and citizenship vary with the color of one's skin, the creed of one's church, the wealth of one's parents, or the birthplace of one's great-grandparents, then the humanities may as well not be taught at all, for the concept has been drained of its essential meaning.

3. Properly defined and correctly taught, the humanities necessarily treat with values. We acknowledge that the word "values" is itself fraught with controversy, the more so when applied to public education, and we cannot still the battles that rage about it. But even a moment's reflection makes clear that these conflicts are both noisier than they need to be and less profound than many suppose. They are generally posed as an irreconcilable choice between opposite extremes: on the one hand, a hypothetical world in which the only values are those that an individual devises for himself and, on the other, a single set of all-encompassing beliefs that should determine every action and shape every idea of all persons. The former is anarchic, the latter totalitarian, and we are persuaded that practically no one would willingly select either for himself, his children, or his fellow men.

The schools necessarily and inevitably impart values, beginning with the values of knowledge, of refined intellect, of certain cognitive skills. Their very structure presupposes other values in the ways that persons behave toward one another in an institutional setting that has hierarchies of status and authority. As agencies of organized society, schools are obliged to reject certain forms of behavior—murder, dishonesty, plagiarism, wanton violence—and thus to condemn whatever values would condone such behaviors. All this is taken for granted by practically everyone, and those few who disagree generally go to great pains to extricate themselves or their children from the schools.

The "values" that we observe to be held by most people, and already embodied in the schools themselves are the values that the humanities address. More difficult issues arise in connection with what may more precisely be termed "ideologies" than "values." People do disagree with one another about the merits of various political and economic arrangements, about the ways nations should treat other nations, about the proper level of common provision in a society, about the desirable distribution of sundry resources, about the nature of the family and the codes of behavior that should govern sexual relationships. People even disagree with one another about the extent to which such issues are legitimate subjects for disagreement!

The schools do not escape such quarrels, and the public schools cannot expect to, for in being "public" they seek to embody a public consensus, that means that in domains where no consensus exists they are inevitably whipsawed by the adherents of rival ideologies. But even here the humanities can help, if only because those learned in the humanities are mindful of values that transcend particular ideologies, are knowledgeable of the past and the eternal and thus perhaps less easily swayed by the arguments of the present, and are possessed of an array of intellectual skills that enable them to see beneath the surface of "viewpoints," to find parallels and commonalities where some see only differences, and to engage in reasoned discourse even with those who at first glance seem to be speaking in other tongues or from alien perspectives. The humanities, in this sense, are anchors for schools—and indeed for societies—otherwise buffeted by the winds of ideology and the tides of self-interest, but they are effective anchors only insofar as we recognize that the weight that gives them stability is the weight of values acquired in centuries of searching after truth.

Those values function as criteria by which individuals—and societies—can weigh alternatives and make choices. Hence teaching the humanities means preparing people to make important choices with the prior understanding that not all of the options are equally sound. "The crucial error," Hutchins wrote, "is that of holding that nothing is any more important than anything else, that there can be no order of goods and no order in the intellectual realm. There is nothing central and nothing peripheral, nothing primary and nothing secondary, nothing basic and nothing superficial. The course of study goes to pieces because there is nothing to hold it together. Triviality, mediocrity, and vocationalism take over because we have no standard by which to judge them."[11]

The humanities can supply the missing standard, but for the teacher to achieve this result with his students the teacher must himself have standards—and know how to apply them. We do not refer only to the technical criteria by which a student's work is appraised—do the sentences parse, are the facts accurate, is the verb correctly conjugated?—but also standards by which the quality of the ideas and the values they reflect can be judged. "Since freedom resides in the operations of intelligent observation and judgment by which a purpose is developed," Dewey wrote, "guidance given by the teacher . . . is an aid to freedom, not a restriction upon it. Sometimes teachers seem to be afraid even to make suggestions to the members of a group as to what they should do."[12] Such teachers, we believe, have no business purporting to instruct others in the humanities. They have surrendered their right to be called teachers. As Carlyle said, "Surely, of all 'rights of man,' this right of the ignorant man to be guided by the wiser, to be, gently or forcibly, held in the true course by him is the indisputablest."[13]

4. The quality of humanities teaching at the secondary level is di-

rectly proportionate to the success of the elementary schools in equipping their graduates with basic academic skills. We alluded earlier to a fundamental incompatibility between sound secondary education and remedial courses in which substantial portions of the high school program are given over to the task of imparting rudimentary skills and elementary knowledge to adolescents so that they can pass proficiency tests. We do not argue against such tests, and we applaud the idea of minimum educational standards that they embody. But if a given educational standard is, say, "sixth grade proficiency" in reading, language arts, and arithmetic, then the sixth grade is the proper place to apply it.

We reject the false dichotomies that some would create between "basic" and "higher order" cognitive skills on the one hand, and between "skills" and "knowledge" on the other. To learn the words on a page without engaging the ideas that they contain is absurd. It is the work of machines, not of the human mind. (As to the obverse, we offer Wittgenstein's insight, echoed and amplified by Leon Botstein, that an "idea" has no existence until it is formulated into words.) Education does not suddenly shift from imparting something called "skills" in the early grades to the development of "wisdom" in the later years. But a well-ordered educational system, in our view, will have a whole succession of "standards," each pegged to a desired level of intellectual attainment, and each functioning as companion or antecedent to the next. It is altogether desirable to develop such standards at the secondary level with respect to the content, knowledge, and sophisticated skills imparted by the several subjects we call the humanities. Such gauges of attainment are certainly more meaningful than the ersatz "standard setting" that takes the form of requiring youngsters to accumulate on their transcripts a certain number of years or units of exposure to one subject or another. But unless those youngsters bring with them to high school the webs of knowledge and skills properly deemed "primary," they cannot reasonably be expected to undertake a "secondary" education—in the humanities or in anything else.

5. High school humanities courses must be intellectually anchored in the scholarly disciplines. Among the many findings of this project, none alarmed us more than the discovery that in a number of high schools the humanities are regarded as a course of study separate and distinct from English, history, and foreign languages. We encountered strange amalgams of interdisciplinary and nondisciplinary study which, their proponents asserted, "used the humanities approach" or took the "humanities perspective." While one can imagine courses in English, history or foreign languages that are outside the humanistic tradition—grammar and punctuation, for example, the rote memorization of facts and dates, or an

introductory language course confined to vocabulary and syntax—it is impossible to conceive of courses "in the humanities" that do not consist of literature, history, philosophy, and the like. Such a course may well be multidisciplinary, as in the "history of ideas," "history and literature," or the examination of an ancient civilization through its poetry, its modes of worship, and its works of art. Skillfully taught, such a course can be a memorable intellectual experience and a humanizing one as well. But secondary education must respect the major divisions into which human knowledge has been classified over the centuries, must be mindful of the distinctive content and intellectual styles of each and—when bringing two or more together into a multidisciplinary course or curriculum—must recognize that this is because they strengthen and reinforce each other, not because they lack value or integrity of their own.

In the main—though this cannot be set forth as a rule—we believe that young people should first make the acquaintance of the several humanities disciplines as separate subjects, and thereby come to recognize their singular strengths, before being confronted with the formidable intellectual task of integrating them. While it can be argued that one should examine an entire edifice before scrutinizing its separate parts, we submit that adolescent learners will gain more of lasting value if they look carefully at the shape and composition of each part before considering the ways in which these are joined together. This will readily be understood by anyone who has taken children to visit a cathedral, which is only a large and pretty building until the guides explain the relationship of chancel to nave, show how the flying buttresses support the roof, recount the stories told in the stained glass windows, describe the wars that were fought, the lives that were lost, and the treasures that were committed to the enterprise, and surround the entire structure with a vision of the soaring faith and profound devotion that energized its construction.

6. The single most important qualification for a teacher of the humanities is to understand and love the subject that he teaches. This means, in the first instance, that the high school humanities teacher must himself be the proud possessor of a sound liberal education, and we cannot improve upon the illustration that Peter Pouncey gives of what such an education ought to look like.

The teacher must also be a serious student of his own subject, with at least an undergraduate "major" in it and preferably an advanced degree. He must have assimilated the intellectual discipline of his own discipline: its major works, its great thinkers, its primary modes of analysis, its own intellectual history, its dominant theoretical and interpretive controversies, and a sense of its scholarly frontiers. If he has done this *and* yearns to teach it to others, one can fairly assume that he is qualified to do so.

Does that mean the prospective teacher should eschew the study of education per se? Not necessarily. To teach in the schools is to enter into the organizational life of a large and complex institution with a history of its own, with ideological and philosophical traditions—and disputes—of its own, with social and political relationships of its own, with diverse technologies, multiple objectives, and demanding constituencies, and with constraints and rules—not always of its own making—that influence it. The wiser and more informed a teacher is about the enterprise of education, the more likely he is to be successful and contented in his work. But the teacher is first and foremost a transmitter of knowledge, and it little avails him to study the apparatus of knowledge transmission until he has acquired the knowledge that he will be transmitting. In the phrase of the moment, it's a "matter of priorities," and if a four- or five- or six- or more-year university education means, as it inevitably does, that choices must be made, then it is clear which ought to take precedence. The implication for teacher educators, policymakers, and school administrators may be self-evident, but we will state it anyway: the requirements that are set for the future teacher, whether by the university in which he studies, by the state that licenses him, or by the school system that employs him, must never discourage or impede him from acquiring the liberal education and disciplinary knowledge without which he cannot legitimately presume to teach others.

7. The good teacher who wants to become a better teacher and who wants personal growth and fulfillment from his work needs to sustain an active intellectual life, which in most cases means participating in an intellectual community that includes his fellow teachers. We agree wholeheartedly with Edwin DeLattre's assertion that "no one can begin to do an adequate job of nurturing those powers [of mind and heart] in others, particularly the young, who is not permanently cultivating them in himself or herself." We endorse as well the two key policy recommendations that DeLattre derives: that what is generally known as "in-service education" urgently needs a thorough overhaul if it is to foster and enrich the processes of permanent intellectual cultivation, and that schools must "encourage, support, and budget for continued study and learning by their teachers, principals and superintendents."

This may appear both familiar and altogether bootless to the reader whose eyes glaze when the words "in-service education" are mentioned, who knows full well that much of what travels under that banner is intellectually bereft and is endured by teachers only because it carries the promise of higher salaries or time away from the students, and who supposes that people who write of an active intellectual life among teachers either do not understand the teacher's burdens or do not appreciate his need to earn additional money in his limited spare time.

We do not defend the current arrangements, save to note that the handful of intellectually vibrant "in-service" programs known to us—one in Virginia sketched by DeLattre, others that we have learned of through the conferences or have had direct experience with—prove that such can exist and that the arid, trivial programs that are today more common in fact can and should be drastically rethought.

For the high school humanities teacher in particular, sound in-service education will ordinarily consist of deepening his knowledge and understanding of the humanities themselves. (Not always. Sometimes the history teacher craves greater knowledge of psychology, or the English teacher yearns to study the architecture of medieval France.) This can happen at many times and in various formats, and it need not always be an organized event or group activity. There is much to be said for the old-fashioned practice of reading a good book on Sunday evening or taking a stack of accumulated journals to the lakeside in July. Nor do we suggest that the teacher's every waking hour must be given to serious matters. Teachers, like everyone else, need diversions, recreations, and genuine vacations.

For the policymaker, however, we have these straightforward suggestions: the job the teacher is paid to do must include regular participation in activities that foster his intellectual growth and deepen his knowledge, which is to say the teacher, like the university professor, must be paid to learn more and thereby to become a better teacher.

We salute the National Endowment for the Humanities and other public and private agencies for recognizing the worth of such activities on the part of schoolteachers and for providing them through such vehicles as summer seminars and institutes, weekend workshops, and presentations by visiting scholars.

At the risk of stating the obvious, we wish to be clear that activities intended to foster intellectual growth and subject matter knowledge are *not* the same as "in-service days" or workshops devoted to matters of school administration and organization. If it is necessary to spend time explaining a new state regulation or the elements of the citywide proficiency test, so be it. But that is not what we are recommending, nor has it much bearing on better high school humanities teaching.

8. Whether the issue is preservice education of teachers, in-service programs with true intellectual content, the development of new curricula, or the recruitment of scholars to give guest lectures on specialized topics, high school humanities cannot be severed from the university.

Perhaps the most gratifying outcome of this project was its success in interesting a number of first-rate university humanities scholars in the quality of secondary education, and in deepening the involvement of some others who were already interested.

It is a familiar lament in education circles, but a true one, nonetheless, that dedicated scholars in the several disciplines have generally ignored the schools and that the only parts of universities that have paid close attention have been the colleges of education. We do not propose here to join the swelling mob of "ed school bashers," for these are as varied a lot as any 1,200 institutions could be and which include a number of people doing solid research and fine teaching. The point, rather, is that the customary arrangement has tended to keep links from forming between the scholars who are the major intellectual custodians and developers of the academic disciplines in which high school humanities courses are rooted and the secondary school educators charged with creating and teaching those courses. It is rather as if the people who do biomedical research and develop new medications and treatments had no contact with clinical physicians, as if musical composers never spoke to performers, or as if weapons designers had no communication with military field personnel. At the very least, one expects that the medical researcher will want his own inquiries to be pertinent to the needs of practicing doctors, and that when he thinks he is onto something he will want it to be tested in clinical settings. When a new drug or device is finally put onto the market, he will assist in various ways to explain it to those who will prescribe it and to train them in its uses, he will want to evaluate its effectiveness among large populations over a long time, and will probably design his next research project at least in part on the basis of the questions left unanswered by his last one. Conversely, the responsible clinician will not only read the latest journals, he will also attend conferences, seminars, and symposia where he can learn from—and talk with, and perhaps give advice to—the researchers.

The parallel with education is not exact, but neither is it irrelevant. The university professor doing advanced research on the history of the Belgian monetary system or recurring themes in the correspondence of Tolstoy is, in fact, producing knowledge in the same fields that high school humanities instructors are teaching. While his findings may not be directly transferred into secondary school courses, if he and his peers pay no attention to the schools several unfortunate consequences will ensue: the curricula will gradually become antiquated, based ever more completely on commercial decisions by textbook publishers and political decisions by school boards and ever less on the current content of the disciplines to which they are nominally related; teachers will have scant opportunity to develop intellectually in their fields; and the college students and graduate students of the future, not to mention the book-buying, newspaper-reading public, will have less and less interest in the subjects and issues that fire the enthusiasm of the scholar.

But the obligation of the scholar and his university to the quality of public education is a moral responsibility as well. It is a solemn obligation to the society that has agreed to institutionalize and underwrite the singular form of leisurely contemplation that is necessary for scholarship itself. The academy is supported by a society that values the fruits of such contemplation, not by one that recognizes any metaphysical right to leisure that inheres in special genius. Two sound ways in which the scholar can mesh his intellectual interests with his larger responsibilities are by translating his scholarship into forms accessible to those who direct and teach in the schools, and by making himself available to assist them in ways they find useful and he finds congenial.

We assert, then, that the university scholar has both a long-term self-interest and a continuing public duty to concern himself with the ways in which "his subject" is approached in the high schools and with the intellectual lives of those who teach it. Further, we suggest, the university has an institutional interest in strengthening the links between itself and the secondary schools, not in allowing them to weaken and break. Finally, it is clear that the intellectual standards that colleges and universities set for admission into their own programs, and the expectations that they communicate to school policymakers and teachers, powerfully influence the content and standards of the schools themselves. Nicholas Murray Butler spoke in 1925 of "the close and intimate association of the secondary schools and colleges in dealing with a common interest and a common task." More recently, that association has seldom been either close or intimate. It needs to become so once again.[14]

9. High school humanities teachers need to become more professional. In those nine words lurk hundreds of problems, issues, and controversies, many of which are thoughtfully essayed by Jon Moline and John Casteen. We do not want to understate their complexity or the difficulty of working through them. But it is agonizingly clear that if no significant progress can be made toward professionalism, schools are going to become more like public utilities, almost entirely regulated by the state, and less like communities of inquiry; the teaching occupation is going to become ever more like an industrial union in a faltering industry; and people with alternatives will neither consider working in public education nor send their own children to public schools.

What does "progress toward professionalism" entail? At minimum, it will have these five characteristics: first, the development of a genuine "career path" in which good teaching yields higher status, greater compensation, and additional authority. Second, more conscientious "self-regulation" by the teaching occupation (including university scholars in the several disciplines), consisting—at minimum—of standard-setting, peer evaluation, and firm handling of incompetence, sloth, and malpractice. Third, more faculty governance of schools, including staff and curriculum decisions. Fourth, a major reorientation of teacher licensure and certification standards, replacing course requirements and similar "paper credentials" with comprehensive examinations of knowledge and performance, akin to the "bar examination" or to the rigorous tests administered by medical "specialty boards." Fifth, the systematic provision—already noted by us—of opportunities for teachers to grow and renew themselves intellectually. We applaud John Casteen's insight that such "professionalization" may occur more readily and appropriately within disciplines and subject specialties or individual schools than in the teaching occupation as a whole, and add that this "model" is particularly well suited to high school humanities teachers.

Should teachers be paid more? Of course, but not if their occupation remains unchanged. More generous salaries should come hand in hand with heightened professionalism. In any case, a number of recent polls have shown beyond peradventure that taxpayers are willing to grant larger salaries to teachers only in conjunction with major changes in the norms, standards, and structure of their occupation.

10. High school humanities teaching cannot significantly improve unless principals (and other school-level administrators) participate actively in the processes of educational renewal and come to see themselves as instructional leaders rather than building managers. No consequential change can occur in a school unless the principal concurs in it, and the surest way to bring about change in a school is to have a skillful principal who nurtures it. Time and again, we encountered teachers, department heads, and curriculum planners with ample energy and sound ideas for strengthening their humanities program who were frustrated, discouraged, and defeated by principals who do not value the humanities, do not understand the ideas, or do not have the courage to make purposeful changes.

If policymakers could do only one thing to improve a school, they would be well advised to hire the best principal they could lay their hands on to direct that school—and then give him sweeping authority. An outstanding principal alone does not make for an effective school, but one almost never encounters a really good school with a weak or ineffectual principal.

Four points about principals must be borne in mind: first, the "job description" should emphasize instructional leadership rather than building management; second, there is little reliable correlation between good teachers and good principals; third, a person with the necessary character, temperament, energy, and intellect can acquire most of the knowledge and skills that he needs for sound instructional leadership; and, fourth, inept principals must not be allowed to remain in those key positions, which means that policymakers must steel themselves to remove from the principalship anyone whose shortcomings cannot readily be corrected.

It would be unreasonable to insist that every high school principal be an expert on the humanities, but the good principal will know enough about them to understand why they are important and what a sound secondary humanities curriculum looks like. He will ensure that his teachers and department heads are thoroughly schooled in their subjects, and he will create a school climate conducive to intellectual growth for teachers and to a sense of intellectual community for everyone.

We see no necessary conflict between these observations and our earlier suggestion that "faculty governance" of schools is a correlate of enhanced professionalism among teachers. Over time, the principal should become more like a college dean and less like a military commander or assembly line foreman. Leadership will still be necessary, but it will be the subtler leadership of an intellectual community rather than bureaucratic control.

The reader may wearily lament that putative reformers of education (as of most things) nearly always deliver themselves of a ringing plea for better "leadership," but that this is far more easily demanded than obtained. We respond that one need only look at the extraordinary leadership today being supplied to educational improvement at many levels— from the schoolhouse to the statehouse—and in many parts of the United States. Though the educational system has many parts whose separate movements should be synchronized, Peter Greer's essay makes clear that there is much that the determined administrator can do by himself to push and tug the part of the system for which he is responsible in the general direction of improved quality.

11. At the secondary level, the humanities are best learned by studying texts, not by reading textbooks. This simple statement, too, has complex and wide-ranging implications, and we do not deny the utility of "readers" and textbooks as frameworks on which courses can be built. But learning the subjects we know as the humanities is more a matter of active participation in a series of intellectual stretching exercises and of direct engagement with the ideas of great thinkers and the works of great writers than of "reading about" them. Throughout this volume, we have argued that the humanities have substance and content, not just method

and application. But the way to learn that content is to be immersed in the study of great works under the tutelage of teachers who value and understand them, not to read what someone else said about them. A student will learn more from studying *Macbeth* than from reading about Shakespeare, more from analyzing the Lincoln-Douglas debates than from reading a textbook account of the causes of the Civil War, more from struggling with the *Aeneid* than from memorizing the idiosyncrasies of the third conjugation.[15]

Nor will it do to justify the reading (or writing) of ephemera and trash on grounds that it is better to read something than nothing, that the student will not be "engaged" in the learning process unless what he reads is "relevant" to his own life, and that one book is as good as another for purposes of illustrating whatever lessons the teacher may be trying to hammer home. As the investigations of Scott Colley and Gilbert Sewall reveal with sometimes painful vividness, a teacher who does not anchor his pedagogical activities in important ideas and worthwhile texts can find himself driven by waves of trivia and topicality against shoals that tear the bottom out of the educational process itself. "We have become so preoccupied with trying to find out how to teach everybody to read anything," Hutchins observed, "that we have forgotten the importance of what is read. Yet it is obvious that if we succeeded in teaching everybody to read, and everybody read nothing but pulp magazines, obscene literature, and *Mein Kampf*, the last state of the nation would be worse than the first. Literacy is not enough."[16] If information is restricted or teaching debased, Dewey recognized, the skill of literacy alone may be manipulated by evil people to control others. That is why totalitarian states are so meticulous about censoring the content of the books that are used in their schools—and why those still fortunate enough to live in democracies must be equally meticulous in developing through their schools the critical intelligence that enables one to resist indoctrination and to understand the real meaning of freedom.

12. We turn, finally, to the curriculum itself. Only the foolhardy would suggest that all schools ought to adhere to exactly the same curriculum, and it is not our place to set forth the details of even an idealized course of study. But decisions must be made as to what shall be taught, and we therefore sketch the essential considerations that we believe should inform those decisions. Our comments, it should be clear, apply to all high school students, not just those who plan to attend college. The qualities of mind that the humanities help develop are qualities that every American youngster should acquire before completing secondary education. Hence while we may not endorse every detail of *The Paideia Proposal* as set forth by Mortimer Adler and associates[17], we subscribe to the

principle that every boy and girl should pursue essentially the same program of study while in elementary and secondary school, regardless of social class, ethnic heritage, or career ambitions. Naturally, not all will begin or end at the same point, nor will they learn at the same rate. But all should have the same opportunity to study the central disciplines, to ponder the great questions, and to develop their skills and knowledge to the fullest. We also welcome the strong support that the National Commission on Excellence in Education has given to toughening and enriching the content of the high school program by urging higher minimum requirements for all in what the Commission calls the "Five New Basics": four years of English, three years of mathematics, three years of science, three years of social studies, and a half year of computer science.[18] We applaud as well the Commission's insistence that "the curriculum in the crucial eight grades leading to the high school years should be specifically designed to provide a sound base for study in those and later years in such areas as English language development and writing, computational and problem solving skills, science, social studies, foreign language, and the arts."[19]

We would alter and extend the Commission's comments in just three ways:

First, the phrase "four years of English" has been spoken so often that it frequently slides off the tongue or past the ear without registering any real meaning. The essential problem with high school English, as Robert Fancher explains with alarming clarity, is not that too few years are spent studying it but that what is studied is too often either soft and trivial or rudimentary and mechanistic, lacking any clear sense of the "humane culture." In too many classes called "high school English," we find students either learning the grammar and vocabulary that they should have learned in the lower grades, or reading stories and books of scant literary merit. We also find far too many students emerging from "four years of English" without the ability to write a cogent paragraph, much less a critical analysis containing well-formulated ideas persuasively stated.

The high school English teacher must be able to assume that his students have attained reasonable mastery of the structure and mechanics of the English language before leaving elementary school. The high school years—all four of them—should then be devoted to ever more sophisticated use of the language as our primary medium for expressing serious ideas, emotions, values, and beliefs. This means careful, critical reading of literary works: prose and poetry, essays and biographies, meditations and plays, sonnets and treatises, short stories and long novels, exegeses and editorials, reportage and fantasy. It also means a great deal of student writing in many modes and genres, complete with editing, revising, and lots and lots of constructive criticism by teachers and others who know what separates good writing from bad. The study of literature, and the practice of writing: that is high school English conceived as part of the humanities.

Second, the phrase "social studies" should be banished from the high school curriculum. What should be taught and learned is history, and this must consist fundamentally of the history of the United States, the enveloping history of Western civilization, and the parallel history of non-Western civilizations. By history we do not mean only—or primarily—the memorization of dates and facts or the identification of wars and political leaders, though these have their place. Properly conceived, history includes the history of ideas, cultural developments, and social, political, and economic movements. It includes the evolution of diverse cultures and the changing relationships among peoples, races, religions, and beliefs. Everything worth learning that is commonly found under the rubric of "social studies" can be taught and learned as history, but only if it is taught and learned in an essentially chronological framework can the student emerge with a sense of how he and his society came to be what they are and where they are at the present time. And only with that understanding of the past can the student reasonably hope to know where and how he would like himself and his society to be in the future—or what is entailed in getting there.

Third, with respect to foreign languages, the National Commission on Excellence in Education courageously—and we think rightly—pointed out that "achieving proficiency . . . ordinarily requires from 4 to 6 years of study and should, therefore, be started in the elementary grades."[20] But it then equivocated, suggesting only that "for the college-bound [student] 2 years of foreign language in high school are strongly recommended in addition to those taken earlier."[21] Our view is clearer and our prescription more demanding: *every* American should become proficient in at least one foreign language, and while this must—as Carlos Hortas explains—begin before high school, it should continue in high school. As with English, if the elementary school equips the student with reasonable mastery of the structure and mechanics of the language, then the high school years can be given over to good literature and to the written and oral expression of more sophisticated ideas. Proficiency in a foreign language means more than knowing how to decipher a street sign and say "please pass the bread." It means grappling with the best that has been written in the language, and learning how to use it to convey one's own best thoughts. That is, after all, what the humanities are about, and what education ought to be about.

We conclude with the words of the late Charles Frankel, as perceptive and eloquent a student and teacher of the humanities as our culture has produced, and with the hope that the questions he raises—the central questions we have sought to address in this volume—will linger in the minds of educators and policymakers long after our own tentative answers have faded:

> What will our country offer its members as a diet for their minds and souls? They are the citizens of a free society. They must make their own decisions about the good, the true and the beautiful, as well as about the genuine article and the fake, the useful and the useless, the profitable and the unprofitable. But their individual minds, their individual schemes of value and structures of belief within which they make their choices, are largely formed by the social and cultural atmosphere, with all its educational and miseducational effects. . . .
>
> No institution within our society, certainly not government, has the capacity to control this cultural and moral environment. We can be thankful this is so. Nevertheless, any citizen—and certainly anyone with public responsibilities or anyone who is a trustee for a tradition of civilized achievement—must ask what part he or she can play in shaping the environment in which we Americans must live and find our being.
>
> What images of human possibility will American society put before its members? What standards will it suggest to them as befitting the dignity of the human spirit? What decent balance among human employments will it exhibit? Will it speak to them only of success and celebrity and the quick fix that makes them happy, or will it find a place for grace, elegance, nobility, and a sense of connection with the human adventure? What cues will be given to our citizens, those who are living and those still to be born, that will indicate to them the values authoritative institutions of our nation, such as our governments, national, state, and local, and our halls of learning, regard as of transcendant importance? These are the questions that I believe are really at issue when we consider the place of the humanities on the national scene. . . .[22]

NOTES

1. National Commission on Excellence in Education, *A Nation at Risk: The Imperative for Educational Reform* (Washington, D.C.: U.S. Department of Education, 1983), 5–6.

2. Robert Maynard Hutchins, quoted by Mortimer J. Adler in *The Paideia Proposal: An Educational Manifesto* (New York: Macmillan Publishing Co., 1982), p. 6.

3. Horace Mann, quoted by Mortimer J. Adler, ibid., p. 5.

4. Report of the Commission on the Humanities, *The Humanities in American Life* (Berkeley: University of California Press, 1980), p. 28.

5. For perhaps the most celebrated and erudite discussion of the limitations of knowledge as a guarantor of virtue—and of the enduring value of knowledge for its own sake—see John Henry Newman, *The Idea of a University* (Oxford: Clarendon Press, 1976), especially discourse 5.

6. Alfred North Whitehead, *The Aims of Education and Other Essays* (New York: The Free Press, 1929), p. 29.

7. John Dewey, *Experience and Education* (1938; reprint, New York: Collier Books, 1968), p. 65.

8. Robert Maynard Hutchins, *Education for Freedom* (Baton Rouge: Louisiana State University Press, 1943), pp. 91–92.

9. Joseph Adelson, "How the Schools Were Ruined," *Commentary* 76, no. 1 (July 1983), 46.

10. We intend to examine a number of these in greater depth through a successor project, named "Challenges to the Humanities."

11. Hutchins, *Education for Freedom,* p. 26.

12. Dewey, *Experience and Education,* p. 71.

13. Thomas Carlyle, *Chartism* (Boston: Charles C. Little and James Brown, 1840), p. 52.

14. The quote is taken from a splendid recent report by the College Board that exemplifies the best of contemporary school-college cooperation in serious matters of academic content and standards. See *Academic Preparation for College: What Students Need To Know and Be Able To Do* (New York: College Board, 1983).

15. Obviously, the student who has never made the acquaintance of the third conjugation cannot get very far with Vergil, any more than the student who does not grasp the overall nature of the North-South conflict in the 1850s can intelligently interpret the statements of Lincoln and Douglas. The point, rather, is that too many high school humanities courses never get beyond tools and chronologies into the texts that give those courses their humanistic value.

16. Hutchins, *Education For Freedom,* pp. 14–15.

17. Mortimer J. Adler, *The Paideia Proposal: An Educational Manifesto* (New York: Macmillan Publishing Co., 1982).

18. NCEE, *A Nation at Risk,* p. 24.

19. Ibid., pp. 26–27.

20. Ibid., p. 26.

21. Ibid., p. 24.

22. Charles Frankel, "Why the Humanities?" in *The Humanist as Citizen,* ed. John Agresto and Peter Riesenberg (Chapel Hill: National Humanities Center, 1981), pp. 4–5.

Conference Participants

Titles and affiliations as supplied by the participants
at the time of the conferences

ATLANTA CONFERENCE (MARCH 14–17, 1983)

Henry Acres, Chancellor, Muhlenberg College, Allentown, PA

Jane Algozzine, Bureau Chief, Language Arts, New York State Department of Education

Jack Armistead, English Professor, University of Tennessee, Knoxville, TN

Stephen Arons, Associate Professor, Legal Studies Program, University of Massachusetts, Amherst, MA

Sharon Ayers, High School French Teacher, Raleigh, NC

Linda Barnard, Chairperson, Humanities Department, Chapel Hill High School, Chapel Hill, NC

Leslie Berlowitz, Assistant Vice President for Academic Affairs, New York University, NY

Ann Beusch, Maryland State Department of Education, Specialist in Foreign Language Education, Annapolis, MD

June Birnbaum, Adjunct Instructor, Rutgers Graduate School of Education, Rutgers College, State University of New Jersey, New Brunswick, NJ

Eve Bither, Assistant Superintendent for Secondary Education, Portland Public Schools, Portland, ME

Jaque Bradford, Public School Supervisor of English Instruction, Knox County Schools, Knoxville, TN

Donald H. Bragaw, Bureau Chief, Social Studies Education, New York State Department of Education.

Phyllis Bretholtz, English/Social Studies Teacher, Cambridge Rindge and Latin School, Cambridge, MA

Nancy Burkhard, CSJ, High School English and Social Studies Teacher, Rome Catholic High School, Rome, NY

Rebecca Burns, High School English Teacher, Kanawha County, Charleston, WVA

Sidney Burrell, Professor of History, Boston University, Boston, MA

Willard Callender, Professor of Education, University of Southern Maine, Portland, ME

Victor Carrabino, Associate Chair for Graduate Affairs, Florida State University, Tallahassee, FL

Carole Chaet, Coordinator, Social Studies Instruction, Cambridge Public School, Cambridge, MA

Mark Christiansen, Department of Curriculum and Instruction, University of Tennessee, Knoxville, TN

Doris Clanton, Director, Instruction Services, The School District of Greenville County, Greenville, SC

Dario Cortes, Professor, Foreign Language, North Carolina State University, Raleigh, NC

Richard Dollase, Director, Teacher Education Program, Middlebury College, Middlebury, VT

Gloria Duclos, Professor of Classics, University of Southern Maine, Portland, ME

Roberta Dunbar, Professor of African and Afro-American Studies, University of North Carolina, Chapel Hill, NC

Robert Egolf, Chairman, English Department, William Allen High School, Allentown, PA

Antonia Ellis, Social Studies Teacher, Longmeadow High School, Longmeadow, MA

George Fraker, Social Studies Teacher, Deerfield Academy, Deerfield, MA

Paul Gagnon, Professor of History, University of Massachusetts, Boston, MA

Harold Garrett-Goodyear, Chairman, History Department, Mt. Holyoke College, South Hadley, MA

Peter Greer, Superintendent, Portland Public School System, Portland, ME

Mary Alice Gunter, Assistant Professor, Department of Curriculum and Instruction, University of Virginia, Charlottesville, VA

Alan Hall, English and History Teacher, Yarmouth High Schools, Yarmouth, ME

Charles Hancock, Professor of Education, University of Maryland, College Park, MD

Katherine Hanley, CSJ, English Professor, College of Saint Rose, Albany, NY

Hazel Harris, Professor of Education/Director of Graduate Studies, Furman University, Greenville, SC

Hazel Hertzberg, Professor of Education, Teachers College of Columbia University, New York, NY

Miriam Hoffman, English Teacher, Millburn Township Public Schools, Millburn, NJ

Marta Impara, Assistant Professor of Education, Florida A&M, Tallahassee, FL

Carolyn Kelly, Coordinator, Language Arts, English, Cambridge Rindge and Latin School, Cambridge, MA

Everett Kline, Chairman, Social Studies Department, Columbia High School, Maplewood, NJ

Geoff Lawrence, English Teacher, Middlebury Union High School, Middlebury, VT

Joan Lescinski, CSJ, English Professor, The College of Saint Rose, Albany, NY

James Liddicoat, Professor of Education, Cedar Crest College, Allentown, PA

Gladys Lipton, Foreign Language Program Coordinator, Anne Arundel City Public Schools, Annapolis, MD

Frank Macchiarola, Chancellor of Schools, New York City Board of Education, New York, NY

Bonnie Maddox, Chairman, English Department, Charleston High School, Charleston, WVA

Arlene Malinowski, Coordinator, Foreign Language Education, North Carolina State University, Raleigh, NC

Barrett Mandel, Associate Professor of English, Rutgers College, State University of New Jersey, New Brunswick, NJ

John McCardell, Associate Professor of History, Middlebury College, Middlebury, VT

Terry Meyers, Professor of English, William and Mary College, Williamsburg, VA

William Monahan, Consultant, Foreign Language/Bilingual Education, School District of Greenville County, Greenville, SC

Robert Monson, Assistant Superintendent for Secondary Studies, School District of South Orange and Maplewood, Maplewood, NJ

Jack Murrah, Associate, Lyndhurst Foundation, Chattanooga, TN
Patricia O'Connell, Maine State Department of Education, Consultant for Gifted and Talented, Augusta, ME
Charlotte Pritt, Writing Program Manager, Kanawha County Schools, Charleston, WVA
Paul Regnier, Assistant to the Deputy Commissioner, State Department of Education, New York, NY
Kevin Ryan, Division of Instructional Development, School of Education, Boston University, Boston, MA
David Schimmel, Professor of Education, University of Massachusetts, Amherst, MA
Jan Schwab, Coordinator, Gifted and Talented Program, Charlottesville High School, Charlottesville, VA
Valerie Seaberg, Coordinator, Main Humanities Project for Rural Secondary Schools, Augusta, ME
Jean Self, History Teacher, Calhoun High School, Signal Mountain, TN
Milton Silver, Project Director, High School for the Humanities, Manhattan Superintendent of High Schools, New York, NY
Sharon Smith, High School Social Studies Teacher, Virginia Beach, VA
Ulysses Spiva, Dean of Darden School of Education, Professor of Educational Leadership & Services, Old Dominion University, Norfolk, VA
Weldon Thornton, Professor of English, University of Chapel Hill, Chapel Hill, NC
John Trimpey, Dean, College of Arts & Sciences, University of Tennessee, Chattanooga, TN
Benjamin Troutman, Director, Curriculum Assessment and Development, Virginia Beach Public Schools, Virginia Beach, VA
Gabriel Valdes, Foreign Language and Bilingual Education Consultant for the State Department of Education, Tallahassee, FL
Charles Vandersee, Associate Professor of English, University of Virginia, Charlottesville, VA
William Watterson, Assistant Professor of English, Bowdoin College, Brunswick, ME
Dennis Younger, Director of Curriculum, Anne Arundel City Public Schools, Annapolis, MD

DENVER CONFERENCE (APRIL 20–23, 1983)

Dwayne Adcock, Coordinator of Secondary Curriculum, Eugene School District, Eugene, OR
William Joseph Alexander, Hillsboro High School Social Studies Teacher, Hillsboro, OH

Neil L. Anstead, Magnet High School Coordinator, Grover Cleveland High School, Reseda, CA

David Arlington, High School History Teacher, Salem, OR

John N. Austin, Professor of Classics, University of Arizona, Tucson, AZ

James M. Barr, Principal, Hillsboro High School, Hillsboro, OH

Alice Barter, Professor of English, Chicago State University, Chicago, IL

Samuel R. Bell, Assistant Professor of Education and Coordinator of Inservice Education, Bradley University, Peoria, IL

Richard C. Benjamin, Assistant Superintendent for Planning and Development, Fort Worth School District, Fort Worth, TX

Robert Berdahl, Dean, College of Arts and Sciences, University of Oregon, Eugene, OR

M. Jean Bressler, Associate Professor of Education, University of Nebraska, Omaha, NB

Naomi Brodkey, English and History Teacher, Evanston Township High School, Evanston, IL

Robert V. Bullough, Jr., Professor of Education, University of Utah, Salt Lake City, UT

Kenneth M. Bumgarner, Assistant to Division Management, Director of Basic Education Office, Tumwater, WA

Robert Louis Chianese, Professor of English, California State University, Northridge, CA

Henry F. Cotton, Principal, Cherry Creek High School, Evergreen, CO

Billie Cox, English Teacher, Mesa Public Schools, Tempe, AZ

Keith Crosbie, Bilingual Coordinator and Foreign Language Supervisor, State of Washington, Olympia, WA

Harrison Davis, Professor of Humanities, Brigham Young University, Provo, UT

Rebecca Duran, Supervisor of Arts and Music Education, Public Instruction, Tumwater, WA

Toni L. Farquhar, Chair, Department of English and Foreign Languages, Boltz Junior High School, Fort Collins, CO

Betty S. Flowers, Professor of English, University of Texas, Austin, TX

Roger E. Foltz, Chairman, Department of Music, University of Nebraska, Omaha, NB

Robert Frazier, Department of Secondary Education, Humanities Education, Arizona State University, Tempe, AZ

Clifford J. Gallant, Professor of Romance Languages, Bowling Green State University, Bowling Green, OH

Norman Geschwind, Honolulu, HI

Donna Green, Member, Mesa Board of Education, Mesa, AZ

Dean Haggard, St. John's College, Santa Fe, NM

Gavin Hambly, Dean, School of Arts and Humanities, University of Texas at Dallas, Plano, TX

James W. Hauter, Superintendent, Metamora Township High School, Metamora, IL

Kay U. Herr, Associate Professor, Department of Foreign Language and Literature, Colorado State University, Fort Collins, CO

Richard H. Hersh, Dean of the Graduate School and Associate Provost for Research, University of Oregon, Eugene, OR

Leo J. Hertzel, Associate Professor, Department of English, University of Wisconsin, Superior, WI

Theodore Higgs, Associate Professor of Spanish and Hispanic Linguistics, San Diego State University, San Diego, CA

V. Pauline Hodges, Associate Professor of Education, Colorado State University, Fort Collins, CO

John Hoge, English Teacher, Catalina High School, Tucson, AZ

Tom Kay, Chair and Associate Professor, History Department, Wheaton College, Wheaton, IL

Thomas Henry Kent, Chair, Department of English and Foreign Languages, Bradley University, Peoria, IL

Francis X. King, Special Projects Coodinator, San Diego Unified School District, San Diego, CA

Joanne Kleist, Curriculum and Evaluation Director, Green Bay Public School System, Green Bay, WI

Evelyn Klinckmann, Assistant Superintendent, Hawaii State Department of Education, Honolulu, HI

Charles Robert Kline, Jr., Associate Professor of Curriculum and Instruction, University of Texas at Austin, Austin, TX

Nina M. Little, Humanities Curriculum Specialist, Omaha Benson High School, Omaha, NB

John Mangieri, Dean, School of Education, Texas Christian University, Fort Worth, TX

Joanne Martin-Reynolds, Associate Professor of Education, Bowling Green State University, Bowling Green, OH

Charles Mayers, Assistant Superintendent, Bowling Green, Ohio Public Schools, Bowling Green, OH

James E. McGlinn, Associate Professor of Education, Ottawa University, Ottawa, KS

Dottie McGrossen, Language Arts Teacher, Ottawa High School, Ottawa, KS

John G. McLevie, Chairman, Department of Secondary Education, San Diego State University, El Cajon, CA

Earlene Mitchell, Hillcrest High School, Midvail, UT

David Oliphant, History Teacher, Wheaton North High School, Wheaton, IL

John A. Orange, Professor of Spanish, Texas Christian University, Fort Worth, TX

Mitchell B. Pearlstein, Consultant, Humphrey Institute of Public Affairs, University of Minnesota, St. Paul, MN

Lora Reiter, Associate Professor of English, Ottawa University, Ottawa, KS

Georgianna G. Robbins, Chair, English Department, Hillsboro High School, Hillsboro, OH

Paul Robinson, Assistant Professor of Secondary Education, University of Arizona, Tucson, AZ

Jerrold Rodesch, Chair, Humanistic Studies and Associate Professor of History, University of Wisconsin, Green Bay, WI

Ruth B. Ross, Assistant Principal, Grover Cleveland High School, Reseda, CA

Howard Scheiber, Director of Writing Programs and Assessment, New Mexico State Department of Education, Albuquerque, NM

Sam Snyder, Associate Professor, Department of Educational Theory, College of Education, University of Toledo, Toledo, OH

Mary E. Stanton, English Teacher, Plano High School, Plano, TX

Sanford Stein, Chinese-Russian Study Center, Toledo Public Schools, Toledo, OH

Larry Strickland, Supervisor of Social Studies, Public Instruction Office, Tumwater, WA

Stephan A. Stuart, Principal, Jemez Valley High School, Jemez Pueblo, NM

Philip E. Thompson, Associate Professor of Education, University of Wisconsin, Green Bay, WI

Miriam Tormollan, English Teacher, Crockett Senior High School, Austin, TX

Robert G. Trauba, Professor of Education, University of Wisconsin, Superior, WI

James Unseth, English Department, Drummond High School, Drummond, WI

Muriel M. Van Patten, Acting Director of School Program Service, Department of Education, Lansing, MI

Larry D. Wilcox, Department of History, University of Toledo, Toledo, OH

Dean Woelfle, High School Social Science Teacher, Pekin, IL

John Wollstein, Asian, European and Pacific Languages Specialist, Hawaii State Department of Education, Honolulu, HI

Victor Leonard Worsfold, Associate Dean for the Arts, University of Texas at Dallas, Dallas, TX

For Further Reading

This highly selective list—augmented by notes at the end of individual chapters—is intended only to provide a starting point for scholars, practitioners, policymakers and interested laymen who want to explore in greater depth some of the many issues raised in this volume.

Adler, Mortimer J. *The Paideia Proposal: An Educational Manifesto.* New York: Macmillan Publishing Co., 1982.
———. *Paideia Problems and Possibilities.* New York: Macmillan Publishing Co., 1983.
Agresto, John, and Peter Riesenberg, eds. *The Humanist as Citizen.* Chapel Hill: National Humanities Center, 1981.
Applebee, Arthur N. *A Survey of Teaching Conditions in English, 1977.* Urbana: National Council of Teachers of English, 1978.
———. *Tradition and Reform in the Teaching of English: A History.* Urbana: National Council of Teachers of English, 1974.
Barzun, Jacques. *The House of Intellect.* New York: Harper Brothers, 1959.
Beesley, Patricia. *The Revival of the Humanities in American Education.* New York: Columbia University Press, 1940.

Bestor, Arthur E. *Educational Wastelands*. Urbana: University of Illinois Press, 1953.

Bigelow, Donald N., ed. *The Liberal Arts and Teacher Education: A Confrontation*. Lincoln: University of Nebraska Press, 1971.

Broudy, Harry S. *The Real World of the Public Schools*. New York: Harcourt Brace Jovanovich, 1972.

Broudy, Harry S., B. Othanel Smith, and Joe R. Burnett. *Democracy and Excellence in American Secondary Education*. Chicago: Rand McNally, 1964.

Burston, W. H. and D. Thompson, eds. *Studies in the Nature and Teaching of History*. New York: Humanities Press, 1967.

Chaffer, John, and Lawrence Taylor. *History and the History Teacher*. London: George Allen and Unwin, 1975.

Chastain, Kenneth. *Toward a Philosophy of Second-Language Learning and Teaching*. Boston: Heinle & Heinle, 1980.

Cohen, Arthur A., ed. *Humanistic Education and Western Civilization: Essays for Robert M. Hutchins*. New York: Holt, Rinehart & Winston, 1964.

Commager, Henry Steele. *The Commonwealth of Learning*. New York: Harper & Row, 1968.

Commager, Henry Steele, and Raymond H. Muessig, *The Study and Teaching of History*. Columbus, OH: Charles E. Merrill, 1980.

Cremin, Lawrence A. *The Transformation of the School: Progressivism in American Education, 1876–1957*. New York: Alfred A. Knopf, 1961.

Dewey, John. *Experience and Education*. Kappa Delta Pi Lecture Series. New York: Macmillan Co. 1938.

Fenstermacher, Gary D. and John I. Goodlad, eds. *Individual Differences and the Common Curriculum: Eighty-second Yearbook of the National Society for the Study of Education*. Chicago: University of Chicago Press, 1983.

Fisher, James A., ed. *The Humanities in General Education*. Dubuque: William C. Brown Company, 1960.

FitzGerald, Frances. *America Revised: History Schoolbooks in the Twentieth Century*. Boston: Little, Brown & Company, 1979.

Gardner, John. *On Moral Fiction*. New York: Basic Books, 1978.

Gilbert, Felix. *History, Choice and Commitment*. Cambridge, MA: Harvard University Press, 1979.

Glazer, Nathan, and Reed Ueda. *Ethnic Groups in History Textbooks*. Washington, DC: Ethics and Public Policy Center, 1983.

Goodlad, John I. *A Place Called School*. New York: McGraw-Hill, 1983.

Graubard, Stephen R., ed., *The Arts and Humanities in America's Schools,* special edition of *Daedalus,* Summer 1983.

Hertzberg, Hazel Whitman. *Social Studies Reform 1890–1980*. Boulder: Social Science Education Consortium, 1983.

Hester, Ralph, ed. *Teaching a Living Language*. New York: Harper & Row, 1970.

Hillocks, George, Jr., ed. *The English Curriculum Under Fire: What Are the Real Basics?* Urbana: National Council of Teachers of English, 1982.

Hofstadter, Richard. *Anti-Intellectualism in American Life*. New York: Vintage Books, 1962.

Howard, James, and Thomas Mendenhall. *Making History Come Alive: The Place of History in the Schools*. Washington, DC: Council for Basic Education, 1982.

Hutchins, Robert Maynard. *Education for Freedom*. Baton Rouge: Louisiana State University Press, 1943.

Kammen, Michael, ed. *The Past Before Us: Contemporary Historical Writing in the United States*. Ithaca: Cornell University Press, 1980.

MacIntyre, Alasdair. *After Virtue*. Notre Dame: Notre Dame Press, 1981.

Miller, Bernard S. *The Humanities Approach to the Modern Secondary School Curriculum*. New York: Center for Applied Research in Education, 1972.

Mitchell, Richard. *The Graves of Academe*. Boston: Little, Brown and Company, 1981.

Mooney, Michael, and Florian Stuber, eds. *Small Comforts for Hard Times: Humanists on Public Policy*. New York: Columbia University Press, 1977.

Parr, Susan Resneck. *The Moral of the Story: Literature, Values, and American Education*. New York: Teachers College Press, 1982.

Postman, Neil. *Teaching as a Conserving Activity*. New York: Delacorte Press, 1979.

Ravitch, Diane. *The Troubled Crusade: American Education, 1945–80*. New York: Basic Books, 1983.

Report of the Commission on English. *Freedom and Discipline in English*. New York: College Entrance Examination Board, 1965.

Report of the Commission on the Humanities. New York: American Council of Learned Societies, 1964.

Report of the Commission on the Humanities. *The Humanities in American Life*. Berkeley: University of California Press, 1980.

Report of the National Commission on Excellence in Education. *A Nation at Risk: The Imperative for Educational Reform*. Washington, D.C.: U.S. Department of Education, 1983.

Report of the Twentieth Century Fund Task Force on Elementary and Secondary Education Policy. *Making the Grade*. New York: Twentieth Century Fund, 1983.

Richards, Jack C., ed. *Understanding Second and Foreign Language Learning*. Rowley, MA: Newbury House, 1978.

Rodriguez, Richard. *Hunger of Memory*. Boston: David L. Godine, 1982; New York: Bantam Books, 1982.

Shulman, Lee S. and Gary Sykes, eds. *Handbook of Teaching and Policy*. New York: Longman, 1983.

Sizer, Theodore R. *Secondary Schools at the Turn of the Century*. New Haven: Yale University Press, 1964.

Stevens, David H. *The Changing Humanities: An Appraisal of Old Values and New Uses*. New York: Harper & Brothers, 1953.

van Essen, A. J., and J. P. Menting, eds. *The Context of Foreign Language Learning*. Assen, The Netherlands: Koninklijke Van Gorcum & Company, 1975.

The Authors

Biographical information supplied by authors in Summer 1983

Leon Botstein is President of Bard College and of Simon's Rock of Bard College. He is a European historian who has published frequently in such magazines and journals as *The New Republic, Harper's, Partisan Review, Salmagundi, The Chronicle of Higher Education, Musical Quarterly,* and *Psychoanalysis and Contemporary Thought.* He is now finishing a study of the musical life in Vienna at the end of the nineteenth century.

Harry S. Broudy, Professor Emeritus at the University of Illinois, is one of the nation's foremost philosophers of education. His ten books include the classic *The Real World of the Public Schools* and *Building a Philosophy of Education.* He has presented over a dozen endowed lectureships.

John T. Casteen, III—formerly of the English Department of the University of Virginia, now Secretary of State for the Commonwealth of Virginia—publishes short stories, essays on education and public policy, and studies in medieval history and Virginia history. He is coeditor of *The Jefferson Papers of the University of Virginia.*

Scott Colley is Associate Dean of Vanderbilt University's College of Arts and Science and Associate Professor of English. A Shakespeare scholar—he is currently editing the New Variorum Edition of *Richard III*—he is also an outstanding, committed teacher. Vanderbilt University honored him with the Madison Sarratt Award for Excellence in Undergraduate Teaching in 1974.

Edwin J. Delattre, who was director of the National Humanities Faculty from 1976 to 1980, is President of St. John's College in Annapolis, Maryland, and Santa Fe, New Mexico. He publishes regularly in a wide range of leading journals and magazines, such as *The Wall Street Journal, The Chronicle of Higher Education,* and *American Educator,* and serves on many national boards and commissions—including the Matchette Foundation advisory board and the President's Commission on White House Fellowships.

Robert T. Fancher earned the Ph.D. in philosophy from Vanderbilt University in 1980 and is now Research Associate at the Vanderbilt Institute for Public Policy Studies. He has taught philosophy at Vanderbilt University, the University of South Carolina, and Seoul National University. As a Henry Luce Scholar, he was Visiting Professor of English Literature at Sogang University in Seoul in 1981.

Chester E. Finn, Jr., is Professor of Education and Public Policy at Vanderbilt University, where he is also codirector of the Center for Education Policy. He has written *Scholars, Dollars and Bureaucrats* and *Education and the Presidency* and coedited (with David Breneman) *Public Policy and Private Higher Education.* He is currently completing a book about private schools for Oxford University Press.

Peter R. Greer, superintendent of the Portland (Maine) school system, has taught in junior and senior high schools and leads one of the nation's most dramatically improving systems. Dr. Greer formerly served as Associate Director of the National Humanities Faculty (1972–1974).

Carlos R. Hortas, chairman of the Department of Romance Languages at Hunter College, is a contributing editor of the *Handbook of Latin American Studies* of the Library of Congress and a member of the Modern Language Association's Standing Commission on the Literatures and Languages of America—of which he was chairman, 1981–1982.

Clair W. Keller taught high school for a decade before joining the faculty of Iowa State University in 1969. He is author of *Involving Students in the New Social Studies* and coauthor (with Richard Bartlett) of an American history textbook, *Freedom's Trail.* He is director of Iowa's History Day and was a member of the National History Day Coordinating Committee. Professor Keller is a member of the Executive Committee of the National Council of Social Studies and President of the NCSS Special Interest Group for History Teaching.

Jon Moline is Professor of Philosophy and Environmental Studies at the University of Wisconsin–Madison. In addition to distinguished scholarly work—represented recently by his *Plato's Theory of Understanding*—he has published articles of policy analysis and is completing a book on practical wisdom.

Peter R. Pouncey has been Dean of Columbia College and Chairman of Columbia's Contemporary Civilization Program and is now President-designate of Amherst College. His book, *The Necessities of War: A Study of Thucydides' Pessimism,* received the Lionel Trilling Award for Columbia University's best scholarly publication in 1981.

Diane Ravitch is Adjunct Professor of History at Teachers College, Columbia University. In addition to over one hundred scholarly and popular articles, she has written three books *(The Great School Wars: New York, 1805–1973; The Revisionists Revised: A Critique of the Radical Attack on the Schools;* and *The Troubled Crusade: American Education, 1945–80)* and has coedited two others, (with Ronald Goodenow, *Educating an Urban People: The New York City Experience* and *Schools in Cities: Consensus and Conflict in American Educational History).* Professor Ravitch is a member of the National Academy of Education.

Gilbert T. Sewall taught history and economics at Phillips Academy and was education editor at *Newsweek.* A regular contributor to *Fortune,* he is author of *After Hiroshima: America since 1945* (with A. Ganley and T. Lyons) and *Necessary Lessons: Decline and Renewal in American Schools.*

Gary Sykes, formerly leader of the Teaching Policy Team at the National Institute for Education, has coauthored two books, *Value Conflicts and Curriculum Issues* (with J. Schaffarzick) and *Handbook of Teaching Policy* (with L. Schulman), edited a special edition of *Educational Evaluation and Policy Analysis,* and testified before numerous state, federal and privately sponsored education commissions, committees, and panels.